The
Statistical Movement
in Early Victorian Britain

The Statistical Movement in Early Victorian Britain

The Foundations of Empirical Social Research

M. J. Cullen

*Lecturer in History, University of Otago
New Zealand*

The Harvester Press Limited

Barnes & Noble Books · New York

First published in 1975 by
THE HARVESTER PRESS LIMITED
(*Publisher: John Spiers*)
2 Stanford Terrace, Hassocks, Sussex
and published in the USA 1975 by
HARPER & ROW PUBLISHERS, INC.
BARNES & NOBLE IMPORT DIVISION
10 East 53rd Street, New York 10022

Copright © M. J. Cullen

Harvester Press
ISBN 0 901759 17 1

Barnes & Noble
ISBN 0–06–491333–3

Designed by Yvonne Dedman

Printed in Great Britain by
Western Printing Services Ltd, Bristol
Set in Linotype Granjon

All rights reserved

To A.R. and I.J.C.

'In most of the accounts which have come under our observation... it is impossible not to discern a kind of foregone conclusion... in quarters where the professed principle is to "exclude all opinion", opinions... are perpetually insinuated.'

Rev. James Shergold Boone, 1838.

Contents

Preface	ix
Abbreviations	xi
Prelude: Social Statistics in Britain, 1660–1830	1
Part I: Government Departments and Social Statistics, 1832–52	
1. The Statistical Department of the Board of Trade	19
2. The Work of the General Register Office	29
3. The Health of the Armed Forces	45
4. Edwin Chadwick and Sanitary Statistics	53
5. The Government and Moral Statistics	65
Part II: The Statistical Societies	
6. The Foundation of the Statistical Society of London	77
7. The Statistical Society of London: the improved society	91
8. The Manchester Statistical Society	105
9. The Other Provincial Societies	119
Conclusion: Social Statistics and the Ideology of Improvement in Early Victorian Britain	135
Notes to Text	151
Bibliography of Primary Sources	189
Index	201

Preface

This book is a revised version of a doctoral thesis submitted in the University of Edinburgh in 1971. Its purpose is to delineate the main features of the statistical movement in early Victorian Britain, a movement which has been noted by many recent historians as one of the distinguishing features of the period. It is not intended to provide an introduction to, and discussion of, the sources for the social statistics of the 1830s and 1840s. My main intention has been to see how the movement organized itself, to assess its achievements, and, from an analysis of the major surveys and writings of the members of the movement, to see if it possessed a distinguishing philosophy. Where it seemed particularly useful to do so I have also tried to comment on the accuracy of the figures collected.

It should also be made clear that this is not a study of all the people who produced works with quantitative material in the period but of those men who coalesced into a movement. This includes the great majority of the significant social statisticians of the time, especially in England, but it does mean that some surveys, even well-known ones, will not be mentioned. Moreover, a few men whose importance only begins in the late 1840s have been excluded. The greatest problem was Edwin Chadwick, who was not a central figure in the Statistical Society of London, but who in most other respects was not untypical of the movement. That movement began in the 1830s, flowered in the late 1830s and 1840s, but then began to wither, or at least change considerably, and may be said to have ended in 1852 when two of its leading figures died.

I have received much assistance from scholars and librarians in my work but in particular I would like to acknowledge the help of Professor M. W. Flinn (who not only supervised the thesis from which this book developed but is in large part responsible for its publication), Mr I. H. Blenkinsop, Miss Margaret Dowling, Professor D. V. Glass, Dr J. R. B. Johnson, and Dr R. J. Morris. In addition, I must acknowledge the permission of the Royal Statistical Society to publish material from its records.

M.J.C.
Dunedin, New Zealand
August 1974

Abbreviations

Apart from standard abbreviations (such as PRO for Public Record Office) the following have been used:

App Mins.: *Appendix to the Minutes of the Manchester Statistical Society*.

Chadwick, Flinn: Edwin Chadwick, *Report on the Sanitary Condition of the Labouring Population of Great Britain* (ed. with an introduction by M. W. Flinn, Edinburgh, 1965). The introduction is referred to as 'Flinn', the report as 'Chadwick'.

Diary: J. E. Drinkwater's diary consisting of the minutes of the committee of the Statistical Section of the British Association for the Advancement of Science from June 1833 to March 1834.

GBPP: Great Britain, Parliamentary Papers.

JRSS: *Journal of the Royal Statistical Society*.

JSSL: *Journal of the Statistical Society of London* (superseded by *JRSS* 1887).

Local Reports . . . England: *Local Reports on the Sanitary Condition of the Labouring Population of England*.

Local Reports . . . Scotland: *Local Reports on the Sanitary Condition of the Labouring Population of Scotland*.

MCSSL: *Minutes of the Council of the Statistical Society of London*.

MLSC: *Minutes of the Leeds Town Council Statistical Committee*.

MSSL: *Minutes of the Statistical Society of London*.

Observations: Bernard Benjamin, 'John Graunt's "Observations"'. With a foreword', *Journal of the Institute of Actuaries*, XC, 1964, pp. 1–61.

PEW: Charles Henry Hull (ed.), *The Economic Writings of Sir William Petty together with the Observations upon the Bills of Mortality more probably by Captain John Graunt* (Cambridge, 1899).

Proc. SSL: *Proceedings of the Statistical Society of London*.

TPMSA: *Transactions of the Provincial Medical and Surgical Association*.

Trans. BAAS: *Transactions of the British Association for the Advancement of Science.*
Un. Serv. Jnl.: *United Service Journal.*

Prelude: Social Statistics in Britain 1660–1830

It is generally agreed that the statistical study of social problems began in earnest in Britain with the work of Captain John Graunt and William Petty in the 1660s.[1] The intellectual origins of this work may remain a matter for debate but it is reasonably clear that the *Natural and Political Observations on the Bills of Mortality* published in London in 1662 represented a new approach to the study of society. At least in intention, if not in practice, the science of 'political arithmetic' was to incorporate the systematic collection of statistical information relating to both social and economic questions. Analysis of that information was to lead to the generation of laws governing the social sciences comparable with those contemporaneously developing in the physical sciences.[2]

If it seems understandable that there would be in Britain in the second half of the seventeenth century a desire to create a science of society there was no obvious reason why this should be tied specifically to the notion of quantification. In fact, even the more general problem of the flowering of science in the Restoration period has produced a host of often mutually exclusive and contradictory explanations. R. F. Jones and Margery Purver have championed the Baconian heritage of empiricism.[3] In the case of political arithmetic this heritage is incapable of explaining the specific form taken by the empirical data. Moreover, there seems a great deal in Webster's argument that the real importance of Francis Bacon to seventeenth-century science was as a kind of totem.[4] Nor is the popular sociological explanation which stresses the role of Puritanism in the genesis of Restoration science any greater help. Merton and other writers in this 'Neo-Weberite' tradition seems to be bordering on the incredible in arguing an identification of industrious empiricism with godliness and membership of the elect.[5] Inevitably, the counter-claim has been made that the roots of seventeenth-century science were to be found in a spirit of individualism, utilitarianism, and hedonism.[6] Even less illuminating is the view that the distinctive feature of the men of the seventeenth century was a craving for novelty, or the idea put forward by G. N. Clark that the dominance of mathematics naturally led to 'the belief that all things can be measured'. This dominance was supposedly 'fixed' in some unexplained way by the importance of music in the seventeenth century.[7]

These theories and others concerned with the same problems tend to be too ingenious and too dependent upon the skilful use of language rather than content. They fail to provide a framework for the kind of case-study in which we are interested. It seems more fruitful to return to the personalities involved to see if any coherence can be given to the origins of social statistics. But here an immediate difficulty presents itself. While it is agreed that the *Natural and Political Observations* was the first work of any significance in social statistics, it is not universally accepted that John Graunt wrote it, rather than William Petty, despite the appearance of the former's name on the title page. The reasons for doubt lie largely in the fact that Graunt was a London merchant who published very little else (and that on other topics) while his friend, William Petty, was a man of wide experience, successful, who wrote many essays and books on political arithmetic. Finally, contemporaries with good sources of information, such as Aubrey and Evelyn, at various times identified Petty as the author.[8]

On the other hand, the list of authorities who have decided that Petty's role in the work was strictly limited is an impressive one and includes all the important economists, demographers, and medical statisticians who have written on the subject.[9] Their argument springs from an underlying distrust of Petty as an intellectual gadfly, a distrust which is backed by the obvious superiority of arithmetical and demographic skills evident in the *Observations* to those demonstrated in the known works by Petty. The most which these writers allow to Petty is that he may have suggested the work to Graunt, helped over a few details, possibly wrote the conclusion, and also persuaded Graunt to insert what has commonly been called a life table.[10]

In allowing this much, Greenwood, Professor Glass, and the others have allowed a very great deal. As professional demographers and economists they are naturally swayed by the mastery of technique demonstrated by the writer of the *Observations*. No one can deny that Petty was a poor arithmetician. Simple problems became complex in his hands,[11] and the practicalities of calculations where 'the algorithm is more operose, and when the stock is all the truth in nature that can be expressed in number, weight, and measure' were luckily scarcely ever entered into his works.[12] Yet to argue from this that Graunt was the principal author, is to attach more importance to technique than to theory, which hardly seems justified, especially at the foundation of a discipline.

The reasons for concentrating on Petty as the founder of British social statistics rest on a firmer base than just the fact that he may have suggested to Graunt the subject of the latter's essay. If Aubrey is to be trusted, Petty was discussing social statistics some three years before the publication of the *Observations*, for he was putting his ideas forward at Harrington's Rota Club in 1659.[13] Unfortunately, very little can now be discovered of this important body and Aubrey cannot be checked, though there is no cause to doubt him. Moreover, a list of Petty's writings dated 6 October 1671 in the manuscripts at Bowood includes the cryptic entry '1660. Observations on the Bills of Mortality'.[14] The presumption must be that Petty had already begun to develop his concept of 'political arithmetic' well before the *Observations* were published. Indeed, another of the Bowood papers, which bears the date 1660–1, is entitled 'Question of an Irish land registry' and warrants detailed examination for it shows how developed Petty's theories were at that early date.

In the paper, he called for 'Accompts of the Inhabitants' in order to discover the occupational structure of the population, the number of people transported in the Civil War–Commonwealth era, and the religious structure of Ireland's population. He also called for a general register of births, deaths, and marriages to collate the parish registers and thus help to reveal the numbers married, the age-structure of the population, the occupational and religious distribution, and the wealth of any particular area.[15] By 1661 Petty had already formulated many of the basic principles and proposed procedures of the early phase of social statistics.

It is to Petty that we must look for the ideas which generated the statistical study of society. William Petty was born in 1623 the son of a small Essex clothier. He received some elementary education but at 14 went to sea as a cabin boy. A broken leg resulted in his being left ashore at Caen, where he studied for some years, probably under Jesuits. Another brief spell in the navy gave way to a much longer period as scholar, inventor, and amanuensis. It was in the last-named capacity that he made the acquaintance of Thomas Hobbes, serving him for a while as a secretary in the mid-1640s. By 1650 Petty was a Doctor of Medicine and a Fellow of Brasenose College, Oxford. Through the aid of John Graunt he became Professor of Music at Gresham College. In 1652 he went to Ireland, where he was to become Surveyor-General, undertaking the famous Down Survey, and then Secretary to Henry Cromwell. This period was the foundation of Petty's fortune. In 1659 he returned to London, managed to ingratiate himself after the Restoration with Charles II, and was active in the embryonic Royal Society.[16]

By 1661, then, Petty was a highly successful man, a man on the make. Nevertheless, he had much to live down. He had served the Commonwealth well and in association with a Cromwell. His actions in Ireland had come under attack from jealous and land-hungry gentry. He had been involved in the now disreputable Rota Club. He had been in contact with Thomas Hobbes. It may well have been Hobbes who set Petty on the path to political arithmetic. The 'arch-atheist' had been interested in the applicability of mathematical methods to social and political analysis.[17] A number of writers have agreed that this had a profound impact on Petty's thought. Lewis S. Feuer has referred to Petty as 'an inheritor of the Hobbesian mantle' while Wilson Lloyd Bevan pointed out many years ago that Petty 'follows Hobbes in assigning to mathematical proof the highest place' and that the only English philosophical writings on a reading list that Petty drew up for his sons were Hobbes's *Logic* and *De Cive*.[18] Most recently Quentin Skinner has ventured the opinion that Petty's political arithmetic 'was built out of studying Hobbes'.[19] In the study of society the primacy which Hobbes gave to geometry at some point became translated in Petty's mind to arithmetic and quantification. In view of the fact that Petty is first reported as spreading his theories after his return from Ireland it would appear feasible that the surveying work in Ireland (with its unavoidable emphasis on the arithmetical aspects of geometry) was crucial in the development of his thought.[20]

Although this hypothesis rests to some extent on pure speculation it has been dwelt on because it goes a long way towards explaining Petty's coyness in not publishing earlier and his desire to test the acceptability of his studies via the less controversial figure of John Graunt. The early members of the Royal Society shared a determination to dissociate themselves from accusations of atheism. As Westfall has noted, 'Thomas Hobbes, who was notorious in the virtuosi's eyes as an atheist, did not apply and was not suggested for membership in the Royal Society.'[21] In the tense political and intellectual atmosphere of 1661–2 Petty could scarcely afford to risk notoriety. He was naturally cautious all his life over publishing his works; most were never published until the Marquis of Lansdowne produced the Petty Papers in 1927, while publication of others was postponed for many years, some not appearing until three or four years after Petty's death.

It seems reasonable to assume that the *Natural and Political Observations* represented more than the product of an off-hand remark as far as Petty's role was concerned. Graunt may have written the body of the work but the general framework and the whole conception were Petty's. The second dedication of the *Observations*, to Sir Robert Moray, President of the Royal Society, suggests Petty's influence with the studied ambiguity of its opening: 'The observations, which I happened to make (for I designed them not).'[22] This is not to dismiss Graunt from his honourable position in the history of social statistics. He was not the true founder but the *Observations* bear the mark of a man skilled in arithmetic, careful, judicious, and full of common sense in his deductions. Without Petty it seems most improbable that Graunt would ever have written on the subject but had it been left to the former the finished product would have been inferior. As it was, social statistics emerged as a well-developed infant.

The *Natural and Political Observations* was an analysis of the London Bills of Mortality, which formed the only readily available source of demographic data.[23] From this unpromising material Graunt extracted a large number of conclusions including, as Hull said, some of the most important facts of vital statistics: the regularity of social phenomena, the excess of male over female births, the approximate numerical equality of the sexes, the high rate of mortality in the early years of life, and the excess of urban over rural death rates.[24] More significant in many ways than the conclusions was the high degree of methodological skill. Before analysing any statistical data Graunt discussed its reliability. In other words, it was realized from the beginning that all social data were to some extent inaccurate, the question being whether they were accurate enough to justify further manipulation. With this insight Graunt was able to revise the figures given in the bills of mortality for the causes of death as well as compare the mortality in various plague years.

The justification for these investigations was given in the conclusion to the *Observations*, very probably written by Petty. Petty stressed the utility of the new discipline, its ability to lead to an understanding of 'true politics' or 'how to preserve the subject in peace and plenty'.[25] Petty was in fact the most significant theorist of social statistics in Britain, at least until the heroic decade of the 1830s, and even then no single figure stood out with his overall vision. But he was also the first expression of a type to be found repeatedly in the history of social statistics: the reformer who saw the collection of facts as an indispensable preliminary to practical and effective reform. The facts he chose to collect, as with later statisticians, were designed to demonstrate the necessity and desirability solely of those reforms which he desired.

In the remainder of his many writings Petty had two main themes which he summarized in his *Political Arithmetic*:

> Instead of using only comparative and superlative Words, and intellectual Arguments, I have taken the course (as a Specimen of the Political Arithmetic I have long aimed at) to express myself in Terms of *Number*, *Weight*, or *Measure*; to use only Arguments of Sense, and to consider only such Causes, as have visible foundations in Nature; leaving those that depend on the mutable Minds, Opinions, Appetites, and Passions of particular Men, to the Consideration of others ... Now the Observations or Positions expressed by Number, Weight, and Measure ... are either true, or not apparently false, and which if they are not already true, certain, and evident, yet may be made so by the Sovereign Power ... Nor would it misbehave Authority itself, to clear the Truth of those Matters which private Endeavours cannot reach to.[26]

Thus the first theme was the familiar one of the role of political arithmetic as a science of society whose conclusions were dependent upon 'number, weight, and measure'.[27] Secondly, for the science to be successfully studied it was necessary that the raw data should be greatly improved. Thus in numerous papers Petty argued for the creation of a central statistical office and often saw himself in the role of chief statistician.

Yet his own achievements in practice were severely limited and he failed to produce any first-rate models or examples. The major features of Petty's exercises in political arithmetic were a somewhat cavalier attitude towards facts and a reliance on over-lengthy chains of deductions from initially dubious material. Although examples of these faults are easy to find, if Petty is compared with his predecessors rather than his successors then he was a master of statistical techniques and a paragon of carefulness. His main ambition was to lay out a grand design. In Kuhn's terms,[28] Petty was a man who tried to establish the paradigms for a new science and also suggested most of the 'puzzles' it would be worth solving. Because he associated population with wealth and power the new science was intended to have demography at its core. Even so, it was not demography as such but a hybrid of all the social sciences using quantitative techniques, and its end was the production of what was later to be called 'useful knowledge'.

To a large extent Petty failed. Walter E. Houghton, talking of the English virtuosi in general, has referred to the period 1680 to 1710 as 'The Decline of the Movement'.[29] In Petty's case there was no one to succeed him and the term 'political arithmetic' became debased. Social statistics were confined within a narrow demographic channel.[30] This is not to deny the real achievements of demography in the late seventeenth and eighteenth centuries. Demography, of all the social sciences, earliest, and perhaps alone, attained the status of what Kuhn would call a 'normal science'. But the men of the eighteenth century were not simply raising higher a structure begun by Petty.

The attempt to describe the situation of states in terms of demographic phenomena received further expression in the late seventeenth century from Sir Peter Pett, Charles Davenant, and Gregory King. Of these three, King was by far the most important. His contribution to demography is well known and his table on the numbers and wealth of each rank in society has gone beyond the realm of historical source to become a historical cliché. But his work was not published in full until the second edition of George Chalmer's *An Estimate of the Comparative Strength of Great Britain* in 1802. King's intentions are not clear but it seems that he too was primarily concerned with gauging the nation's power. The demographic sections are renowned for their accuracy but it must be wondered how far this was due to luck.[31]

King's work, together with that of Edmund Halley two years earlier, indicates that the reduction of political arithmetic to demography was an almost instantaneous process. Halley was particularly significant for he made the first serious attack on a problem suggested by Petty and Graunt – the construction of an adequate life-table. Halley was the first writer in English to place this in the context of life insurance and annuities. There was little impact on practical insurance schemes until the mid-eighteenth century but his work did generate one of the most popular classes of early demographic investigations. Halley was the only seventeenth-century writer to understand that the construction of an accurate life-table depended upon the concept of a stationary population. Either a stationary population had to be used or the figures adjusted in such a way as to allow for this criterion.[32] Halley 'had realized an important truth, which did not become part of even expert knowledge for more than a century'.[33]

Halley started a long line of investigations. During the first 80 years or so they were not particularly numerous – perhaps a dozen major works. Even so, they followed a distinct pattern, though it must be emphasized that the practical effects of these early writings on the principles of life insurance were limited. Eighteenth-century schemes were dependent more on rough and ready guesses than life-tables[34] The first life-insurance business to base itself on recognizably modern actuarial methods was the Society for Equitable Assurances for Lives and Survivorships which began in 1762.[35] Thus the importance of the writers from Abraham de Moivre to Richard Price lies rather in their increasing competence and their development of new, if not always better, life-tables.[36]

Price was the only one of these writers to give a great deal of space to the problem of the reliability of the available life-tables and other demographic data.[37] The strongest doubts were usually expressed by those writing specifically on the bills of mortality. However, as early as 1729 in a general description of London, William Maitland included a short section on the bills in which he reckoned that apart from the 29,722 burials mentioned there were 3,038 Dissenters who did not appear because they were not buried by ministers of the Church of England. A little later Thomas Short argued that the parish registers had been inadequate ever since the rise of organized Dissent.[38] By the middle of the century a rough consensus existed on the faults of the parish registers and the bills of mortality, a consensus expressed by William Heberden in 1759. As he pointed out, the bills included baptisms only and thus omitted all Roman Catholics and nearly all Dissenters as well as those who died before baptism and many of the lower classes who were never baptized in any case. Much the same criticisms applied to the figures for burials, which also failed to include those carried out of London for burial.[39]

In the 50 years from 1780 to 1830 some signs of expansion and diversification in social statistics began to appear. A national census was instituted, medical statistics unevenly but discernibly broadened into wider but more immediately applicable areas, new techniques of statistical analysis were discovered, while available techniques were applied to previously unquantified issues. Finally, the whole question of the inadequacy of available vital statistical data was reopened. Yet seeds were often laid down which were long in germinating and even failed for lack of nourishment so that replanting had to occur later. The range of material to be studied is wide – too wide to be properly encompassed within the short space allotted to it in this work.

In medical statistics the period opened with William Black's *Observations Medical and Political, on the Smallpox*,[40] which was both the culmination and full flowering of previous trends and a work of originality. Black was judicious for his time in the use of statistical material: a familiarity with the sources was combined with some scepticism as to their value and reliability as well as a desire to avoid the defect of many earlier writers who 'have obscured their works in a cloud of arithmetick and calculation. Therefore the reader must have no small portion of phlegm and resolution to follow them through with attention; they often tax the memory and patience with a superfluity of figures, even to a nuisance'.[41] Of particular value was a postscript wherein Black discussed the defects of the London Bills of Mortality. In a splendid phrase they were described as 'Gothic ruins, which it is wasting time to prop and plaster.' His own solution was a system of civil registration plus a septennial census.[42] His suggestions were by no means impracticable but they were ignored. However, a few years later he sketched a plan for a national census.[43]

Black's last important work was perhaps the first application of the statistical method to insanity.[44] He had few early imitators though Andrew Halliday produced a survey of the extent of insanity in Scotland.[45] Another area in which a few studies appeared was the health of the armed forces. The outstanding figure here was Gilbert Blane who first wrote on the diseases of seamen in the late 1770s and was to carry on for many years charting the progress of the health of the navy and supporting improvements on the basis of experimentally justified remedies (such as the use of lemon juice).[46] The army was not so well served but one work of note was contained in part of a mammoth study on the occurrence of diseases in India by James Annesley published in 1828.[47] Annesley was later to co-operate with the Statistical Society of London on the health of the army in India.

Blane in particular was an example of a type which began to increase in numbers towards the end of the eighteenth century: the man who used quantification to justify the introduction of particular reforms. Major Greenwood stated many years ago that all 'the pioneers of Social Medicine based most of their arguments on statistical reasoning'.[48] This was particularly true of John Heysham at Carlisle, who collected vital statistical data for that town and then campaigned for public health reforms.[49] Another example was John Haygarth of Chester.[50] At Manchester Thomas Percival took a leading role in the creation of the Manchester Board of Health in 1796. These and other cases were, however, scattered and uncoordinated. The achievements in a practical sense of the provincial medical statisticians must remain open to serious question and it would be difficult to argue that, in the main, the first decades of the Industrial Revolution saw any significant growth of medical statistics beyond a continuation and elaboration of the trends of the previous century. It was in other ways that the period 1780 to 1830 was crucial.

One of the strangest of these was the introduction of the term 'statistics' into the English language. This was to become a vogue word in the 1820s and later, yet its meaning was only just becoming fixed and the process of changing definition was to go on to the end of the nineteenth century if not beyond. 'Statistics' was almost certainly first used in English in 1770 in W. Hooper's translation from the German of a book by J. F. von Bielfeld.[51] Following German practice the term was defined to mean the science which 'teaches us what is the political arrangement of all the modern states of the known world'.[52] It may, therefore, be compared with the much earlier 'statist' for politician or statesman. It was von Bielfield's opinion that Gottfried Achenwall (1719–72) had been the first to make the subject a separate science under the title of 'statistics' and his opinion was repeated for many years thereafter.[53] The Danish mathematician and historian, Harald Westergaard, described this as an over-simplification. Achenwall was the popularizer of the term but the notion of a systematic comparative study of states went back to Hermann Conring of Brunswick, a contemporary of William Petty.[54] The discipline was otherwise known as 'staatenkunde' and in some form or other could, of course, be traced back to Aristotle.[55] But during the eighteenth century it became a serious academic discipline in Germany with its own rules of procedure. However, at the beginning of the nineteenth century a dispute broke out between those who advocated the use of a synopsis in tabular form ('tabellenstatistik') and those who opposed the drift towards a quantitative emphasis.[56]

It is not apparent that the dispute greatly affected the course of development of the term 'statistics' in Britain. After Hooper's early use there was a gap until 1787 when a book by a German of the 'tabellenstatistik' school, E. A. W. Zimmerman, was published in English.[57] At the same time an Englishman travelling in Europe acquired a taste for 'statistics' and determined upon preaching the German science to his countrymen. His book was not published until 1790 but it still marked a stage in the absorption of a new word into the language.[58] The next year 'statistics' was firmly established in English by the publication of the first volume of Sir John Sinclair's *Statistical Account of Scotland*. This was not a work of statistics in the modern sense but it was one in a looser version of the old German sense. Sinclair defined statistical enquiries as those 'respecting the Population, the Political Circumstances, the Productions of a Country and other Matters of State'.[59] Sinclair was so taken with the term and the idea it incorporated that he talked of sending 'Statistical Missionaries' round the country.[60] His advocacy was soon effective and the 1797 edition of the *Encyclopaedia Britannica* described 'statistics' as a 'word lately introduced to express a view or survey of any kingdom, county, or parish'.[61] This definition shows the impact of the *Statistical Account* for it was something of a debasement of the German usage.

Somehow over the next 30 or 40 years it became more and more accepted that statistics involved at least an element of quantification. As early as 1801 Benjamin Capper criticized Sinclair for being 'too voluminous' and himself included a section of 'statistical tables'.[62] But the definition of the word remained, in Daniel Boileau's phrase, 'the knowledge of the existing political state of a country'.[63] Boileau, however, also stressed a concept that was to come to prominence: 'statistics' were not dependent upon politics but were merely 'facts'.[64] It was the union of the two ideas (brevity, possibly by the use of tables, plus objectivity) put forward by Capper and Boileau which may have determined the shift towards quantification. Statistics were facts in a condensed form which revealed the condition of a state. Yet as late as 1842 J. R. McCulloch rejected the idea 'that everything in statistics may be estimated in figures'.[65] The contents of the *Journal of the Royal Statistical Society* would suggest that it was not until the present century that 'statistics' came to mean solely numbers and the methods of analysing numbers. In the early 1830s the term was still in a state of flux, for while it had normally acquired a quantitative connotation this was still subsidiary to the main definition as 'that department of political science which is concerned in collecting and arranging facts illustrative of the condition and resources of a state'.[66] Bisset Hawkins in 1829 was decidedly advanced in defining medical statistics as 'the application of numbers to illustrate the natural history of man in health and disease'.[67]

Hence in the early 1830s a clear definition had yet to emerge. Even insofar as quantification was used the techniques of statistical analysis were (outside actuarial science) relatively undeveloped. One technique of particular interest was the use of graphs and other visual representations. These had a strange history for they appeared in a well-developed form as early as the 1780s yet fell out of use again and virtually had to be reinvented in the 1830s and 1840s. Their first use was entirely associated with one man, William Playfair. Playfair was born in Dundee in 1759, the younger brother of the more famous John Playfair.[68] His first publication to include graphs was *The Commercial and Political Atlas* of 1787, in which the graphs were largely of British exports and imports to and from various places.[69] Eleven years later he produced his *Lineal Arithmetic*, a more complicated work with 37 coloured graphs.[70] By 1801 Playfair came close to suggesting that statistical works should be limited to quantitative data.[71]

Unfortunately his example was not followed. H. Gray Funkhouser found no mention of Playfair's writing by a British statistician until Jevons in 1879.[72] In the first 50 volumes of the *Journal of the Statistical Society of London* graphics appeared only fourteen times.[73] It was still a long time before graphs were widely used. In 1835 Charles Ansell produced some graphs of age-specific mortality and sickness rates recording the experience of various friendly societies.[74] The same year John Rickman, the census-taker, also graphed age-specific mortality rates but did so by cramming no less than twenty lines into one small graph.[75] Technical leadership had passed to the Continent and in Britain graphic representations were to remain crude and scarce throughout the 1830s and 1840s.

Progress, therefore, was very uneven in graphical techniques in the period 1780 to 1830. One achievement of those years is worth noticing: the institution of the national census in 1800. It has usually been assumed that the first census was connected with the publication in 1798 of Malthus's views on population and subsistence.[76] It now appears more likely that insofar as one man was central to the story it was John Rickman. In 1796, the 25-year-old Rickman wrote an essay in favour of taking a census which, Professor D. V. Glass has discovered, was reprinted in 1800.[77] Rickman's arguments were rooted in the confused and dangerous internal and external situation of the mid-1790s. More accurate information would enable the government to form more effective policies, particularly with regard to the recruitment of the armed forces. The census, Rickman believed, would show a substantial population increase, thus demonstrating the nation's growing prosperity and allaying domestic discontent.

Rickman sent his paper to his local M.P., George Rose, who communicated it to Charles Abbott. But Abbott did not take up the idea until four years later, at the end of 1800. It seems unlikely that Abbott had been spurred to action by the publication of the paper in June of that year. For one thing the scheme put forward by Rickman was neither that originally proposed by Abbott nor that incorporated in the ensuing Act.[78] While Abbott saw the potential of a census for 'ulterior uses in matters of War and Finance' his main arguments were concerned with the economic crisis following the disastrous harvest of 1800.[79] Parliament had resumed in November 1800 to take measures to combat the situation caused by what the King's Speech referred to as 'the present high price of provisions'.[80] Eight days after the resumption Abbott presented his Bill, arguing that a census was necessary to assess food requirements 'not only for the uses of the current year (for which it must necessarily come late) but also for the year that is to follow'.[81] The short term character of the reasons for taking the census are apparent. The Bill was passed on the last day of 1800 and the census taken on 10 March 1801. Rickman obtained the post of supervising the census, just recognition of the fact that without his advocacy Abbott might not have made the connection between a harvest failure and counting heads.

The machinery Rickman controlled was perhaps as well oiled as could be expected. In England and Wales the overseers of the poor, and in Scotland the schoolmasters, were to make returns of the numbers and occupations of the people (the latter in three categories) as well as obtaining from the clergy lists of the baptisms and burials for each tenth year from 1700 to 1780 and for every year from 1781 onwards.[82] That the census was inaccurate in the direction of not insignificant under-enumeration is well known but we have little idea of the size of the error. It is generally agreed that the next three censuses, which Rickman also supervised, were more accurate in total (though Professor Glass enters a caveat that the change from the occupations of persons in 1801 to the occupations of families in 1811 probably increased the error under that head). Nor was the census of age in 1821 likely to have been very accurate. Moreover, Professor Glass may be being over-optimistic about the 1801 census of occupation since Rickman later stated that there had been a confusion of persons and families in the returns which made them useless.[83] Nevertheless, the foundations of a decennial census were laid, even if the death of Rickman and the institution of civil registration made the 1841 census a quite different event (at least for England and Wales) from those of 1801 to 1831.

The census was not the only innovation of the early years of the nineteenth century in social statistics. National criminal statistics began to be published by the Home Office in 1810.[84] Scottish figures first appeared in 1812 but regular returns did not start until the figures for 1832.[85] The background to the initiation of the returns for England and Wales has not been studied in any detail but there is little doubt that the explanation is to be found in the contemporary controversy over capital punishment with reformers like Sir Samuel Romilly campaigning for a reduction in the number of capital offences. In 1809 Romilly was forced to withdraw a motion in the Commons for returns of the numbers committed for trial and their sentences, upon a government excuse that it was not possible to provide the returns at that time.[86] The next session Romilly introduced bills to remove capital punishment for some types of theft.[87] As part of the campaign Romilly successfully moved for the same returns that he had called for the previous year.[88]

It was out of the particular issue of capital punishment, therefore, that national criminal statistics were born. Once the figures were available arguments could begin over their significance. By the time of the 1828 Select Committee on Criminal Commitments and Convictions it could be agreed that most of the apparent increase in crime based on the rise in commitments was due to changes in the classification of criminal offences and to more effective enforcement rather than an actual increase in crime.[89] The Select Committee on the Police of the Metropolis came to the same conclusion.[90] With these and other defects it was clear that the official statistics of crime presented ample scope for improvement.

The official statistics of education were rather different for they were never put upon a regular basis during the period covered by this work. Official surveys and private ones co-existed and were perhaps of equal importance. But the three national surveys – 1818, 1833, and 1851 – were all 'official' in one sense or another. The private enquiries pre-date 1818 by some years though as early as 1804 the Society for Bettering the Condition of the Poor proposed a national investigation to the government.[91] The earliest work was undertaken by bodies like the British and Foreign School Society, the West London Lancastrian Association and even the St Giles's Irish Free School. For some reason there was a flurry of such surveys in 1813 though the results did not become widely publicized until the 1816 Select Committee on the Education of the Lower Orders of the Metropolis.[92] In the same year the Select Committee on Children Employed in Manufactories provided a forum for non-metropolitan societies and their endeavours.[93] These two committees were the first of a series on education which reached their apex in the 1818 Select Committee on the Education of the Lower Orders. It was that committee, chaired by Brougham, which decided to institute a national survey of the means of education. Circulars were sent to all the parochial clergy in England, Scotland, and Wales.[94] The returns were digested and printed in 1819.[95] Since the sources used were biased, the basis of the returns unclear (attendance or number on the books, the inclusion or otherwise of dame schools), and there are no other surveys to be used as a check, the accuracy of the figures must be considered highly suspect. Except for a private sample survey carried out by Brougham in 1828 little further happened until the flood of enquiries which forms part of the statistical movement proper.

Crime and education statistics were supplemented by other early exercises in social statistics such as those connected with the health of factory children which were uncovered by the 1816 factory committee. But these were spasmodic and of little value. It was in the long-established discipline of actuarial statistics that the most work was done in the 1810s and 1820s rather than in any more recently mapped areas of social enquiry. Concern grew about the existing vital statistical data and the deductions made from them. In 1810 and 1813 Francis Baily rejected William Morgan's book on contingent annuities as inaccurate.[96] In 1815 Joshua Milne, actuary to the Sun Life Assurance Society, produced perhaps the best study of vital statistics until Farr. In it he took the material collected by John Heysham and deduced the Carlisle tables of mortality which were sometimes used thereafter in place of the more popular Northampton tables.[97] But even the Carlisle tables came under suspicion a decade later when Parliament examined the state of the friendly societies. While the Carlisle tables were the best yet produced John Finlaison, the government's chief actuary, felt that there were no completely reliable tables of mortality.[98] Finlaison, Milne, and the other critics carried the committee with them and the report concluded that the rates of mortality and sickness in England were not 'sufficiently well ascertained to justify a Parliamentary enactment of any particular set of Tables'.[99] Another committee two years later recommended in very vague terms 'the adoption of measures for making an accurate and extensive collection of facts' for the construction of tables.[100]

More precise solutions were also forthcoming. Francis Corbaux wanted a legally enforceable registration of births and deaths.[101] He was followed by Bisset Hawkins who now saw in addition the possibility of registering the causes of death.[102] All saw the major defect of the parochial registers as their exclusion of Dissenters – a defect which would have to be remedied if the registers were to be of any value in correcting the Northampton and other life-tables. For John Rickman, by 1830 an obstacle to any form of innovation in vital statistics, a non-ecclesiastical registration of births and deaths could not be established in England.[103] But it was not up to Rickman for the Dissenters, or at least some of them, were riding a growing wave of reform which had repealed the Test and Corporation Acts in 1828, was soon to strengthen their electoral power by the 1832 Reform Act, and hopefully would sweep away their other grievances. Within six years of Rickman's statement one of the key institutions of the statistical movement, the civil registration of births, deaths, and marriages, had been created.[104]

The body responsible for administering the new registration was the General Register Office which was also empowered to make an annual abstract of the number of births, deaths, and marriages in England and Wales. In fact under the guidance of its chief statistician, William Farr, the office became one of the most important government departments from the point of view of the production of statistical studies of social problems. The other main bodies involved in this work were the Board of Trade, the War Office and the Admiralty, and the Poor Law Commission (though other departments were also producing social statistics, notably the Home Office and, from 1839, the Privy Council Committee on Education). The civil servants who directed these studies were often closely associated in outside organizations such as the Statistical Society of London, the Central Society of Education, and the Health of Towns Association. Most significant, however, was the fact that running through the publications of these men and their associates there was something like a common set of social attitudes leading to the advocacy of certain types of social reform.

It is now time to examine the statistical movement in early Victorian Britain.

[PART I]

Government Departments and Social Statistics 1832–52

[1]

The Statistical Department of the Board of Trade

The Statistical Department of the Board of Trade was founded in 1832 to improve and collate the growing number of returns made to Parliament in a routine manner or called for by individual M.P.s. In an era such as that of the great reform period of 1828–46 it was likely that an attempt would be made to provide a central agency for the generation of statistics demanded to support arguments over the necessity or otherwise of particular reforms. Apart from this, Lucy Brown, in her excellent study of the Board of Trade in the 1830s, has suggested a cogent reason which may have influenced official thinking. There was a great need for reliable information on provincial Britain, especially its trade and manufactures. Parliamentary debates had shown serious ignorance at the official level on the extent and nature of economic distress. While in office Sir Robert Peel, among others, had had cause to complain of the impossibility of obtaining information.[1]

The extent of the deficiency was perhaps brought home to the Board of Trade when James Deacon Hume, Secretary to the Board, was sent on a tour of observation through the principal seats of manufacture.[2] But the spur to action probably came from another official, William Jacob, the septuagenarian comptroller of corn returns.[3] In early 1832 he circulated a paper on statistics within the Board. The paper was returned to him but fortuitously is available to us, for in December 1834 and January 1835 he read it to the newly-formed Statistical Society of London since it was of general as well as departmental interest. The paper is revealing of the attitudes of the Board of Trade and the governing Whigs which led them to favour statistical studies. As Jacob explained,

> little statistical information has been collected, and that chiefly by the industry of the two Houses of Parliament, but that little has been so mingled with a vast mass of irrelevant, or unimportant, or tiresome details, and is scattered through such a number of

ponderous folio volumes, that it has presented an appalling labour to all but the most indefatigable inquirers. It is true that, of late years, accurate indexes have been framed to the parliamentary papers, which have given better facilities for references than were before afforded: but at the same time the number of the annual volumes have continued to increase, so that even with those helps, they present an array that requires courage to encounter.[4]

Jacob's complaint might well be echoed by the historian of the nineteenth century. But Jacob went further and put forward a classic argument which serves to tell us that behind much of the statistical movement that was evolving in the early 1830s lay more personal political motives. In the troubled situation of 1832 it was somewhat more than relevant to suggest that 'the best mode of allaying disquietude and of diffusing contentment on the subject of public affairs is an open and clear disclosure of their condition and management'. The prophylactic effect of statistical studies was so significant that Jacob repeated the point: 'A more general diffusion of accurate knowledge regarding the state of public affairs would tend to check that excitement and party spirit which has often been created by misrepresentation or exaggeration, and has produced an annoyance to the government, and at least a temporary disaffection of the public mind.'[5]

It would be premature at this time to try to delve deeper into what was meant by such loaded terms as 'diffusing contentment' and 'accurate knowledge' but the general drift is apparent. Given a full knowledge of the condition of the country, assent to the obviously correct principles of the existing government was a foregone conclusion. What was needed was a Statistical Department of the Board of Trade. Consequently it was decided to approach the Treasury.[6] It was explained that the purpose of the department would be 'to obtain and systematically arrange returns upon the Wealth, Commerce, and Industry of the United Kingdom'. Material covering the previous ten years was to be gathered together while it was hoped that by methods akin to those of the first four censuses (the letter was vague on this point) the department would be able to provide estimates of the produce of agriculture, mining, and industry. More specifically, there already existed grandiose if nebulous plans for the study of the currency, crime, insolvency, mendicity, education, county rates, church rates, poor rates, the distribution of funded property, savings banks, the tonnage using canals and artificial docks, as well as colonial and foreign topics.[7]

In its consent to the creation of a department the Treasury ignored this formidable list and simply agreed with the need for good information and the value of saving money by rationalization.⁸ George Richardson Porter was appointed to be in charge of the work for an initial period of three months.⁹ The man first approached was Charles Knight, at that stage at the peak of his precarious career as publisher to the Society for the Diffusion of Useful Knowledge (and hence well known to Lord Auckland, President of the Board of Trade).¹⁰ Knight recommended Porter, who had written a section on life assurance for one of the SDUK's publications, the *Companion to the Almanac*.¹¹ Porter, born in 1792, was a brother-in-law of Ricardo's but the significant fact about him was his membership of Henry Brougham's SDUK which brought him into contact with other members of the charmed circle of the Whig-Liberal intelligentsia who were to dominate the parliamentary enquiries and statistical investigations of the 1830s. Dr Brown has noted that Porter's own views were not necessarily settled in their final form in 1832 since in 1830 he had published a book on the sugar industry dedicated to the Marquis of Chandos and the standing committee of West Indian planters and merchants.¹² But the book said little or nothing in favour of protection and was an obvious attempt to salvage Porter's sugar-broking business, particularly by persuading the industry to adopt a patent he had taken out in 1828.¹³ Certainly, once Porter was inside the Board of Trade he 'emerged as a free-trader'.¹⁴ His views became so notorious that when he died suddenly in 1852 Disraeli remarked that his death 'was occasioned, I suppose, by the accession of a Protectionist Ministry'.¹⁵ A Liberal wit might well have replied that the truth was not greatly different since Porter had died of the aftermath of a gnat's sting.¹⁶

In 1832 all this lay in the future and it was not even clear whether the new section was planned to be permanent or not. Reorganization on a permanent footing did not take place until the end of 1833 by which time a Parliamentary Select Committee on Public Documents had considered the best means of providing information 'with a view to Economy, facility of Access, and clearness of Arrangement'.¹⁷ Its major recommendation was the extension of the Statistical Department in order to create a central statistical office.¹⁸ The recommendation was not immediately carried out since there was a conflict over who should head the office. Poulett Thomson, Vice-President of the Board, wanted J. R. McCulloch, his old tutor. Also in the field was John Marshall, Joseph Hume's candidate,¹⁹ who was preparing a voluminous summary of the parliamentary papers (published in 1833).²⁰ He had earlier written a large volume on the statistics of the British Empire published in 1825 under the aegis of a non-existent 'London Statistical Society'.²¹ Marshall was not in favour with the Whigs and Poulett Thomson was overruled. Porter was appointed, with Rawson of the Corn Department being transferred as his assistant.[22]

Like Porter, Rawson was to be very important in the statistical movement. Born in 1812, educated at Eton, at 17 he entered the Board of Trade, the post no doubt obtained because of the connections of his late father who had risen from obscurity to being an oculist to the Prince Regent and the dukes of Kent and Sussex in the late 1810s.[23] In 1830 the younger Rawson also became private secretary to the Vice-President of the Board of Trade, a post he continued to hold until 1841. In 1842 he left England to begin a long career in the colonial service which culminated in the governorships of the Bahamas and Windward Islands. On his retirement in 1875 he renewed his connection with the Statistical Society and was in the chair when Charles Booth gave his first paper to the Society in 1886. He did not die until 1899.[24]

The first action of the reorganized Department was to attempt to take over from the Home Office its responsibility for criminal statistics, which Porter had coveted since November 1833.[25] It was suggested that it would be desirable to obtain more accurate information than had been available hitherto on the number of persons committed for trial and the nature of their offences. A draft form of returns drawn up by Porter was sent with the letter.[26] Although ultimate control remained with the Home Office and its official in charge, Samuel Redgrave, Porter was successful in 1834-5 in getting the criminal statistics improved. But, as he pointed out to Adolphe Quetelet, the Belgian statistician, when the first returns appeared, 'I am by no means satisfied with these tables except as the beginning of improvement.' He hoped (a wish fulfilled) that the following year (1836) he would be able to give information on the education of criminals as well as extending the new tables to Scotland and Ireland.[27] He had already written, in May 1835, to Lord John Russell along these lines and obviously Russell concurred.[28]

It was one of the few successes of the Department. By the time of the permanent formation in early 1834 it was perhaps clear to Porter and his colleagues that there were narrow limits to what could be achieved by a government body. The evidence had been building up since the foundation of the Department in 1832. The surviving letter-book of the Department gives a clear picture of the failure of the high hopes of early 1832. Porter seems to have settled in and begun work in earnest in June 1832. Letters were sent to the National Debt Office, the Excise, the Stationer's Company, the Lord Mayor of London, the West India Docks, and the Treasury to obtain various returns.[29] These were mainly of a minor nature and the first hint of an intention to carry out the more grandiose schemes suggested in March did not come until the end of August. The Waterford Chamber of Commerce was the first to be approached (Ireland may have been chosen because there had been no account of Anglo-Irish trade since 1825). In his letter Porter explained that he wanted returns from the principal town of each area to form an impression of the industry, wealth, and resources of the surrounding county as well as of the condition of the population. He wanted the first returns to be retrospective to 1820 with quarterly returns in future, covering a wide variety of social and economic phenomena.[30] Over the next month similar letters were sent to eight other Irish towns, and also to Manchester and Birmingham. The immediate result of all this in the first volume of published papers (the *Tables*) was one small return from Waterford and one from Limerick, though Manchester sent returns some months later.[31]

Nevertheless, not all was black. Both the British and Foreign School Society and the National Society acceded to requests for their past annual reports.[32] But Porter was now wary of Chambers of Commerce. In December 1832 he wrote a 'private' letter to the secretary of the Glasgow Chamber of Commerce stating that before he wrote an official letter he would like to know on what points information could be provided and what other sources of information might be approached. He received a reply recommending James Cleland's works on Glasgow, which were useful but too limited for Porter's purposes. He wanted a retrospective account, regretted that the Chamber of Commerce would not supply it, and wondered if the Town Council could be of assistance.[33] In fact, Cleland proved the only source of value.[34] Porter also had a degree of success with Sheffield where the master cutler responded (in part) to a request for data.[35] In fact, insofar as Porter did get material on the provinces, he had to rely on scraps from individuals. The third volume of the *Tables* included data on Leicester and Bradford, in both instances from 'a principal Manufacturer' in each town, and on Newcastle from 'a Merchant'.[36] The most complete returns, however, were the Manchester ones mentioned above which covered vital statistics, savings banks, wages, prices, and cotton mills.[37]

A pattern was beginning to emerge in the annual tables with the inclusion of statistics from three different types of sources. First, and by far the largest, was the reproduction of other official data with occasional additions not found elsewhere from such sources as the Inspector-General of Imports and Exports, the Colonial Office, and the Home Office. Secondly, information was collected from certain institutions of a semi-official character. Bethlem, Greenwich, St Thomas's, St Bartholomew's, and St Luke's hospitals were tapped as sources of supply for the level of wages and prices. But for the provincial scene Porter was forced to rely, as he wrote to the Collector of Customs in Liverpool, on the 'co-operation of many intelligent and well-informed gentleman in various parts of the Kingdom'.[38]

Expectations from this third source were usually higher than the realities justified. Porter first wrote to Charles Pope of the Bristol Customs in August 1833 on the suggestion of the Collector of Customs there.[39] Pope indicated his willingness to co-operate but in January 1834 Porter wrote that he had had no reply to a letter sent four months previously.[40] Men like Pope seldom volunteered themselves for the tasks Porter expected them to carry out. Benjamin Gott of Leeds, for example, had been mentioned to Porter by Gott the younger when Porter was in Leeds in September 1833. Gott did not come up with anything. Despite occasional returns the scheme to provide provincial statistics must be accounted a failure. The government was not prepared to pay for a nationwide system of paid agents so Porter had to try to follow J. R. McCulloch's advice to have 'half a dozen Clelands'. But he did not succeed.[41] In fact, from early 1834 Porter seems to have largely dropped the plan. Gradually the correspondence registered in the letter-book of the Department became less frequent: eight letters in the first three months of 1836, one the next July, then a gap until January 1838. The last letter was dated August 1838 despite the fact that most of the book was still to be used.

This last letter itself shows the collapse of the final attempt to carry out a large scale plan. In May 1836 it was decided to try to obtain returns on the state of agriculture for the whole country. Bedfordshire was chosen as a test area and questionnaires were sent to 126 parishes. Returns came back from the clergy in no more than 27 cases and the project was abandoned. The little data that was obtained was printed in the first volume of the *Journal of the Statistical Society of London*. Porter consoled himself by appealing at the 1839 meeting of the British Association for the Advancement of Science for the systematic collection of agricultural statistics.[42]

The end of the grandiose scheme of March 1832 and its later elaborations did not of course mean the end of the work of the Statistical Department. The annual *Tables* grew in volume from year to year. Nor were they limited to collating into one volume statistics available elsewhere but in scattered form throughout the blue books. In the *Tables* for 1839, for example, there were 114 tables of criminal statistics, 87 of which derived from local police returns in London, Liverpool, Hull, and Dublin; while there were 79 tables on hospitals, including many on the duration of sickness and other medical questions.⁴³ The main fault of these tables is their apparent aimlessness: everything was printed that came to hand. Thus in the *Tables* for 1845 there appeared a particularly detailed set of tables on crime in Manchester, down to the amount of money taken from drunks by the police and returned to them when sober, the number of public houses with musical entertainment, and the number licensed to keep billiard and bagatelle tables.⁴⁴ The importance of such work in the government's mind may be gauged from the fact that when a replacement was needed for the promoted Porter in 1847 the man chosen was Albany Fonblanque, editor of the *Examiner*, a man who had no statistical experience.⁴⁵ The admittedly politically biased Disraeli saw Fonblanque as 'an imbecile as a man of business'.⁴⁶

The collection of much useless material was accompanied by an inability to provide useful, even necessary, statistics. As Lucy Brown points out, 'there is no sign' in times of need such as 1839 and 1842 'that the Government had a firmer knowledge of the economic situation in the provincial centres than it had ten years previously'.⁴⁷ Dr Brown puts much of the failure down to a certain 'narrow vision' inherent in the 'intellectual attitude dominant in the Board of Trade'. There is much in this and it is apparent that within the field of economic statistics Porter and his associates could not put forward a proper plan of action.⁴⁸ But in social statistics, even allowing for the fact that all social statisticians of the 1830s and 1840s had a 'narrow vision' it is clear that the failure was one of means. By the end of our period this failure was publicly recognized. In 1850 the then President of the Board of Trade admitted that the Department was 'susceptible of a great deal of improvement'.⁴⁹ The 1854 report on the Board analysed the reasons perceptively. The Department had been unable to become a central statistical office providing all the facts required by Parliament because of the delay in some of its publications (necessitating motions for returns which would give priority to one section of documents), because of the 'want of proper adaptation of the form of others to the requirements of the present day', because of the sheer bulk of the annual publications, which daunted readers, and because of the existence of other departments, both old and new, for social problems which retained their independent statistical functions.⁵⁰ Much of the responsibility for failure, therefore, lay outside the competence of Porter and the Statistical Department. Despite the 'narrow vision' Porter's major book, the *Progress of the Nation*, suggests that given the opportunity and the means the Department would have achieved more.⁵¹

Progress of the Nation was in many ways a scrappy book. The sections on vital statistics were dull and lacking in originality, frequently very uncritical of existing source material and (justifying Dr Brown) seemingly more concerned to chart progress than to discuss the situation in depth. Yet, in the 1851 third edition, these sections had greatly improved, indicating that part of the problem had been simple ignorance. For all his limitations Porter was interested in collecting better social statistics, notably statistics of crime and education. By early 1834 he may have had doubts about the possibilities within the existing Board of Trade.

Porter was not alone in the Board in realizing this, nor was he the only one to wish to extend the scope of statistical enquiries. In January 1834 Poulett Thomson was in Manchester and held a conference with James Phillips Kay of the infant Manchester Statistical Society. Kay was told that there was no chance of the government adopting an extensive scheme of enquiry. The organization required was beyond the means of government,[52] the electors would not stand the expense, and in any case Britain was a free country in which such governmental snooping would be resented and resisted. Thus it was better for voluntary associations to take up the task. That there was a task was obvious: the late session of Parliament had shown, in Poulett Thomson's view, a great deal of ignorance the remedy for which was statistical surveys in order that 'vague generalizations and personal impressions should, as far as possible, be avoided'.

Thomson put forward a plan for statistical surveys which gives a clear indication to add to Jacob's paper of what had been initially intended when the Department was set up. It was suggested that districts of similar type should be covered so that

> the number, age, sex, employment and wages of each member of the family might be ascertained – the number of those employed in each family – the number of families unemployed in the district – the number dependent on the Parish or receiving aid from it – the state of the dwellings as far as convenience – the number of children educated ... the number who can read ... whether the inmates are members of any Benefit Society – subscribers to any Library or Mechanics' Institute – or have any amusement ...

In addition note would be taken of the prices of clothes and provisions, the consumption of meat and 'ardent spirits', and the use of cheap publications.[53] Despite the breadth of subjects suggested for enquiry a coherent if limited view of society can be discerned in Thomson's suggestions, stressing both environmental and moralistic approaches to the problems of society.

Poulett Thomson was trying to achieve privately what he could not achieve publicly. This was typical of the relationship between the activities of the reformers in government and their involvement in private societies and royal commissions and select committees. The same men tend to recur in all three avenues leading to the generation of social statistics. G. R. Porter was to become the leading member of the Statistical Society of London while also feeding information to other reformers involved in commissions and committees.[54] William Farr was another example of a man who had recourse to the Statistical Society of London when the confines of the General Register Office proved too limiting. But throughout the period from 1838 to 1852 that office was one of the most important sources for social statistics and Farr used his position to argue for a wide range of public health reforms.

The Work of the General Register Office

Mid-1837 may be taken as the time when England and Wales (but not Scotland) entered the modern era of vital statistics for it was then that the Registration Act of 1836 came into force. Under the Act a General Register Office was to index and collate the returns of births, deaths, and marriages from a two-tiered system of registrars and superintendent registrars. Registration of births was not compulsory but the registrars could seek information which then had to be supplied. Registration of deaths was compulsory. The superintendent registrars were to make quarterly returns to the General Register Office and the Registrar-General was to make an annual abstract of the number of births, deaths, and marriages to be laid before Parliament.[1] The Act did not apply to Scotland – attempts to pass Bills for Scotland failed in 1834 and 1835 and Scotland was not to have civil registration until 1855.

It had been intended that the Act should go into effect on 2 March 1837 but the delay in the formation of the new poor law unions made it expedient to postpone implementation until 1 July.[2] By that time the General Register Office had five men in the permanent establishment. Lord John Russell's brother-in-law, T. H. Lister, 'a very good novelist who cared nothing for the subject' according to Edwin Chadwick,[3] was Registrar-General. Thomas Mann was the senior clerk and there were three other clerks. William Farr was in charge of the statistics branch but was not placed on the permanent establishment until mid-1839. Under him there was initially only one clerk, two more being added in January 1838 and five more by the time of Lister's death in 1842. The return of the employees in the whole office in 1847 implies that a drastic reduction in the establishment took place when Major George Graham succeeded Lister. Twelve clerks out of the 68 appointed up to Lister's death were 'reduced' whereas none appear to have suffered that fate among the 16 appointed up to April 1847. Moreover, Graham made no appointments in his first year, and only two in the following two years.[4] Lister was probably mainly responsible for the early over-expansion. He must be suspected of taking on a large number of clerks, especially in the records and indexes branch, who were of good Whig connections but superfluous to requirements.

At the end of 1846 the office comprised four officers: Graham, Mann, and two inspectors. Beneath them were four branches – correspondence, accounts and register books, records and indexes, and statistics – each headed by a first clerk, though Farr had the additional and unusual distinction of the courtesy title, 'Compiler of the Abstracts'. Farr headed a team of three senior clerks and 10 juniors plus 10 temporary clerks working on the rearrangement of the 1841 Census statistics by registration areas. Altogether the office had four officers, 17 first and senior clerks, 30 juniors, and eight messengers on the establishment plus Farr's 10 temporaries, six sorters of transcripts, one labourer, four transcribers, and seven indexers not on the establishment. This relatively large piece of centralized administrative machinery (by the standards of the time) had grown by a process determined by patronage, population expansion, the continuing accumulation of records, the 1841 census (which was supervised by Horace Mann), and an expansion in the office's activities which remained unsanctioned by statute. The local network consisted of 621 superintendent registrars and 2189 registrars. Altogether, it cost nearly £73,000 in 1846.[5]

The quality of the local officials is not easy to ascertain. Criticism was not long in arising. Edwin Chadwick, whose plans to control their appointment and the work of the new office had been foiled,[6] found some of them intolerable. Chadwick singled out a 'Calvinistic Dissenter' in Manchester who favoured the separation of Church and State, a 'socialist' in Birmingham, and an itinerant nonconformist preacher, anti-corn law lecturer, and temperance man in Leeds.[7] *The Times* also took exception to the local officials in reporting the case of a woman prosecuted for failing to give the particulars of birth when requested. It luridly made an issue of the idea that a 'coarse and greasy district registrar' should ask questions 'which circumstances might make of the most delicate and distressing nature'.[8]

The local officials, greasy, socialist, or otherwise, were chosen by the Boards of Guardians on the basis of guidelines issued by the General Register Office. These guidelines were vague, the major requirements being solvency and residence (even the latter could be waived).[9] Of the 2193 registrars appointed by the end of 1838 just under half were poor law officers (1021, including 416 medical officers). The remaining 1172 comprised 111 medical men, 262 in other professions, 437 'in trade', and 362 'others'. The registrar at Nailsworth (Gloucestershire) was an auctioneer and appraiser, secretary to a loan society, agent of a savings bank, treasurer to the 'Society for the Prosecution of Felons', and a general house agent.[10] Jobbery probably played a part in many appointments: the superintendent registrar of St Luke's, Leeds was the son of John Wilks, the man most responsible for the passage of the Registration Act as well as vestry clerk of St Luke's.[11] It is not surprising that after Major Graham came to power doubts about the quality of the registrars led to the appointment of four inspectors.[12] By 1846 two were on permanent establishment. How much they improved efficiency is a moot point, given the regrettable lack of departmental records.

One of the inspectors' main tasks was to find out how well the registration of births was being accomplished. Apart from the exclusion of Scotland (and Ireland) the main defect of the 1836 Act was the voluntary nature of births registration, the result of a last-minute amendment in the Lords. The deficiency was widely recognized but could not be remedied until Anglican resentment against civil registration had substantially diminished. In fact few changes occurred in the administration of civil registration in its early decades as a result of officials' discovering previously unsuspected defects. In 1836 the statistician supporters of civil registration wanted a compulsory system covering the whole of the United Kingdom. This, with concessions to regionalism, is what was created by stages over the succeeding generation.

The problem of births registration was in some ways one of public relations for the General Register Office. It was necessary, in order to justify the system, to prove that civil registration was more complete than parochial registration. It was also necessary to be able to argue that room for improvement would always exist while births registration was voluntary. The first annual report maintained such a balance, showing that in the fourth quarter of registration the births total was running about one-fifth ahead of that for the parochial system: this, despite the fact that baptisms just before and after the introduction of civil registration may have been higher than usual as a result of a campaign by some members of the Church.[13] The office could report a 'considerable and progressive advance' to superiority over the old system despite difficulties of novelty, indifference, ignorance, and 'extensive and stubborn opposition'.[14]

Little further was said in the second report and by the third Lister and Farr were able to state that the 500,000 per annum mark had been passed in 1839–40.[15] But the fourth report estimated that 'several thousand' births were still unregistered and Parliament was reminded that completeness was impossible without compulsion.[16] The extent of under-registration was taken up in earnest in the sixth annual report in conjunction with an analysis of illegitimacy rates in various countries. In Europe, illegitimacy rates in various countries were two to nine times as great in the capital city as in the country at large, whereas in England the rate for London (3.2 per cent) was less than half the national figure (6.7 per cent).[17] Despite various disturbing factors it was difficult for Farr to avoid the conclusion that there was a considerable under-registration of illegitimate births in the larger English cities, especially London.[18] In fact only one of the registration districts of London had a rate above the national average and the 10 lowest figures for the country were all returned by London districts.[19] The highest rates tended to be recorded where people had the greatest difficulty in concealing their private affairs, the lowest where it was very simple to do so.

Moreover, for 1838–45 the registered birth rate per thousand women aged 15 to 44 was 109.2 for London compared with 134.3 for the country as a whole.[20] If we assume an under-registration for London of 20 per cent and no other under-registration in the country, then the birth rates per thousand fecund women would be raised to 136.5 and 140 respectively. Professor D. V. Glass, using more sophisticated methods, has estimated that registration in the period should be multiplied by 1.094 to arrive at births.[21] Applying this multiplier to non-London births for 1841–5 and allowing for 20 per cent under-registration in London gives national figures of 10.1 per cent under-registration, 148 births per thousand women aged 15 to 44 and a crude birth rate of 35.2 per thousand. If we adopt the round figures of 10 per cent under-registration outside London, and 25 per cent for London we obtain an overall under-registration for 1841–5 of 11.3 per cent, a crude birth rate of 36.3 per thousand and fertility rates of 148 per thousand women aged 15 to 44 in London, and 152 per thousand in the country as a whole.[22]

There are endless permutations but a tentative conclusion may be suggested. Professor Glass's suggested multiplier for 1841–5 (and, one suspects, for 1846–50) is probably too low, as he himself indicated. An under-registration of 10 per cent or slightly more for the whole country for the first period seems likely. For London the under-registration was probably nearer 20 to 25 per cent with a sliding scale of adjustment down to nearly complete registration in rural areas. If fertility levels remained unchanged then we may deduce that under-registration was still at about nine per cent in 1846–50 and six per cent in 1851–5.[23] Much of this under-registration would arise from the illegitimate births of a segment of the urban lower-class population which largely remained outside the scope of government. The marriages of this group were often *de facto* insofar as they had any permanence and the resulting children were illegitimate and unregistered. Even where the marriages were formally legalized there was probably a weaker tendency to bother with registration.

More births would of course mean more deaths (via infant deaths) so that it is doubtful whether deaths registration was quite as complete as the 98 per cent figure claimed by Farr in the first annual report.[24] But under-registration of non-infant deaths was certainly negligible and the new system was clearly far more accurate than the old. Thus Farr and his colleagues were able to concentrate on what they considered to be the most serious weakness of the early registration of deaths, the incompleteness and inaccuracy of the information supplied under the head 'cause of death'. The problem divided itself into two parts. Firstly, medical practitioners were urged to fill in the forms since a few did not bother to do so. Secondly, Farr had to devise some means of classifying the material. For the former he relied, in the first annual report, on emphasizing the benefits of registering the causes of death as well as printing an open letter from the leaders of the medical profession[25] which had previously appeared in medical journals and was backed by editorials.[26] The letter was reprinted in a circular sent to all physicians, surgeons, and apothecaries in July 1845 and subsequently published in the seventh annual report.[27] There was still a hard core of opposition, for the *Medical Times* in an editorial reported receiving several letters against registration and called for co-operation.[28] It was backed by *The Times*, which reversed its earlier scepticism.[29] The exhortations faded away as did, presumably, the few recalcitrant doctors.

More serious, from both the contemporary and historical standpoints, were the obstacles encountered in devising a satisfactory means of classification. Doctors might fill in the forms but what they filled in could be vague and meaningless. Returns also had to be compared if the great scheme of investigating disease – specific rates of mortality was to be carried out. Farr set about the job immediately in the first annual report with a new statistical nosology. The most common nosology in use at the time was that of William Cullen, the great Edinburgh physician of the third quarter of the eighteenth century. Farr saw it as not only outdated but ill-adapted to statistical purposes. The basic principle which Farr tried to establish was that unclear distinctions should be abolished. This was a necessary precondition for Farr, who referred to his plan in one of those striking phrases which are strewn across the early reports:

'classification is another name for generalization, and successive generalizations constitute the laws of the natural sciences.' The desire for uniformity took precedence over completeness since in the first half year of registration *some* cause of death had been assigned for 141,607 out of 148,701 deaths.[30]

In the appendix to the fourth report the material presented in 1839 was modified and the original statistical nosology was refined and extended.[31] Farr explained that he had no basic dissatisfaction with the early registration but wished to make improvements in detail. The new nosology received a mixed review in the *London Medical Gazette*, which criticized ambiguities in some of the names as well as some of the causes.[32] Farr, however, persevered with it and the circular of July 1845 offered a free copy of the nosology on request and enclosed a book of blank death certificate forms which included spaces for primary and secondary causes. These circulars were sent to the registrars for distribution.[33] There are signs of decreased concern after this, partly because there were fewer inadequate registrations and partly because Farr's interest shifted – he became less single-minded about the analysis of the causes of death.

In the seventh annual report Farr was able to compare civil registration with the burial registers for the years 1838–40. In 1838 the burial registers were deficient by a margin of 14.6 per cent which increased to a constant level of nearly 15.4 per cent for the next two years. Civil registration was justified.[34] Farr had never doubted this, even over the registration of the cause of death, where it was agreed that there was a greater margin of error. With slight reservations we may also agree that the totals were nearly complete. The cause of death is a different matter since, given the state of medical science in the 1840s, there would be a considerable amount of misdiagnosis. It is instructive to note that a recent study of the causes of death assigned respectively by clinicians and by pathologists after a post-mortem, showed that both gave the same underlying cause of death in only 45.3 per cent of the deaths though only one-quarter of the cases involved disagreements over facts and there was a tendency to compensatory errors.[35] Perhaps, therefore, Farr's statistics of the causes of death should be treated with caution.

Farr probably realized that the statistics were useful only in broad outline for he seldom utilized the minute medical and geographical sub-divisions which in the earliest reports appeared in the massive following tables. These reports stand as a testimonial to one of the great medical statisticians. William Farr was born in 1807, the son of a Shropshire farm labourer. His parents migrated to a local village to become servants and at the age of two Farr was adopted by the local squire, an elderly bachelor. The move was advantageous for at an early age it brought Farr his first patron. In 1826 he was indentured to a Shrewsbury physician. In 1829 he went to Paris and stayed there for some time. In 1832 he gained the licence of the Society of Apothecaries, his only formal qualification, after attending classes at University College, London. For a while he was a house surgeon at the Shrewsbury infirmary but after his marriage he set up practice in London. Probably he was not very successful. However, he was involved in a number of literary ventures including editing journals and was responsible for the statistical work in Sir James Clark's book on consumption in 1835. His success, then, was dependent upon patronage but his varied background ensured a great sympathy for and understanding of human problems, especially those of the lower classes. Furthermore, in 1837, after only three years of marriage, his first wife died of consumption.[36] Behind the reports, with their insistence upon the quantity of needless suffering and early mortality, may lie unrevealed personal emotion.

The range of subjects covered in the reports is very wide indeed. The breadth of erudition displayed astounds the over-specialized scholar of the late twentieth century, the battery of epigrams overwhelms the historian attempting to sift and summarize the material in the more important sections. To summarize is, in fact, to do an injustice to Farr, the assistants he so brilliantly directed, and even George Graham who, as the second Registrar-General, gave him able backing. There is little dross in the early reports, which entitle Farr to wider recognition and a place among the small band of truly excellent practising social scientists of the nineteenth century.

Farr's works, little read today, may even have been little read in his own time. The annual reports and appendices for which he was responsible (whoever signed them), do not arouse antiquarian interest or figure among desert island literary survival packs.[37] There are no entries under his name in dictionaries of quotations. Yet, had he had the flair for publicity of a Chadwick, a Simon or a Kay-Shuttleworth some at least of his more striking phrases might have found a place. An undated remark provides the basic key to Farr's ideas: 'There is a certain relation between the value of life and the care bestowed on its preservation.'[38] There are many other phrases worthy of being singled out: 'diseases are the iron index of misery';[39] 'the aggregation of mankind in towns is not inevitably disastrous';[40] 'To save the life of one human being is meritorious; but here are thousands to be saved in every part of the kingdom from sickness and untimely death';[41] 'man's course is determined by opinion; and opinion uninformed by science is full of delusions, wayward and prone to exaggeration';[42] 'knowledge will banish panic'.[43] They are signs of one of the best Victorian rationalist reforming minds in full operation. Further than this, Farr was one of the clearest exponents of a considered environmentalist theory. He believed that poverty and despair were the result of poor living conditions and that their inevitable concomitants were high rates of disease. These could be partially reduced by sanitary measures but otherwise would have to wait upon rising standards of living. Farr never succumbed to the *monodeism* of a Chadwick.

Like many great social scientists Farr did not develop these theories principally as a result of his investigations; rather, he followed certain types of investigations because he was convinced by these theories. In a long and revealing passage in the first report he makes this apparent. Moreover, the work he carried out to prove his theories and its subsequent publication was not, strictly speaking, sanctioned by the 1836 Act, as was noted in the instance of the causes of death in the second annual report.[44] This barrier was at first circumvented by the device of the 'letter' which Farr 'wrote' to the Registrar-General and which was then reprinted as an appendix to the official report. It is in the letter in the first report that Farr issued his manifesto:

> Diseases are more easily prevented than cured, and the first step to their prevention is the discovery of their exciting causes. The registry will show the agency of these causes by numerical facts, and measure the intensity of their influence. The annual rate of mortality in some districts will be found to be 4 per cent., while in another set of circumstances, which the registry will indicate, they do not live more than 25 years. In these wretched districts, nearly 8 per cent. are constantly sick, and the energy of the whole population is withered to the roots. Their arms are weak, their bodies wasted, and their sensations embittered by privation and suffering. Half the life is passed in infancy, sickness, and dependent helplessness. In exhibiting the high mortality, the diseases by which it is occasioned, and the exciting causes of the disease, the abstract of the registers will prove, that while a part of the sickness is inevitable, and a part can only be expected to disappear before progressive social amelioration, a considerable proportion of the sickness and deaths may be suppressed by the general adoption of hygienic measures which are in actual but partial operation. It may be affirmed without great risk of exaggeration, that it is possible to reduce the annual deaths in England and Wales by

30,000 and to increase the vigour (may I add the industry and wealth?) of the population in an equal proportion.[45]

This is not the voice of a man seeking answers to new questions but that of a man wishing to state accurately his theses about the nature of urban society and demonstrate them to the public by irrefutable, government-collected statistics. With only six months' material to hand Farr was prepared to state that, all else being equal, mortality increased with density and that where density and affluence were equal then mortality depended upon the effectiveness of waste disposal. Unfortunately, his own tables showed that the densest areas were not always the most unhealthy, a fact that Farr interpreted to mean that mortality could be reduced by artificial agencies.[46]

The next year he returned to the subject armed with a complete year's figures which enabled him to elaborate upon the 'true causes' of high mortality. Again the blame was laid on overcrowding and insanitary conditions which could be countered to a considerable extent by effective sewage disposal and by the 'dilution of inevitable exhalations'.[47] Farr realized that social reform could best be carried out if a sound economic rationale could be provided. He therefore came up with a scheme for recycling sewage for manure, which was later to be taken over by Chadwick, who was always adept at inventing other people's ideas.[48] Farr went further in 1840 and tried to design statistically controlled experiments which would enable him to separate out of the influences of sex, location, climate, seasons, and epidemics on mortality.

The expansion of subjects was continued in the third annual report with a long discussion of violent and sudden deaths, an examination of the influence of seasons on mortality, of mortality differences by sex, deaths in London hospitals, age-specific rates for various causes of death, urban-rural differentials, influence of locality and occupation, and epidemics. He also extended the brief analysis, in the second report, of the age at marriage.[49] The discussions of violent and sudden deaths were paradigms of the Farr method. Firstly, Farr demonstrated that violent deaths were often related to occupation. Then, while conceding that some violent deaths were almost unavoidable, he reeled off a list of reasons and questions directed towards the assertion that mortality could be greatly reduced. If some mines and factories were better than others then all could be improved. Mines could be better ventilated, people who work at heights should not drink, research might make cotton and linen less combustible, fireguards should be used, poisons and drugs should be harder to acquire and be kept out of the reach of children, people should learn to swim. Other violent deaths could be averted. Suicide and murder were often committed as imitative acts and thus newspaper stories of violence should be discontinued for it was highly questionable whether 'the advantages of publicity counterbalance the evils attendant on one such death'. High suicide rates were also associated with unhealthy areas and could be reduced by pure air and exercise.[50] In any event there should be much deeper research into the circumstances surrounding any sudden death.[51] What is striking about all this is not so much its humanity as how little the tediously collected and collated statistics were required. The real function of the General Register Office was to be another government-sponsored pulpit for reforming ideas.

In the fourth annual report Farr was able to complete one piece of research which he had touched on the previous year. With the results of the 1841 Census to hand he tabulated all deaths by age, sex, and successively small units of area, down to the sub-district level. One other feature was an essay on the growth of population notable for its anti-Malthusian approach.[52] The last principal point of interest was a discussion of the numbers that marry and remarry.[53] Otherwise there were no major innovations.

The following year, 1843, was one of crisis. It was a crisis of vague dimensions in retrospect but the office was under the impression that there was a move for the repeal of the Marriage and Registration Acts and a nervous collection of newspaper clippings was made to add to those previously collected.[54] Understandably, the fifth annual report is something of a tour de force. The investigation into marriage and remarriage continued.[55] The seasonal influence on mortality was summarized into a neat little law which stated that the annual mortality equalled twice that of the spring plus the autumn and equalled twice that of summer plus winter.[56] Neat but useless, and therefore no justification for government expenditure. What was a justification was Farr's glittering centrepiece, the discussion of mortality tables and the presentation of English Life Table No 1. This was fanfared by a history of life-tables in which the nations of Europe were exhorted to channel their chauvinism into a rivalry for the production of the best official statistics.[57] The methods used in the calculation of the table as well as its terminology and potential utility were explained. This last gave Graham and Farr the opportunity to compliment the middle classes on their 'favourable reaction...on the highest departments of science, and on the physical condition of the people' since England led in actuarial science.[58] The supporters were rather blatantly being rallied.

Actuarial applications were only one aspect of the life-table. It was also seen as representative of the age, of the Victorians, triumphant in their enlightened, reforming attitude to social conditions just as their forbears had conquered the ignorance of the heavens. In that rationalist dawn of the social sciences Farr could foretell the future on the basis of laws supposedly as immutable as those of Kepler and Newton. He predicted that 9398 out of each 100,000 born in 1841 would be alive in 1921, a prediction he likened to Halley's confidence in the return of the comet:

> What new Halley of the vast realms of aether in which that comet disappeared? Upon what grounds did he dare to expect its reappearance from the distant regions of the heavens? Halley believed in the constancy of the laws of nature... Although we little know the labours, the privations, the happiness or misery, the calms or tempests, which are prepared for the next generation of Englishmen, we entertain little doubt that about 9000 of the 100,000 of them will be found alive at the Census in 1921.[59]

It was quite inconsistent with the notion that mortality could be reduced but that inconsistency was immediately set down in print. While their necks were still craned towards the golden future promised by the Registrar-General the sewage was lapping round the feet of Englishmen. Thanks to the Office, this problem too could be solved. By the study of differential rates of mortality useful information was given 'not only to those professedly engaged in sanatory and statistical inquiries, but to the inhabitants of the respective districts, who are really the parties most interested'.[60] A modest claim compared with an earlier one that stated bluntly that the barrier to ascertaining 'the influence of external causes upon health and longevity, has now been overcome in this country by arduous labours of scientific inquiries, and by the conjoint enumerations of the ages of the population and the registration of Births and Deaths'.[61] To prove the claim there were graphs of life-tables for England and for Surrey, Liverpool, and London (with an enormous age-axis but still the first graphs to appear in the reports),[62] 28 pages of deaths by ages, and 100 pages of deaths by cause, age, and locality.[63] In what was by now an established pattern many people were shown to fall short of their allotted life-span from remediable causes. Instead of 70 years they had but 26 to 45 and so were deprived of

> years of childhood and youth principally – years of toil too and poverty perhaps, but of life – years also of manhood in its prime, wisdom in its maturity, virtue in its height of usefulness and glory. The facts... will be confirmed by the still more extended data

which are every year accumulating under the present system of Registration. In the mean time enough has been advanced to direct public attention to the 'hidden pitfalls', which had so long lain concealed, which destroy every year thousands of lives, and which it is believed admit, to a considerable extent, of removal by the judicious application of sanatory measures.[64]

Clearly no man of heart or sense could fail to support the Office in its endeavours.

This was Graham's first full report, though written by Farr. It was a ham performance of heroic dimensions wringing out every last drop of sympathy and support for the Office. Like most ham performances it concealed inadequacies. Farr's work may not have added as much to knowledge about the causes of death as he claimed though it may have proved things to non-specialists about which they were previously dubious. One must take a very hard look at Farr's insistence that 100 pages of tables on the causes of death formed the indispensable statistical concordance to the local administrator's text-book. Nor is there a great deal of evidence to demonstrate that the early reports had a major effect on the public conscience. They seem to have lacked the immediacy which gave Chadwick's 1842 Sanitary Report its great impact though, of course, Chadwick and others used the registration data to support their arguments.

Moreover, as Farr's writings became more scientific the reports were to that extent decreased in the universality of their appeal. The fifth report may be taken as the dividing line. The part intended for the general public, that part which was published over Graham's name, is full of generalized statements of little substance designed to prove the worth of the Office. The problems of the causation of death, which had originally dominated Farr's research, were stated to have been solved. On the other hand, Farr's appendix included a splendid treatise on life-tables which must have been incomprehensible to all but a handful of readers. The application of the theory of differences and interpolation to the construction of life-tables was treated in an elegant passage.[65] Only after this did Farr proceed to less technical questions. High infantile mortality (said Farr, dealing with new questions) could be controlled by better training of nurses and midwives.[66] Other mortality differentials were generalized into equations showing Farr's shift from practical to theoretical questions, from application to methodology. Life could be expressed in terms of seven parameters – drink, food, medicine, clothing, firing, lodging, and cleansing. Income divided by the cost of these multiplied by the mean physiological duration of life equalled life expectancy. A general identity for mortality and density of population was also calculated. Hence the density variable was controlled to reveal the impact of other factors.[67] Farr, challenging Chadwick, put forward his own solutions to high urban mortality rates: more hospitals, better sewage disposal, and the equalization of poor rates and other local taxes in large local authorities.[68] In this way poverty, which caused widespread 'depravity of mind and habits', would be eliminated, although it would require generations.[69]

The report concluded in what can best be described as a proto-Booth-style survey of living conditions in London. Circulars were sent to the registrars of the 125 registration districts of London in October 1842. Their primary purpose was to compare areas of high mortality (down to the street and house level) with the drainage, density, occupations, earnings, food, firing, and moral habits of the people in those areas. The 120 returns obtained by the end of October were reprinted but the lack of a framework in which they could be placed for useful comparative purposes rendered abortive one of the most interesting projects launched in this period.[70]

Despite this failure the fifth report represents both a turning and a high point of the first decade or so in the life of the General Register Office. A slight loss of momentum is discernible after this. Farr did not settle down in the early years to a routine of producing annual statistics on the same problems but tended to move on to further questions once he was reasonably satisfied with the reliability of his answers. In the sixth report, as we have seen, he dealt mainly with foreign returns, especially those on illegitimacy. He furthered his work on life-tables and added tables of insurance premiums for males and females of different ages. Little space was devoted to other topics, including the analysis of the causes of death.

The last two topics worked themselves out within the next three reports. In the eighth report Farr carried out an excellent dissection of the Northampton Tables which were still used by most insurance offices.[71] As for the causes of death it was clear that Farr had lost interest, at least temporarily. There was little comment in the sixth report and in the seventh and eighth the figures were given for London only. By the ninth report they were not included at all but were reserved for the weekly publications for London and were not included again in the parliamentary reports until 1857.

Attention had shifted to three topics: education, marriage, and methodology. The first was covered by the proportion of people signing the marriage registers with a mark: this Farr took as an index of literacy. The seventh report dealt in part with this and Farr produced statistics on it for many years.[72] As for marriage itself Farr demonstrated in the eighth and ninth reports a close correlation between marriage rates and economic fluctuations.[73] The main significance, however, of the reports of these years lies in their treatment of the methods of collecting demographic data, in itself an indication of Farr's loss of enthusiasm for his first concerns. He was like an intelligent boy with a building set he had had for some time. Kit No 1 was fun and absorbing for a time but its possibilities had been exhausted and he now wanted more advanced kits with which to build more complex models.

In the seventh report the extras requested were registers of migration and annual revision of the census lists,[74] the recording of the age of the mother at marriage and at the birth of her children,[75] and the extension of civil registration to Scotland and Ireland.[76] Farr also designed a complete new kit with a rearrangement of the 1841 census material for Kent in which the population was enumerated by sex and the districts by number of houses, area, and land-type acording to successively smaller units of registration districts, sub-districts, and parishes. The same geographical divisions were gone through by sex and age and then the divisions were changed to parliamentary cities, boroughs, and counties and the processes repeated. Finally, the population in institutions was counted and classified.[77] Part of this work was continued in the very long (462 pp.) appendix to the ninth annual report. In it were the rate of increase, population, deaths, and death-rates by registration divisions, registration counties, and districts; population by sex and number of houses by districts and sub-districts from the census of 1841, and the population by age and sex in the parliamentary counties for the census years 1801–41.[78] Farr's 10 temporary junior clerks had earned their money.

The concentration on improving the methods of collection and presentation of demographic statistics was shown in the tenth annual report not by any new material but by the total absence of Farr's usual appendix. The report was restricted to 13 pages of abstracts and official comments which set the model for the next few years.[79] Farr, with Horace Mann, had moved on to preparing directly for the 1851 Census which was to be a showpiece for mid-nineteenth-century English demography. The early phase of civil registration had come to an end.

It was an end which was more like what the beginning ought to have been than the beginning actually was. The brief tenth report of 1849 is what might have been expected from the clause in the 1836 Act laying down the requirement for the presentation to Parliament of an annual abstract. Instead, the 'annual abstract' had grown to mammoth volumes of up to 500 pages which collectively formed one of the nearest things to a periodical encyclopaedia that has ever been issued by a British government department. In this chapter we have mentioned but a few of the many questions touched on or fully discussed in the reports and only the barest outlines of those studied have been given. Farr's multi-faceted endeavour was a source of both strength and weakness. Strength in that it entitles Farr to be regarded as the greatest British statistician of his time. Weakness in that the Office could not properly perform the functions of 10 sociology departments and a number of research units on its own, nor was it meant to. For the historian all the data is of value but for the contemporary the resources and arguments may have been spread too thinly over too many causes to have had a great impact on public consciousness. It is not the Registrar-General's annual reports which spring to mind when one thinks of the formative influences on the development of the reforming social conscience of the mid-nineteenth century. Nevertheless, Farr was, like the statistical movement as a whole, a part of the drive to convert the political nation to a particular set of reforms. Moreover, his work did provide ammunition for other forces in the battle and therefore may have contributed to what small victories were won by the end of our period.

[3]

The Health of the Armed Forces

The General Register Office was not the only official source of vital and medical statistics in the early Victorian period. Apart from the familiar example of the great public health enquiries (discussed in the next chapter) there appeared a series of reports on the health of army and navy personnel. The army statistics take precedence both in timing and expertise. Their genesis is clear. The first report was on the health of the troops in the West Indies. This had been giving cause for concern for some time and in 1834 the Deputy Inspector-General of Army Hospitals, Sir Andrew Halliday, wrote to the Secretary of State for War.[1] Halliday claimed in a pamphlet of 1839 that he was responsible for the idea of the reports. This claim should be placed in the context that the pamphlet was an attack upon the choice of people outside the Army Medical Department to prepare the reports. Halliday felt his department would have made a better job. This is doubtful for, as Halliday himself admits, the public had a low estimation of the department. Nor was Halliday the only person to urge summarization of the medical officers' returns. Sir James McGrigor, Director-General of the department, had repeatedly called for a digest to be made of the folio volumes of returns starting in 1816.[2]

Nothing might have been done had not a specific issue arisen – the alleged unhealthiness of the lower floor of the officers' barracks in the Bahamas – which resulted in a medical board being set up in October 1835.[3] Underlying this seemingly trivial matter was the whole question of the causation of disease on foreign stations and the best means of reducing the high mortality among officers and men. At the same time the adequacy of the diet of the troops was under consideration (having first been discussed in the West India Commissariat in September 1835).[4] Consequently in October 1835 the Secretary of State for War, Viscount Howick, determined upon an enquiry into the health of the troops, designed to reduce the loss of life.[5] Henry Marshall was placed in charge of the operation.

Marshall was a man of some 60 years of age. His father had been a relatively poor inhabitant of Stirlingshire. Marshall the younger studied medicine at Glasgow, afterwards joining the navy and then, in 1805, transferring to the army. For a man of little social standing he rose high, to the post of Deputy Inspector-General of Army Hospitals in 1830.[6] Over the next few years he published a number of articles on army statistics in the *Edinburgh Medical and Surgical Journal*. Marshall did not anticipate an official survey for in a paper on the French infantry he expressed the hope that the Statistical Society of London would study the vital statistics of various classes in society.[7] Nevertheless, he had already used the manuscript returns of the medical officers and was an obvious choice to head Howick's proposed enquiry.

But Marshall's role was quickly reduced to a supervisory one by his transference to Edinburgh in 1836. The bulk of the work was undertaken by Lieutenant Alexander Murray Tulloch, whom Howick had brought in from outside the medical department. Like Marshall, Tulloch had distinguished himself in the previous few years by a series of articles on army statistics. Born in 1803 at Newry, he came from a Jacobite family. He was initially intended for the law and began his practice in Edinburgh (presumably after studying there). He quickly threw this up, joined the army and was posted to India. There he immediately attacked the inadequate diet of the troops and other abuses.[8] On his return to Britain he began to express his ideas in some anonymous articles in the *United Service Journal*.[9] One of these criticized the existing system of military pensions. Much of the technical part of the argument revolved around the exact number of deaths among the troops and Tulloch called for detailed studies of the 'mortality at each station occupied by British troops'.[10] The article demonstrated an impressive grasp of actuarial methods. In a later number Tulloch raised the question of mortality among officers.[11] The major motive was an actuarial one but Tulloch favoured investigations 'from the statistical point of view' which would help to improve the condition of the troops and reduce the high levels of morbidity and mortality. He hoped that others 'of due competence and authority' would take up the burden.[12]

Howick decided that Tulloch had the due competence and gave him the authority. That his worth was appreciated is shown by his promotion to captain in 1838, major in 1839, and lieutenant-colonel in 1844.[13] With Marshall in Edinburgh Tulloch assumed direction. From April 1836 he was aided by Thomas Graham Balfour, an assistant-surgeon in the Army Medical Department. Balfour was another Scot who had recently graduated in medicine from Edinburgh and was, much later, to become a leading member of the

Statistical Society of London.[14] Manuscript drafts of a few of the parliamentary papers indicate that Tulloch did the basic writing with comments and corrections from Balfour (who undertook much of the tabulation). Marshall was responsible for the overall design of the reports (which was fixed in the first one).[15] His contribution, therefore, was crucial and in particular it should be noted that he drew up the classification of diseases used throughout the reports.[16]

It was more than two years before the first report was published. This was due to the strange belief on the part of some in authority that publication of the morbidity and mortality rates of the troops in the West Indies would constitute a danger to security in the event of war.[17] It was not until mid-1838 that publication was authorized and the delay removed something of the interest in the report. As early as June 1836 Marshall and Tulloch had finished their preliminary research on the Windward and Leeward Islands. They had concluded that more fresh meat was required in the army rations, which prompted the War Office to recommend an increase.[18] However, the Treasury was not fully convinced and some salt rations were retained.[19]

Hence there was still much to argue about in the first report if only to justify the reforms already introduced. It is deceptively mild and uncommitted at first sight (by the standards, that is, of the argumentative parliamentary papers of the time). In his introduction Tulloch stated that it was

> principally confined to such points as can readily be solved by the test of facts and figures. Observations as to treatment, speculations regarding the contagious or non-contagious nature of particular diseases, or any reference to medical theories except where they can be made the subject of calculation, would obviously be quite foreign to the purpose of a Statistical Report.[20]

The remark puts Tulloch within the framework of the statistical movement of the early Victorian period with its much professed antipathy to '*opinions*'. Yet within that framework there was a great range of carefulness in the treatment of evidence. Tulloch and Marshall shared William Farr's notion of statistics as 'an essential means of acquiring the requisite information upon which to found practical measures for the amelioration of the condition, and for promoting the health'.[21] They were also close to Farr's end of the spectrum in their technical competence and intellectual honesty.

Like Farr, Tulloch had controversial points to make but of all the statisticians perhaps Tulloch was the least vehement, the most measured in his writing. The report itself was divided into six sections. The first was by far the longest and was in four parts dealing respectively with the Windward and Leeward Command, the Jamaica Command, the Bahamas Command, and the Honduras Command (the last two very briefly) with regard to sickness and mortality. Each part began with a description of the topology and climate of the area to provide a background for possible local variations. Tulloch then dealt with the number of troops, their duties, accommodation, and rations. The very high rate of mortality led into a discussion of the various causes of death.

The second section in each part was on invaliding but the available statistics did not allow Tulloch to go very far into the problem.[22] The third section was an even briefer discussion of the numbers in hospital.[23] It was the fourth section which contained the most radical argument of the report. This section was concerned with the influence of age and length of residence on mortality. Returns were available only from 1830 but this was sufficient for Tulloch's needs. He was able to compare age-specific mortality rates for the Windward and Leeward and Jamaica Commands with the English figures according to the Carlisle tables. There had been an impression that mortality decreased with age among the troops. Tulloch showed that this was untrue and that mortality increased faster among the troops (except for the 40 to 50 year olds in Jamaica, many of whom were invalided out and therefore did not appear in the returns). Tulloch was well pleased by this reversal of accepted belief by his statistics: 'we trust they will be sufficient to displace hypothetical opinions, which have principally originated in the want of accurate statistical information'. As Tulloch pointed out, the error had arisen from the preponderance of youthful deaths in absolute terms, a preponderance which vanished once the returns were reconstructed on an age-specific basis. The conclusion resulted in the recommendation that it was best to send out young troops once they were fully trained.[24]

It was a natural progression to consider the effect of length of service (that is, acclimatization). Though it was not easy to separate out, Tulloch showed that in Jamaica, where 'of all others the benefit of residence has been most strongly insisted upon', mortality among those resident one year was 77 per thousand, two years 87 per thousand, and over two years 93 per thousand. He could not control for the influence of age and while it is not clear whether he understood this problem Tulloch did note that the correlation would have been more marked had it not been for the inclusion in the new arrivals of a number of old soldiers who quickly died.[25] Other statistics were not so conclusive but did not suggest the opposite and Tulloch felt justified in arguing that length of residence did not reduce mortality except during epidemics when newly arrived troops might suffer excessively.²⁶ The results had already gone to Howick, who was sufficiently convinced to announce that in future regiments would stay three years in the West Indies and not up to ten or eleven as had been the case in the past.²⁷

The other reform, which we have already noted, was the increased ration of fresh meat. This followed from Tulloch's success in proving his case by the clever expedient of separately analysing the mortality of officers. Had there been no difference then it would be legitimate to deduce that 'no improvement either in the comfort, diet, or accommodation of the soldier, would be likely to effect any material improvement in his health.' But it was not so. Mortality among officers was half as high as among the troops in the Windward and Leeward Command and two-thirds in the Jamaica Command. In the former the officers' susceptibility to diseases of the lungs and stomach and bowels was much lower than the troops generally. The same effect was nothing like so marked in Jamaica, a contradiction which Tulloch turned to his advantage by arguing that it demonstrated that the high rates of the men could not be due to intemperance or night duty. The argument was supported by reference to the high rates for non-commissioned officers who did not perform night duty and were presumably less intemperate. Tulloch's thesis on the difference between Jamaica and the Windward and Leewards was a little forced but he managed to carry his point. Moreover, he had carried it by an early use of differential mortality rates of a class-based type (using the term loosely though, in retrospect, it applies in a more precise sense as well).

On the basis of the statistics Tulloch felt confident in asserting a number of conclusions. Some shibboleths could be demolished: high temperature was not very important since the various stations fluctuated widely in their mortality but little in temperature; nor was excess moisture the villain since no pattern could be discerned (though Tulloch conceded the two combined might have some effect); miasma 'wafted' from South America was no more likely than local 'exhalations' from the soil. Indeed, apart from very high localities Tulloch could not 'point out any practical rule to be followed in the choice of healthy localities for the troops'.²⁸

Tulloch had overstated his case against the suspicion of marshes (though that is to criticize with hindsight), had been a little less than rigorous in his treatment of the mortality of officers, and the nosology bequeathed to him by Marshall was a very inefficient analytical tool. Yet, in the context of other statistical works, it was a masterpiece, if a masterpiece demonstrating some of the assumptions and attitudes of the statisticians. Apart from Sir Andrew Halliday, obviously eating sour grapes, the work was very favourably received. The best praise of all was imitation: a lengthy summary was read to the Statistical Society of London, which set up a committee to process data from the East Indies along the lines laid down by Tulloch.[29]

Tulloch continued his work with a report on the health of the troops in the United Kingdom, the Mediterranean, and British North Amerca wherein his skill was further demonstrated. In studying the dragoons in the United Kingdom he found that their mortality was higher than that of the civilian population of similar ages. Tulloch neatly explained this by urban-rural differences since the troops were garrisoned in towns.[30] In the report on the Mediterranean he cast further doubt upon the accepted notions of the causation of fever by examining the lack of relationship between marshy soil or excessive vegetation and the occurrence of fevers.[31] The point was made even more sharply in the report on West Africa where mortality from fevers was very high, especially in Sierra Leone, where no less than 410 per thousand of the white troops had died on average per annum.[32] The reports were now becoming predictable and had little to add.[33] A proposed summary never appeared though a draft was prepared and is to be found in the Tulloch papers. But Tulloch and Balfour also prepared, a few years later, a report on the period 1837-46 for some stations.[34] The returns had been improved and comparisons were made easier by the growth of non-military vital statistics, especially Farr's reports.

The army reports had by this time been joined by similar reports on the health of the navy, which had made it possible for comparisons to be made.[35] A few months after Tulloch and Marshall began work the question had been raised in the Admiralty and after consultations with the head of the Army Medical Department the navy's Physician-General, Sir William Burnett, recommended the idea.[36] There were difficulties over the estimated cost and in the end it was proposed that one surgeon and one clerk should be employed.[37] The officer initially employed died after a few months and was replaced by John Wilson. He found it necessary to reorganize the enquiry and begin again since the initial plan had made no provision for tracing the sick from the ships to the hospitals (thus greatly reducing the number of cases). It was also felt that the method of computing the strength of the squadrons led to an overestimate of the total population. The combination of the two errors would have given 'an exaggerated view of the health of the Navy'.[38] Wilson, who had joined the navy in 1813, was yet another Scot.[39] It was not until 1825 that he graduated in medicine (from Edinburgh with a thesis on dysentery). In 1827 he wrote a book on the causation of fevers in the West Indies which was sceptical of existing theories but was in no way quantitative. One notable feature, however, was a cautiousness and humility of approach shown when he said, 'it is easier to demolish an old structure than to rear a better one in its stead... It may be found... I have only substituted one error for another'.[40]

This caution was evident in the official reports (and any lack of numeracy was, at least in the details, made up for by somebody else doing the arithmetic). Many defective returns were found and if Wilson was not satisfied that the deficiencies could be made up then the particular ship concerned was struck out of the totals for whatever period was necessary. Moreover, though returns of mortality were reasonably accurate, invaliding returns were not and with transferences from ship to ship and ship to shore double-counting must have occurred. It was also difficult to trace all cases on shore, while the short service of a ship in any one place created further obstacles in the way of assessing the effects of climate and location. Ages were indeterminate in the returns. In the tables of the sick and hurt no mention was made of rank so that no controls could be introduced to compute the differences in diet or other environmental factors.[41] Nevertheless, Wilson had felt confident enough in a preliminary report to state that the figures gave 'a very gratifying view' of the health of the navy.[42]

The introduction to the first published report was a catalogue of the great improvements which had taken place in the navy: the reduced spirits ration, the use of lemon juice, the better water, improved diets for the sick, the cleansing of the ships, and, most recently, the institution of ships' libraries, which marked the passing of the belief that the 'debasing, and destructive effects of savage ignorance, is thought essential to the character of a British seaman.'[43] Both the moralism and its irrelevance to the statistics shows that Wilson shared some of the features of the civilian statisticians. Moreover, despite his ability and care, he did not realize that few conclusions could be safely drawn from the statistics even on such a simple matter as the overall level of mortality. In the second report he was to note with some surprise that the South American station appeared healthier than the English Channel.[44] The result might have convinced Wilson that the South American figures were meaningless but it did not. He was more concerned by this time with proving that the navy was healthier than civilian life since he could not think of anything 'so well fitted to popularize the service'.[45]

The second report was even more of a statement of faith that the 'spirit of improvement, every where active, will not sleep in the Royal Navy'.[46] While the figures may not be entirely reliable the great magnitude of the improvement which had occurred cannot be denied: according to Wilson the annual mortality in 1779 was one in eight, in 1811 one in 32, and in 1830-6 one in 72 of the establishment.[47] Wilson gave credit to the changes in diet and water but also stressed the value of the attention paid to 'the intellectual, religious, and moral improvement of seamen'.[48]

The resumption of the reports in the late 1840s marks the emergence of a different type of statistician, perhaps narrower in outlook, definitely more competent technically. In 1849 the first of a new series of naval health reports was published under the direction of Alexander Bryson. Bryson was a man of wide experience. Born in 1802 he had studied at Glasgow and Edinburgh, joining the navy in 1827.[49] In the late 1840s he distinguished himself by establishing the separate existence of yellow fever and the effectiveness against it of some prophylactic measures, including the use of quinine and the immediate transfer of ships where yellow fever had broken out to colder regions.[50] The first report followed Wilson's plan, though, significantly, without obeisance to the ideology of improvement.[51] The second report was quite different for Bryson had had time to reorganize. The antiquated Cullen nosology used by Wilson (and rejected by Farr) was dropped and various other technical changes made.[52] However, a plan to tabulate the efficacy of methods of treatment had to be abandoned because it would have been impossible to control the experiment.[53] The importance of the report lies in the concluding discussion on the causes of disease.[54] One argument stands out: Bryson rejected swamp miasma as the cause of dysentery and instead hypothesized the existence in rivers of 'infusorial animalcules of a poisonous nature, or... minute organic germs'.[55] This cautiously revolutionary pattern was repeated in the third report.[56]

Bryson's work lies beyond the immediate scope of this book. But it and the writings of Wilson, Tulloch, Marshall, and Balfour bulk large in the general corpus of investigations into the diseases of different occupations of the early Victorian era. They were justly welcomed in their time if largely forgotten since. Their faults were obvious: poor nosologies and deficient statistical techniques (techniques which were not significantly improved until the end of the nineteenth century). Yet they were a necessary beginning and by the standards of the time were far from incompetent or unscientific. They led to immediate changes in governmental practices in the interests of improving the health of the armed forces. Perhaps most importantly, they formed a considerable part of a movement which hoped to improve society by detailed study of its problems.

[4]

Edwin Chadwick and Sanitary Statistics

The annual reports of the General Register Office by William Farr and the reports on the health of the armed forces are by no means the most well-known aspects of government involvement in vital statistics in the 1830s and 1840s. It is rather the name of Edwin Chadwick which is likely to spring to mind when the statistical study of public health questions is under consideration. Since the appearance of biographical works by R. A. Lewis and S. E. Finer, Chadwick's place in all the text-books has been well established – a difficult but brilliant man who laid the foundations of the modern sanitary revolution by an unusual combination of energy and expertise.[1] There is indeed some danger of exaggerating his achievements. He was not the only able man in the public health movement and his abrasiveness, egotism, and lack of tact all too often caused him to alienate powerful allies. Chadwick's essentially sectarian approach to the public health issue was frequently less than useful. Nor were his surveys as scientific as is usually thought. Yet he will remain forever associated with the public health movement because of his responsibility for producing one if not two of the three great official enquiries into the cesspool that was British urban life in the early Victorian era.

Chadwick's interest in public health is usually seen as being derived in some way from his association with Jeremy Bentham, which received early expression in an article written for the *Westminster Review* in 1828 on life assurances.[2] Although, at the beginning of the article, the author briefly urges that the government improve the data on vital statistics it would be using excessive hindsight to see this as the real beginning of the 'sanitary idea'. This may rather be seen as occurring in 1836 when Chadwick became involved with the Registration Bill then before Parliament. It seems likely that as part of a political bargain with Lord Ellenborough Chadwick obtained the insertion of the cause of death in the mortality registers.

Initially, this was probably not for reasons connected with public health but as a method of placating the medical profession, which was after Chadwick's blood because of the administration of the medical provisions of the Poor Law Amendment Act. In addition, Chadwick hoped to bribe the medical officers by offering them appointments as registrars of births and deaths.[3] However, Chadwick seems to have quickly realized the potential of the new registers. He was at least partly responsible for William Farr's appointment and obviously hoped to control him. In particular, Chadwick had some plan whereby Farr's office would collate medical statistics, including figures on epidemics.[4]

Farr bluntly informed Chadwick that the Poor Law Commission was too busy and inexperienced to do much for medical statistics. Farr saw no reason at all for interfering and sent Chadwick an article in the *British Annals of Medicine* (of which he was editor) suggesting that the Poor Law Commission should have nothing to do with the administration of the Registration Act.[5] Chadwick dropped the matter for a while but the continuation of severe epidemics caused him to reactivate his plans since the prevalence of fever was having an effect on the volume of claims made on the poor law authorities. Chadwick decided to send out questionnaires to the poor law medical officers in London while his three medical experts, Southwood Smith, Neil Arnott, and J. P. Kay, undertook local surveys.[6]

These three men's reports were of crucial importance in the genesis of the famous 1842 report for two reasons. Firstly, their conclusions were determined by the miasma etiology of disease, which was to become something like an obsession at Somerset House. Thus disease could be eliminated or at least reduced by the removal of the sources of 'putrefactive decomposition', a piece of wisdom which 'until lately... has been little understood'.[7] The advantages of the erroneous miasma theory, which in some ways can be regarded as isomorphic with germ theories, was that the remedies were necessary public health measures: sewage disposal, pure water, rubbish collection and so on. Chadwick was never to deviate from this theory in his public health writings in the 1840s.

The second aspect worthy of note occurred in Southwood Smith's report on the causes of sickness and mortality among the poor. He argued that some of the mortality and sickness was due to 'improvidence' which could only be altered by bringing them 'under the influence of the inducements to forethought and method.' But more significant were factors 'which can be avoided by no prudence, and removed by no exertion, on the part of the poor.' These were the lack of sanitary facilities.[8] Thus an environmentalist explanation emerged of the 'condition of England question.' The time was ripe for the marshalling of a broader volume of evidence to back the emerging public health movement. But it was not until after the fifth annual report (which contained a more statistically based survey by Southwood Smith) that Bishop Blomfield moved in the Lords for a full enquiry into the sanitary condition of the labouring population.[9] The Poor Law Commission was placed in charge and delegated the task to Chadwick. This made up for his increasing lack of influence in the normal affairs of the Commission.[10]

Before Chadwick's report was ready he had been upstaged by Robert Aglionby Slaney. Slaney wanted to see more results than were coming forth from Chadwick and therefore obtained the appointment of a Commons select committee on the health of towns.[11] The proceedings of this committee were modelled very much on Slaney's 1838 committee on the education of the working classes. Its enquiries were not to break new ground. Its purpose was to read into the parliamentary record the opinions and even sections of the writings of carefully selected experts. It thus became a national gathering of some of the provincial statisticians plus the Somerset House doctors. The pattern was established immediately, with Southwood Smith as the first witness assenting to the truth of passages from his own reports:

> Slaney – 'In the second paragraph, after adverting to the want of forethought and prudence, you state, "There are evils of another class, more general and powerful in their operation, which can be avoided by no prudence, and removed by no exertion on the part of the poor. Among the gravest, and at the same time most remediable of these latter evils, is the exposure of certain noxious agents generated and accumulated in the localities in which the poor are obliged to take up their abode, and to the pernicious influence of which they are constantly and for the most part unconsciously subjected"; that is your opinion?'
> Southwood Smith – 'It is.'[12]

This charade continued throughout most of Southwood Smith's evidence and that of the other witnesses. Neil Arnott was treated in a similar fashion, as were a number of representatives from statistical societies which by this time had carried out surveys of the condition of the working classes. Because of such work London, Liverpool, Leeds, Manchester, and Glasgow received particular attention. It would be difficult to argue that there was any objectivity in the examination of witnesses from these areas: the committee was as biased as any of the time and its mode of procedure had a certain superficiality. Yet it would be a mistake to dismiss it as Chadwick tried to do.[13] Chadwick was annoyed at Slaney's interference, and his propaganda against the committee's recommendations went so far that Slaney was ordered to stop work on his enquiries and was only reprieved by the change of government in 1841.[14] Chadwick's antipathy was intensified by the fact that between 1839 and 1841 he had become converted to the belief that the solution lay in external drainage and sanitation rather than in the improvement of the actual houses themselves.[15] Slaney's report was heretical in that it recommended worship of the false god which Chadwick had so recently renounced – a general building act to regulate the quality of dwellings erected for the working classes. Chadwick may have been piqued by the fact that the committee pre-empted his notion of a general sewerage act including boards of health, commissioners, and inspectors. The committee also proposed a general improvement act to obviate the necessity for separate local improvement acts.[16]

It is apparent that Chadwick should not be given credit for ideas which had been expressed elsewhere and at an earlier date. Nevertheless, his single-minded adherence to the sanitary idea in the years 1839 to 1842 resulted in the production of a piece of propaganda of the first importance. The report was not only largely his own work but was issued over his name since one of the Poor Law Commissioners did not wish to take responsibility for it.[17] It is a masterpiece of persuasion, subtly blending fact and fiction. The whole thrust of the argument was designed to prove that national salvation lay through water-fed sewers sweeping away the miasma, accompanied by rubbish collection, pure water, and centrally supervised district medical officers.[18] That the complexities of public health could be reduced to such simplicities of cure immediately arouses suspicion.

These doubts are not allayed by a closer examination of the report. It is vast but repetitive. It begins with a section on the general condition of the residences of the poor which is no more than a string of quotations from the local reports most congenial to Chadwick.[19] This was followed by a long section on the state of drainage and the water-supply and other 'external' arrangements which forms a key part of the analysis.[20] Again there was a heavy reliance upon quotations which supported the miasma theory that Chadwick was determined to prove. Quotation after quotation is used to prop up this thesis, which had reached its absurd but logical extreme a few years earlier when one writer claimed instances of graves being opened whereupon men 'dropped down and expired upon the spot'.[21]

Chadwick's particularly gross selectivity in the use of evidence should not pass unnoticed. This is most clearly demonstrated in the treatment of the great Edinburgh expert on social medicine, W. P. Alison. In Chadwick's report Alison is mentioned twice. The first time when Chadwick is referring to a report by Neil Arnott in which Alison is noticed in passing as accompanying them on a tour of inspection[22] and the second when a paper of his is very briefly cited to show that population increases in parts of Glasgow had not been matched by the growth in housing.[23] As a reference to the leading Scottish expert on the topic this was derisory. Alison's sin was that he refused to accept Chadwick's over-simplifications. Alison had published a major study of the problem of poverty in 1840 as part of a campaign to get the Scottish poor law reconstructed. In it he had argued that poverty and destitution were the primary sources of disease and that intemperance was relatively insignificant since those most afflicted were children, while the poor drank less than the rich. Drunkenness was a result rather than a cause of poverty.[24] In the local reports in 1842 Alison explicitly criticized the miasma theories of the Chadwickians. Alison saw that cleanliness was desirable and necessary but not sufficient and would need to be accompanied by a general improvement in the standard of living of the lower classes.[25] To reduce the impact of this argument Chadwick straddled it with two articles by Arnott pushing the miasma line and denying Alison's conclusions.[26] Furthermore, Chadwick ignored Alison's report in the summary.[27] Examples of this sort begin to make the 1842 report look more like the 1834 poor law report.

The former may also be compared with the poor law report in that large sections which we might expect to be quantitative are non-quantitative. In view of the amount of statistics in the 1842 report, that may seem a startling assertion. But it is justifiable in the sense that the first two sections relied for their proofs of the miasma theory on qualitative or pseudo-quantitative statements: 'The greater number of cases of fever in June is in a great degree to be accounted for from the extremely filthy state of those places where it has been worst,'[28] or, 'it is equally certain that both health and life are frequently sacrificed by the constant damps and unwholesome smell'.[29] There is some statistical material in the third section on 'internal economy and domestic habits'.[30] But the standard was not very high, even for the time. For example, in one table all deaths from lung diseases among milliners and dressmakers were put down to 'ignorance of the want of ventilation'.[31] However, the section on occupational diseases is perhaps one of the best, though still vitiated by Chadwick's dogmatism.

The third section was basically another set of impressionistic assertions carefully selected from the local reports and connected by Chadwick's commentary. It was in the fourth section, on 'the comparative chances of life in different sections of the community', that the bulk of the statistical analysis appeared. Chadwick obtained returns of ages at death from those superintendent-registrars who were also clerks of poor law unions and therefore his to command. The deceased were divided into the conventional three social classes of the time – gentry and persons engaged in professions and their families; 'persons engaged in trade, or similarly circumstanced' and their families; and 'labourers, artisans, and others similarly circumstanced' and their families. Errors were possible since the registration books did not distinguish between masters and journeymen. Chadwick felt that where mistakes had been made the effect would be to increase the apparent life-span of the labouring classes.[32] One of the local reports had been considerably more sceptical about the data but that scepticism did not find its way into the main report.[33] This is not surprising, for the statistics satisfactorily indicated large differences in the average age at death of the three classes. In Truro the average ages at death were respectively 40, 33, and 28; at Derby, 49, 38, and 21.[34] At Leeds the figures were 44, 27, and 19; at Liverpool, 35, 22, and 15.[35]

It was impressive evidence but not as conclusive as Chadwick tried to make out. His own tables showed the enormous infant mortality among the lower classes. If we exclude deaths under 20 then the average ages at death in the nine areas in his summary tables were 65, 55, and 51 in the three classes.[36] The gentry and professions retain their clear advantage but the differential between the two other classes is decreased. Perhaps the working classes' chances were inflated by inclusion of some of the middle classes (though that assumes Chadwick's hypothesis to be true) but against this must be set the fact that social mobility favoured longevity in the middle classes. Upwardly mobile members of the working classes who died young figure in the third group whereas if they died at an advanced age they would figure in the second. Perhaps more important was the differing age-structures of the two groups. If, as seems likely, the working classes had been reproducing faster than the middle classes then that fact alone would cause them to have as a whole a lower average age at death even if life expectancies were the same. This trend would be accentuated by large-scale immigration of young adults from Ireland and the countryside since Manchester, Leeds, Liverpool, and two London poor law unions accounted for some 72 per cent of the sample. Given these constraints on the interpretation of the figures Chadwick might well have concluded that there was no significant difference between the life-expectancies of the middle and lower classes in adulthood.

But Chadwick preferred to use indices which dramatized the issue. He presented more figures in the fourth section to refute Malthusianism by showing that high birth and death rates were associated in poor areas.[37] This was an argument taken from Farr's fourth report but not acknowledged.[38] Further statistics were produced in the next two sections to illustrate the cost of excessive sickness and mortality but they were seldom more than summaries from isolated pieces elsewhere. One table tried to differentiate between the ages at death of miners and non-miners in the same area. It is unfortunately of no value since the percentage of deaths for the non-miners adds up to 154 per cent even though no figures were included for two of the eight divisions of ages.[39] Elsewhere the drop in naval mortality over the previous 50 years was used to show that mortality could be reduced (hence, by implication, the very different conclusion that it could be reduced by Chadwickian methods).[40] All this suggests that as a statistician Chadwick was inferior to many of his contemporaries.

His fault was his determination, marked even for his period, to prove a preconceived theory. As he explained to the Statistical Society of London, he used the index of the average age at death rather than the crude death rate since the latter would 'cause the extent of the evils which depress the sanatory condition of the population, and the mortality consequent on those evils to be under-estimated'.[41] Chadwick had discovered the stationary population fallacy – that is the fallacy of assuming that crude death rates can be immediately translated into life expectancies.[42] There was nothing new in this discovery but one would not think so from Chadwick's paper. He suggested instead the use of his favourite index, the average age at death. This was a relatively constant measure, he thought, little affected by migration. He also poured scorn on those misguided souls who, for example, had ascribed fever on board ships to infection from a sailor who had recently been in a gaol where an epidemic had occurred.[43] Chadwick's microscope had miasma painted on the end of it.

His dogmatism could equally be seen in the passage where he stated that the general effect of migration would be to raise the average age at death.[44] This was untrue since migrants were overwhelmingly young adults who not only soon produced children whose deaths greatly lowered the average age at death, but left behind a population biased towards the elderly, thus raising the average age at death in the migrant supplying areas. The net result was to exaggerate urban-rural differentials. Chadwick turned this argument on its head by objecting that there was nothing inevitable about high infant mortality rates.[45] This was to confuse the issue of whether large numbers of infants had to die with that of whether or not they actually did so. It was the latter which made the index of average age at death unreliable since its use ensured that differing age-structures would give different results even if the age-specific rates of mortality were identical.

The paper was typical of Chadwick, not only in its methodological weaknesses, but also in the way in which he placed his arguments in the context of an attack, and frequently a misinformed attack, on the actuarial profession. This served to antagonize potential allies unnecessarily and F. G. P. Neison was moved to protest. That protest (initially made in discussion after Chadwick's paper) was to lead to the production of a separate paper refuting Chadwick.[46] The use of the average age at death was 'fallacious in principle' and 'contradictory' in use. For Neison the 'whole question turns' on differing age-structures. For example, according to the 1841 census, 14.5 per cent of the population in Bethnal Green was under five while in St George's Hanover Square the proportion was only 8.6 per cent. The average age at death in Bethnal Green was 25.80 years, in St George's Hanover Square 31.23 years. But had the population in St George's had the same age-structure as that of Bethnal Green the average age at death would have been 27.25. Thus the true advantage was 1.45 years not 5.43. By the crude method Marylebone appeared to have the advantage over Bethnal Green by 3.32 years whereas standardization changed this to a *disadvantage* of 1.28 years. The centripetal tendency of standardization was the norm: the difference before adjustment between Kensington and Liverpool was 32.39 years to 20.67, afterwards it was 26.71 to 22.25. Taking seven cities and five counties the range was 20.67 to 38.42 years whereas when all populations were standardized to London the range was 25.07 to 31.48 years.[47] The deduction that Neison correctly made was that Chadwick's index did 'not give any indication of the sanatory condition of a community.' The same objection was made to the crude death rate.[48] For Neison all indices in vital statistics had to be adjusted to a standard age structure.[49]

The recommendation came too late to have much effect on the public health movement which reached its climax of propaganda activities in the years 1843-4 with the work of the Royal Commission on the State of Large Towns and Populous Districts and the formation of pressure groups such as the Health of Towns Association. In any case Chadwick was too powerful a figure for a relative newcomer such as Neison to undermine. That Neison's paper went unremarked outside a narrow circle is shown by the use in the 1848 Public Health Act of an arbitrary crude death rate of 23 per thousand as the point at which local public health boards had to be formed.[50] Meanwhile, between 1843 and 1845, the third of the governmental enquiries had taken place. The Royal Commission of those years marks the broadening of the public health movement to incorporate a much wider range of persons than the statisticians and a few others who had dominated it until the time of the publication of Chadwick's report. Nevertheless, some of the statisticians made a contribution and a part of the commission's work was quantitative in character. Its instructions were to discover the causes of disease and the means of improving the public health with reference to drainage, sewerage, and the provision of water supplies.[51]

Most of the evidence was directed towards means of improvement which perhaps suggests a misplaced confidence in the imminence of legislation. But Southwood Smith was brought in to do his by now familiar performance on the fourth annual report of the Poor Law Commission and the effects of fever on the lives of the poor.[52] W. A. Guy gave evidence as the recognized expert on the effects of employments on health.[53] The main body of statistics, however, came in the appendix. There was, for example, a report on Liverpool by W. H. Duncan. It was a fair indication of the advantage that the public health reformer had in the mid-1840s over people working ten years earlier. Farr's returns enabled Duncan to show the effect of over-crowding on mortality and the greater expectation of life in the country.[54] Enumeration of the number of courts and cellar-dwellings, which had been begun by the Manchester Statistical Society, proved that half of the working classes lived in them.[55] Analysis of the maps prepared by the Commissioners of Sewers suggested that the working classes (three-quarters of the total population in Duncan's reckoning) had just over one-third of the total mileage of streets and one-sixth of the mileage of sewered streets.[56] Farr's reports on the causes of death showed the high incidence in Liverpool of deaths from fevers, consumption, and 'convulsions', which, Duncan argued, were the result of 'impure air'.[57] It was also possible to infer rough correlations between the number of deaths from fevers and the proportion of cellar dwellings, lack of sewerage, and high density.[58] The conclusion that Duncan drew was a paradigm of the belief of the statisticians in reform within the existing structure:

> Of course no one but a Utopian dreamer can expect that – where there is such a wide difference in the command of the necessaries of life as must always exist between one section of the community and another – any sanitary regulations will succeed in reducing the mortality of the poor to the same level with that of the wealthier classes; but after making every allowance of this kind, will any candid mind refuse to admit that, in the case of Liverpool, a large balance must still remain to be charged to the account of the physical causes which have been pointed out.[59]

Equally impressive were some of the other local surveys in the report, in particular those by Rev. J. Clay (chaplain at the prison) on Preston and Thomas Laycock on York, which all led to the same sort of conclusion about the possibilities of reducing sickness and mortality. The series of local reports was expanded in the second report of the commission. John Roberton submitted a paper on the causes of death in Manchester 'authorized by the Statistical Society of Manchester'.[60] Perhaps the most important was that by Lyon Playfair on Lancashire. In a section summarizing much of what had gone before, he examined the physical causes of disease to show the extent of the 'removable causes'.[61] But then, via a discussion of the administration of opiates to children, Playfair takes up the other part of the question, the 'moral causes of disease'.[62] These included the 'ignorance of domestic economy among the poorer classes' which resulted in early marriage. Playfair graphed the relationship between pauperism and mortality and argued that it was inverse in that, between 1838 and 1843, the year of highest pauperism was that of the lowest mortality. Hence he inferred that bad times meant the lack of means for the 'indulgence of vicious and costly propensities'.[63] Here the argument was turned back upon itself in a somewhat inconsistent manner since Playfair further argued that the 'low state of the system produced by continued exposure to the physical causes of disease creates an appetite for stimulants, which gradually lowers the moral as well as the physical condition' so that 'the physical causes of disease indirectly become the causes of crime'.[64]

Playfair was to a large extent repeating Chadwick's ideas in the *Sanitary Report*. But Chadwick was not alone in this type of belief and it is vital to recognize that throughout the public health movement there ran a strong vein of theory about the relationship between the individual and the environment, a theory which was central to the statistical movement. There was a continuing dialectic about the relative importance of the moral responsibility of the individual – poor and degraded in the conventional view of the working classes – as against those factors over which he had no control, environmental influences which had depressed and eventually destroyed his character. This dialectic was not so much an argument between members of the statistical movement, nor a development from one position to another, as an ideological tension which existed within each statistician. At any one time the statisticians would sound more or less moralistic or environmentalist according to the wider topic under discussion. They were at their most moralistic on poor laws, at their least on some aspects of public health and education.

In the field of public health this dualism was inherent in much of the evidence before, and the conclusions of, the Select Committee on the Health of Towns in 1840. At its crudest it could lead to the statement (not by a statistician) that 'bad air ... involves the necessity of taking something as a stimulant'.[65] Miasma theory plus a false view of alcohol as a stimulant did not produce a very subtle view of life. The representatives of the statistical movement were more complex in their attitudes. Southwood Smith was given no chance to go beyond his brief exposition in the fourth annual report of the Poor Law Commission; but Joseph Fletcher[66] wanted to see building regulations and other sanitary reforms to prevent the 'most 'frightful disorders' which were consequent upon the poor being so 'feeble morally, and ignorant to secure their own interests.' Crime, said Fletcher, was generated as much by 'the filthy and miserable habits of these town populations as by their own ignorance.' However, he was unwilling to agree that intemperance was due to 'actual distress' since the workers of Manchester were paid enough if only they drank less, while the 'want of comfort at home' arose from 'moral causes' such as the wife's working.[67] The definition of 'moral causes' may seem a little peculiar but Fletcher had oscillated carefully between them and 'physical causes'.

With evidence like this from the statisticians, Slaney's committee was able to conclude that the physical environment of the working classes degraded their character and produced 'crime, disease, and discontent', thus 'counteracting in great measure (as regards the younger portion of the population) those moral and religious impressions which they might otherwise receive from education where it is afforded to them'.[68] It was too much to expect the committee to stress the other side of the equation since this would have lessened the force of its propaganda.

Chadwick expanded upon, but in no way originated, the environmentalist argument that sanitary reform would produce a more stable and thrifty working class. Overcrowding was seen as 'a cause of extreme demoralization and recklessness, and recklessness, again, as a cause of disease'.[69] But Chadwick was still sufficiently the Chadwick of 1834 to allow a large measure of influence to 'the powerful operation of depraved domestic habits'.[70] Both moralistic and environmentalist conceptions were inherent in the statement that many new convicts arrived 'in a state of disease from intemperance and bad habits' and were improved by 'the effect of cleanliness, dryness, better ventilation, temperance, and simple food'.[71] This contrasted with the non-convict poor who were likely, in the words of the Birmingham committee, whom Chadwick quoted at length, to indulge in 'improvidence and thoughtless extravagance', buying steaks and chops. The women grew up 'totally ignorant of all those habits of domestic economy' which were soon to be preached to the starving Irish.⁷² The great bulk of the *Sanitary Report*, however, was devoted to Chadwick's idiosyncratic version of the environmentalist case. As with the 1840 committee the reason is obvious – it was a necessary condition for public health reform. The same dialectic between moralism and environmentalism occurred when the statisticians turned to what they called 'moral statistics'.

[5]

The Government and Moral Statistics

One of the distinguishing characteristics of the statistical movement is the very use of the term 'moral statistics'. It is a term which gradually disappeared during the nineteenth century: its popularity in our period underlines the importance of moral preoccupations in the movement. At its heart lay two or three broad subjects: crime, education, and, less frequently studied, religion. Of these three the most work was done on education, both by government agencies and the private societies. In the case of the former the two main sources are the 1833 survey of schooling facilities and the 1851 educational census though various useful data can be found scattered through the annual reports of the Privy Council Committee on Education and of the factory inspectors (particularly Robert Baker of Leeds).

The survey of 1833 derived from the Earl of Kerry's successful motion in the Commons calling for returns showing the state of education.[1] The responsibility for implementing the motion was passed to John Rickman who decided to use the overseers of the poor to carry out the survey despite his earlier belief in 'the gross amount of the dullness of all probable overseers'.[2] Information was sought on the number of infant schools, day schools, and Sunday schools and the numbers educated in each.[3] The survey had many obvious defects. The overseers were not required to carry out a street by street survey, so that some small schools were probably omitted. More seriously, there was double counting, notably in the lack of distinction between those who attended both day and Sunday schools and those who attended one type only. It is not clear how the attendance figures were derived but it would seem that they were taken from the numbers on the books, which could be a very different figure from the average or total normal attendance. These inadequacies were remarked upon even before final publication, particularly by the secretary of the British and Foreign Schools Society.[4] Widespread dissatisfaction with the Kerry returns was also a factor in causing the statistical societies to make their own local surveys.[5]

The culmination of these local surveys and other sources for educational statistics was the 1851 census. Before this was taken the Statistical Society of London had set up a census committee, which included William Farr and G. R. Porter as well as other leading fellows. Its report in March 1850 recommended that schedules should be sent to all head teachers requiring a return of the average numbers in attendance at each school with a statement of the age and sex of those on the books while the enumerator was to put each school into one of three classes.[6] This represented a considerable departure from the corresponding report in 1840, which decided that education should be left to 'special investigation' which could also cover the quality of instruction.[7]

Since, as in 1841, the General Register Office was in charge of the census it seems likely that the report was received sympathetically. The relevant Act at first seemed to make it possible to introduce the educational census by the back door. The Home Secretary had the final authority and the Registrar General was to issue 'such Forms and Instructions' as the Secretary 'shall deem necessary'. As if to open the door wider it was further enacted that the enumerators were, in addition to their usual duties, to 'take an Account of all such further Particulars as by the Forms and Instructions which may be issued under this Act they may be directed to inquire into'.[8] With this opportunity offered George Graham suggested the inclusion of censuses of religion and education.[9] Initially, both were to be compulsory in the same way that other parts of the census were.[10] But clearly the new schedules lay outside the spirit if not the letter of the Act. Stanley argued in the Lords that the Secretary of State was not empowered 'to put every question he thought fit, under a penalty for non-compliance.' Objection was made in particular to the 'most inquisitorial' schedules on private schools.[11] But it was the religious census which, naturally enough, aroused greater suspicion. The Bishop of Oxford was moved to quote Canning to the effect that 'nothing was so fallacious as facts except statistics'.[12]

The government were forced into a partial retreat and the religious and education censuses became voluntary. Horace Mann of the General Register Office was in charge and was now able to proceed even though 'some persons in authority' were still trying to persuade people not to co-operate.[13] Stanley had one major victory in that the questions on the number and salaries of the teachers and the income and expenses of the school were not required to be filled in by 'strictly private' schools.[14] The public schools were asked to give this information as well as the numbers on the books, the numbers 'in actual attendance' on 31 March 1851, the ages of the children, the numbers learning various subjects, the tuition fees, and a few other points.[15] Less detailed schedules were addressed to evening schools. Sunday schools, and literary and scientific societies.[16] The schedules, over 70,000 all told, had been distributed before the final verdict on the meaning of the Act and this may have helped in the decision to proceed.[17] The numbers who initially failed to make returns totalled 'several thousands' and a year was spent in follow-up work on these schools with Mann badgering the enumeration officers and they, presumably, badgering the schoolteachers. In the end Mann put under-enumeration at no more than about five per cent.[18] This is not impossible, for each enumerator dealt with a small area averaging a little more than two educational institutions (and the enumerator had to make a house to house survey in connection with his other work).

Given the figures and the returns for 1818 and 1833 Mann argued the progress of education had been at a 'far from unsatisfactory rate.' This left unanswered the question of whether existing provisions were adequate, and if not why not. In both the religion and education censuses Mann followed similar procedures at this point. He had to estimate how many 'ought' to be at school. The method used was a peculiar one but perhaps no worse than any alternative. It tried to take account of the fact that universal education over a 10 or 12 year period was not a practical standard, without falling into the equally vulgar error of assuming that whatever was was what was possible. A standard of one-sixth of the population on the books of the schools was now taken to 'ensure an adequate amount of education, at a proper school age, for the whole of the English people'.[19] Mann was aware that there was no way of knowing the share of various groups in the existing averages and that the available attendance figures implied that the 'unpleasant choice of evils lies between a wide extent of inefficient schooling and a limited extent of more effective teaching, contemporary with a certain portion, also limited, of utter ignorance'. The former was the more likely.[20] At this point Mann reverted to the by now standard argument that a 'desirable standard' was met only if the further criterion was satisfied that those 'already under education were in schools *efficiently conducted*'.[21] An examination of the curricula and other factors, however, indicated that, despite improvements, 'the actual *present* state of many schools must be far from satisfactory'.[22]

It remained, therefore, to account for the failure to reach the practicable ideal. Least important was the lack of school accommodation.

A more diffuse reason put forward was the poverty of the parents but Mann opted for a thoroughly moralistic argument in rejecting this. By 'poverty' Mann took people to mean 'the incompatibility of the child's instruction with some personal indulgence of the parents' and cited G. R. Porter to the effect that the working classes spent nearly £50,000,000 on 'intoxicating liquors'. More telling was the observation that 'free schools, well conducted, may be found half-empty' though Mann did not think it necessary to consider the place of the child in the family economy of the poor.[23] He was by now working himself up to a full denunciation of England's barbarian hosts. Mann's third cause was the Dickensian one of a 'numerous body' of criminal and destitute children (no attempt was made to quantify the assertion). But the 'grand cause' was the *indifference* of parents' who had culpably failed to see where their true self-interest lay. Mann allowed a little for 'a perception of the really trifling value of a proportion of the education offered for their purchase', but shoddy goods were less important than irrational market resistance. This resistance sprang from the generally un-Smilesian attitudes of most parents who saw their 'own social *status* as the standard.' For working-class parents this came to mean that they considered their children would gain a more 'useful' education outside school than inside.[24]

It was self-evident to Mann that such a philosophy was wrong. Once again a 'statistical' report went beyond its terms of reference into questions of social policy and Mann proposed remedies. The first was 'intellectual recreation' for the working classes so that education would be more useful. Mann does not say who should provide the facilities but the mention of mechanics' institutes, reading clubs, and local libraries points to the middle classes encouraging the independent artisans. Indeed, the independent artisan quickly made his expected appearance in the proposal that 'various social duties and responsibilities' (mysteriously undefined) should be 'devolved' upon the parents. Finally, the schools should be improved so that they 'can scarcely fail to attract the children'.[25]

After examining the various types of schools[26] he returned to the subject to consider the respective positions of the 'voluntary party' and those favouring state intervention. Mann's strong bias in favour of the latter quickly asserted itself when he referred to the voluntary party's reasons 'by which they think their position is maintained'.[27] For the state interventionists rather different language was used. They relied on 'certain prominent facts in everyday experience' and 'contended that our need is much too urgent for delay.' State interference was justified since the results of poor education were '*social injuries*'. Nor did interference mean the end of voluntary effort, as experience in the United States showed.[28] Mann then negotiated the differences between the various factions of interventionists in such a way as to imply that he was most probably in favour of local rates for secular teaching only.[29]

In the final section of the report Mann committed himself to an archetypal statement of the contradictions which so frequently occurred in the statistical movement. He acknowledged that 'it is not here that any opinion is to be expressed' yet felt that he might 'be permitted to reiterate a doubt', that is, express an opinion.[30] The form of this statement goes back to the foundation of the statistical movement in the early thirties. What Mann reiterated was not so much a doubt as a balancing of the polar moral view he had previously given vent to with an environmental theory which withdrew from the poor the blame for their failings. Mann 'reluctantly allowed that they have only too much reason for their apathy' since they were forced to live in 'impure and miserable homes'. He was arguing that the good society in one aspect could not be created until the good society in all aspects existed. That would not come about without 'vigorous endeavour' to lessen 'that social wretchedness which blights all educational promise'.[31] Thus the easy moralism of his earlier arguments was replaced by a characteristic tension between moralism and environmentalism, leading to a summons to action to the wealthier classes to create the preconditions for a more moral world.

The 1851 education census was a backward-looking document in that its aims and philosophy were typical of the statistical movement of the 1830s and 1840s. Dr J. R. B. Johnson has argued that the social conflicts of those years became less bitter in the fifties so that the sense of urgency in the campaign for elementary education was lost.[32] This may help to explain the lack of interest shown by contemporaries and historians in the education census.[33] Until relatively recently a similar fate befell Mann's other masterpiece, the 1851 religious census. It was perhaps inevitable that historians would eventually turn to this source for the place of religion in Victorian society. The first to examine the 1851 religious census in some detail was K. S. Inglis and he has been followed by David M. Thompson and W. S. F. Pickering.[34]

The religious census of 1851 was unique. It was not repeated because of the ensuing conflict over its methodology and results, particularly the use of the index of church attendance as the measure of religious influence. This favoured the Nonconformists, who wished any future census to be conducted on similar lines. But the supporters of the Church of England wanted a census of religious profession which would favour them. The simple resolution of this conflict was to drop the idea altogether.[35]

The idea itself was not new. For many years individual religious organizations had tried to claim for themselves larger congregations and a more important position than their rivals. Occasionally, fuller surveys were conducted and published – for example, by the secretary of the Glasgow Church Building Society in 1836.[36] The statisticians to some extent took the matter up, most notably at the British Association meeting in Newcastle in 1838 when tables were prepared following the presentation of the local education report.[37] The Leeds municipal survey included statistics on church accommodation. There were also individual papers, such as those by Rev. Edgell Edgell in 1838 and Rev. George Weight in 1840.[38] But in general the statisticians shied away from the topic. Such reluctance was natural since the question was surrounded by controversy and ideological passions. Yet the statisticians wanted information – the extent of religious influences was part of the extent of moral influences. Hence the census committee of the Statistical Society of London proposed that the census in 1841 should include religious profession.[39] The recommendation was not repeated by the 1850 census committee.[40] In default of further evidence we must presume that the idea was primarily due to Horace Mann.

His experience with the religious census paralleled that with the education census. Objections were made and it became voluntary. Afterwards the results were attacked, particularly by the Bishop of Oxford.[41] It is obvious that the religious census, even more than the education census, was fraught with considerable technical difficulties. It was a combined census of attendance and accommodation. The latter was straightforward enough but the former was not. The day of the census was 30 March 1851, a day associated with secular festivals in some parts of England, a day, too, when the weather may have been worse than usual.[42] More serious was the allegation that the Dissenters had packed their churches.[43] Perhaps this may be ignored as mere prejudice but defects inherent in the census and in Mann's treatment of it cannot be dismissed so lightly. As Thompson points out, the returns say nothing about the social composition of the attendants. Moreover, the report fails to provide a precise identification of some denominations while Thompson has found examples of duplicate returns. Added to this were arithmetical errors and a confusion of actual and average attendance. Even more alarming is the lack of differentiation between the general attendance and that of the children from the attached Sunday school since Mann assumes the returns were limited to the former.[44] Finally, there was the problem of separating the number of attenders from the number of attendances. Many people attended more than once a day and Mann tried to allow for this by assuming that the number of attenders equalled the morning attendances plus half the afternoon attendances plus one-third of the evening attendances.[45] Thompson rightly argues that such a formula ignores local variations, particularly those associated with alternative patterns caused by a church not opening three times a day. It also altered the figures fundamentally in favour of the Church of England since it was the Anglicans who had most attendances in the morning but very few in the evening compared with the Dissenters. In any case, the division between Anglicanism and Dissent was not as rigid as the tables imply since there is evidence that many people simply went to whichever church happened to be open at a convenient time.[46]

But, at least for the historian, the 1851 religious census was not a 'useless experiment'. The published figures are open to considerable suspicion: Thompson's work on six villages and towns in the Midlands shows that actual adult attendance at morning services ranged from 47 to 64 per cent of the published figures.[47] As a guide to the extent of religious observance in the mid-nineteenth century the published report therefore needs to be supplemented by research into the original schedules, which remain, except for Thompson's limited survey, virgin soil.

Yet that in itself is significant, for the collection of quantitative material of dubious value, processed in an inadequate fashion, was not an uncommon feature of the statistical movement. Mann's report was also typical in that he used it to express opinions. After a brief introduction he began with a 20 page religious history of England from the Druids and their 'creed of mingled mystery and terror' through to the Glorious Revolution.[48] He then passed to the growth of the different churches and their beliefs. For the Church of England this was a story 'displaying by what wonderful – almost unparalleled – achievements, in the way of self-extension, she has lately proved her inexhaustible vitality'.[49] That Mann was an Anglican is obvious, that he was liberally inclined was as quickly revealed. He avoided discussing the doctrines of Roman Catholicism at all but simply charted the growth of toleration.[50] His descriptions of the sects were generally sympathetic.[51]

Mann's strong religious faith suffuses the whole report. The aim was to discover the numbers 'destitute of spiritual teaching'.[52] We do not hesitate at the belief that all should receive education but it must also be understood that Mann was saying that all should be under some religious influences, that there should be enough accommodation to seat all who could be expected to attend at any one time.

For Mann 'the most important fact which this investigation as to attendance brings before us is, unquestionably, the alarming number of non-attendants.' This was a class issue: 'the middle classes have augmented rather than diminished that devotional sentiment and strictness of attention to religious services by which, for several centuries, they have so eminently been distinguished.' Even the previously lax landed classes had been swayed by bourgeois ethics so that 'regular church attendance is now ranked amongst the recognized proprieties of life.' But what of the '*labouring* myriads', all too many of whom spent their lives in religious indifference if not worse? The middle classes could not ignore the perils of a situation where those 'most in need of the restraints and consolations of religion are the classes which are most without them'.[53]

Mann put forward a number of reasons for the 'alienation of the poor from religious institutions.' One was the existence of class distinction in the churches and he argued that efforts should be made to overcome 'the prejudices of the working classes' (note which class was prejudiced).[54] Mann thought little of the suggestion that one reason was the indifference of the churches to the social condition of the poor.[55] The third possibility was anti-clericalism, which might be overcome if the ministers were 'less removed in station and pursuits' from the working classes.[56] The final reason often put forward was poverty 'or rather, probably, ... certain conditions of life which seem to be inseparable from less than moderate incomes', the 'vice and filth' of the poor's 'degraded homes'. This could be contrasted with the fact that some of the 'religious character by which the English middle classes are distinguished is the consequence of their peculiar isolation in distinct and separate houses'.[57] As with education, therefore, so with religion, sanitary reform was needed for moral reform. But the moralistic argument was also present in Mann's theory that the main problem was a 'genuine repugnance to religion itself.' The poor were heathen. The only answer was missionary activity, for a religious nation would not come about 'until the dingy territories of this alienated nation are invaded by *aggressive* Christian agency'.[58] With education to refine taste and reveal the social realities and religion to control conscience and instil notions of duty then a society would be founded of 'temperate, industrious, and provident' men.[59] It was the recurring dream of the statistical movement.

The nightmare was the existence of a considerable amount of crime, the most obvious index of moral degradation. But the criminal statistics lacked accuracy and comprehensiveness so that throughout our period the statisticians tried to improve them.[60] Within the government the main activist was G. R. Porter who succeeded in getting the previously very brief returns for England and Wales drawn up 'Upon a New and More Enlarged Plan' in 1835, a reform which was soon extended to the Scottish statistics. The returns were now classified according to county, offence, length of sentence, and sex of the offender.[61] But Porter was not able to gain full control of the returns and their publication, which remained with the Home Office. Nevertheless, he soon managed to get included in the returns a classification of the educational attainments of the criminals.[62]

The last addition was a useful one in terms of the ideological concerns which will be examined later but on a more practical level the returns remained very incomplete. Their most glaring defect is the fact that they cover only commitals for trial. Thus there was no way of deducing the number of offences. At the same time the tables included commitals for many minor offences confused with those for major crimes. In this way they fell between two schools, being neither a measure of all crime nor of serious crime but of the number of persons apprehended for those offences where trial rather than summary conviction occurred. For these reasons one recent writer on nineteenth-century crime found the statistics of little use.[63] Gatrell and Hadden, however, feel that too much has been made of the defects in the returns and that they can be used to analyse trends in criminal behaviour.[64]

The early Victorian statisticians seem to have agreed with both views. While attacking the reliability of the statistics they nevertheless used them for extended analyses. This made it all the easier to continue to believe in certain hypotheses even where the figures suggested they were false. Thus Samuel Greg of the Manchester Statistical Society argued that the old tables were totally unreliable except for the most violent crimes.[65] Commenting on the new tables, Henry Romilly wanted the classification of offences changed to a basic division between offences against private persons and offences against the public, though this led to just as much confusion in the details.[66] The problem of classification was taken up most fully by Arthur Symonds in a paper read to the Statistical Society of London in 1836. Symonds contended that if the tables were to get to the roots of crime they must be classified in such a way as to show the different sorts of motives. The official tables were set out according to objects and means rather than motives. Apart from this the exclusion of summary convictions was a fundamental fault and this error was compounded by the inclusion of acquittals. Finally, Symonds sought information on the occupational background of criminals as well as more detailed geographical divisions than the counties.[67]

Symond's criticisms were often telling even if his proposed classification suggests more about social attitudes than anything else. The official in charge of the Home Office returns, Samuel Redgrave, was aware of some of the deficiencies. He usually wrote an introduction to the annual figures in which he analysed the changing patterns of crime. For this he had never had any relevant training. He had entered the Home Office at the age of 14 and was primarily interested in art and architecture.[68] But he was responsible for further improvements in the figures in the 1850s and his comments were often sensible.[69] Over the years he argued that there were two types of crime: a mass of nearly constant or slowly-changing crime often committed by professional criminals, and a much more variable amount which fluctuated with the economic fortunes of the poor.[70] By the standards of the time Redgrave's reports were remarkably free of personal comment. It can be seen that in the discussion of criminality the major role was taken by the statistical societies which burst into prominence in the 1830s.

[PART II]
The Statistical Societies

[6]

The Foundation of the Statistical Society of London

The creation of a number of statistical societies throughout Britain in the 1830s is perhaps the most important institutional aspect of the statistical movement. The first society to be formally founded was that of Manchester in 1833. The Statistical Society of London, now the Royal Statistical Society, dates from March 1834.[1] Yet there is a sense in which the larger society can claim seniority of age as well as prestige since its roots go back to June 1833 and the third meeting, at Cambridge, of the British Association for the Advancement of Science. At that meeting, in somewhat irregular circumstances, a Statistical Section was added to those covering the natural and physical sciences. It was not a foreseen or planned event but one due as much to chance as to the conjunction of a number of men of similar minds and previous acquaintance who had an interest in statistics.

The new section's parent body, the British Association for the Advancement of Science, had been formed in 1831 as an association to gather together British scientists in annual meetings in major provincial cities. It was designed partially to fill a need that could not be met by the London based Royal Society and partially in imitation of foreign, in particular German, models, at a time when British scientists were becoming worried about their poor position in the European race for knowledge.[2] Though not particularly active in the formation of the Association,[3] the eminent mathematician, Charles Babbage, was consulted as to the nature of the subjects which ought to be discussed at the first meeting at York, as he had attended similar meetings in Germany. In fact various letters in the Babbage papers indicate that some of the more eminent scientists held aloof from the first meeting: perhaps they felt it was somewhat beneath them since it originated in a provincial philosophical society.

The success of the 1831 meeting resolved all doubts and the British scientific establishment, including Babbage, attended in force the second meeting at Oxford in 1832. It was at this meeting that there came a harbinger of what was to occur the following year. At this point in his career Babbage's restless mind had temporarily lighted upon the problems of industry.[4] In addition, he was determined to raise the status of the professional scientist in society. To Babbage the final proof of the existing low state of the prestige of the scientist had been demonstrated the previous September when Henry Brougham had offered Babbage the Order of the Guelph in recognition of his scientific work. The offer turned out to be of the third class only and Babbage, a man who never took such trifles lightly, refused it on the ground that the offer reflected on the place of science in society.[5]

For Babbage the situation could best be remedied by involving the wealthy and the influential in the scientific world. Consequently, at the Oxford meeting Babbage, rather tactlessly, rose after a paper on fossil remains to express the hope that

> attention should be paid to the object of bringing theoretical science in contact with that practical knowledge on which the wealth of the country depends ... I trust we may be enabled to cultivate with the commercial interests of the country that close acquaintance which I am confident will be highly advantageous to our more abstract pursuits.[6]

The seeming narrowness of the appeal to the commercial and industrial bourgeoise may be misleading for in later versions of his thoughts at that time Babbage was to explain that he also wished to include the landed classes and the governing elite – 'the landed proprietors or those members of their families who sat in either house of parliament' as he put it in his autobiography,[7] 'the influential class comprised of civil servants, members of Parliament – all the men who are involved in public affairs' as he described them in a private note for Adolphe Quetelet in 1853.[8]

The additions, in the later versions, to the account in the official report of the 1832 meeting probably accurately represent Babbage's intentions. What we may be suspicious of is the hindsight which allowed Babbage to see that what was needed for the wealthy and influential was some section with wider terms of reference than those existing in 1832.[9] The evidence suggests that Babbage's notions of how to fill the gap were unformed in 1832 since, according to the official report, he did not put forward any concrete proposals. In any case his speech fell flat and nothing came of it at Oxford.

The next meeting, in June 1833, was at Cambridge, at that time dominated in science by Trinity men like William Whewell. Whewell had invited to the conference Adolphe Quetelet, one of the most important scientists in Europe and certainly its leading statis-

The Foundation of the Statistical Society of London 79

tician.[10] Quetelet brought with him to Cambridge reports of his statistical studies on suicide and crime.[11] He went, with this material, to see Richard Jones, the professor of political economy at King's College London and another friend of Babbage's.[12] Jones decided to hold a meeting in his room in Cambridge that evening of a number of people interested in statistics so that Quetelet could discuss his work. At this point Jones was visited by Babbage who was informed of what had happened and invited to the meeting. According to Babbage he 'had just left him when it occurred to me to profit from this event. I returned to Mr. Jones and proposed to him to contact all the members who took an interest in statistical researches in order to form a statistical section'.[13]

What Babbage was proposing was irregular since the section was to be formed before sanction was obtained from the general body. Therefore the scheme had to be carried out with a degree of panache. Babbage 'would announce the formation of the new section as a fait accompli and demand a bill of indemnity to cover the irregularity'.[14]

The prestige of Babbage and the others involved allowed them to get away with it. That such prestige was needed was due to the dubious reputation of statistics among the scientists as a subject involving political discussion. As the president of the British Association, Adam Sedgwick, put it in his concluding address, the new section would have to follow strict rules for 'if we transgress our proper boundaries, go into provinces not belonging to us, and open a door of communication to the dreary world of politics, that instant will the foul Daemon of discord find his way into our Eden of philosophy'.[15]

Sedgwick's fears were not without foundation, as a closer examination of the clique who were responsible for the new Statistical Section shows. Initially a small meeting was held at which were present T. R. Malthus (in the chair), Quetelet, Rev. George D'Oyley, Jones, Babbage, W. H. Sykes, Dr Somerville (of Oxford), and John Elliot Drinkwater. D'Oyley, the rector of Lambeth, and Somerville were of no great importance in the later stages (except that Somerville's stepson, Woronzow Greig, was the first secretary of the London Statistical Society). Malthus, Quetelet, Jones, Babbage, Sykes, and Drinkwater may, therefore, be regarded as the crucial group.

Of these Babbage was the most important. We have already noted some relevant facts about him.[16] But one aspect of his career, which has not been emphasized so far, is that from about 1829 to about 1835 he was deeply involved in Liberal politics. His first major venture was his chairmanship of the election committee for William Cavendish in the 1829 Cambridge election.[17] In 1832 Babbage took a further step and tried to find a seat for himself.[18] He proved a little too much of a prima donna for selection committees and failed. This was not the end of Babbage, the parliamentary scientist. A month before the meeting at Cambridge he was approached to stand 'especially in the interests of the middle class of people' should David Ricardo withdraw from Parliament.[19] In fact Babbage stood again for selection in the summer of 1834 and as late as January 1835 held hopes of election.[20] Thus the period of Babbage's highest involvement in statistical ventures was also the period of his foray into Liberal politics.

Babbage's closest associate in much of this political activity was John Elliot Drinkwater. Drinkwater was a rising man in Whig-Liberal circles. He was the son of Colonel John Drinkwater and was born in 1801. In 1816 he went to Westminster as a King's Scholar and three years later proceeded to Trinity College Cambridge, taking a first in 1820. In 1821 he was entered at the Middle Temple and two years later graduated Fourth Wrangler at Cambridge. Failing to get the desired fellowship he went to France and returned in 1827 to take up a legal career.[21] He was introduced to Babbage by William Whewell in 1824[22] and by 1827 the two were on particularly friendly terms. Drinkwater had aided Babbage in the Cambridge election of 1829 and in the ventures of 1832. He was also heavily involved in the Society for the Diffusion of Useful Knowledge, writing lives of Newton and Galileo and investigating the feasibility of starting the Penny Cyclopaedia.[23] With these connections it is not surprising to find that by 1833 Drinkwater had embarked upon a civil service career becoming legal counsel to the Home Office (and hence drafting many of the Whig reforms of the next few years). He was one of the assistant commissioners for the 1833 Factory Commission and had completed his controversial report on Yorkshire, justifying the factory system, some three weeks before the Cambridge meeting.[24] He was also one of the Municipal Corporations Commissioners.

Drinkwater's political commitments are obvious. Colonel William Henry Sykes is a more shadowy figure though he was long to remain involved in the statistical movement. He was born in 1790 and entered the Bombay Army at the age of 14. He rose to the rank of captain before returning to England in 1820 and then spent four years travelling (during which time he got married). In 1824 he went back to Bombay and was appointed 'Statistical Reporter to the Government'. The post was abolished at the end of 1829 in a wave of retrenchment and after carrying on his labours on his own account for another year Sykes returned to England at the beginning of 1831.[25] Little is known of his views at this stage in his life but his report on the British Association meeting of 1835 implies that he was a typical statistician of the time in seeing statistical studies as a part of the process of 'improving' society.[26] He was to contribute many papers to the British Association and the Statistical Society of London, mainly on Indian statistics.

Also interested in Indian statistics was Richard Jones. He had been a member of the same circle as Babbage in their student days at Cambridge.[27] Jones was curate at Brasted (Kent) from 1826 until 1833 when he became professor of political economy at King's College London. Though a Liberal in politics he was in one sense a lone wolf among the political economists of his time since he was against general laws and more in favour of massive data-accumulation than of the essentially deductive approach of the classical school to which Nassau Senior and Ricardo belonged.[28] In his introductory lecture at King's College he had remarked that

> it is not pleasant to reflect how little has been done in England to systematize statistical inquiries, or to preserve and spread the information which statistics can give us ... We may hope surely, that mankind and their concerns will soon attract interest enough to receive similar attention [to the physical sciences]; and that a statistical society will be added to those which are advancing the scientific knowledge of England.[29]

Of the founders of the Statistical Section Jones was perhaps the least committed ideologically and the most interested in statistics for their own sake.

That any interest at all should be shown in statistics by Malthus is not remarkable. Malthus's many works on population and political economy had, despite their subject matter, been marked by a notable lack of quantitative data. Rather, they were paradigms of the deductive method favoured by contemporary political economists. No doubt he was pulled into the scheme as a readily available elder statesman of political economy. But there may have been more to Malthus's role than this for within a few days of the Cambridge meeting he was writing to Quetelet seeking answers to questions on vital statistics, notably on fertility, fecundity, and the wages and food of the poor.[30] Shortly before his death he sent a paper to Babbage for his comments.[31] One might wonder whether Malthus was working on a revision of his most famous work backed by a greater wealth of detail, a project cut short by his death.

The group of Englishmen which took advantage of the opportunity presented by Quetelet's visit shared one outstanding characteristic which cannot go unemphasized. They were far from being a band of intellectual young turks launching an attack on the citadel of orthodoxy. Rather, in broad terms, they came from within that orthodoxy, already, with the exception of Drinkwater, men of middle age or older and of high standing in intellectual, particularly Liberal intellectual, circles. The statistical movement began, as it was to remain (though less definitely so), a movement of the reforming establishment, Whig to Liberal in politics, non-Benthamite (yet not consciously anti-Benthamite).

The original group met under Malthus's chairmanship on the morning of 27 June 1833 at the Cambridge meeting of the British Association. Quetelet communicated to the meeting the results of some of his researches into the proportion of crime at different ages and in different parts of France and Belgium. Sykes offered for use his work on the statistics of the Deccan and Babbage made some remarks on what, from the description, appears to have been the normal probability curve and its application to social phenomena.[32] With this success behind them the group adjourned to gather together interested people for a larger meeting that evening.

Over 30 assembled, including such important men as Earl Fitzwilliam, Sir Charles Lemon, and Henry Hallam (the Whig historian). Jones enjoined the meeting not to narrow the planned field of investigation at the genesis of the section's labours and suggested that the first order of business should be to draw up heads of enquiry as well as a list of desirable researches. He further indicated that it might be possible to obtain government co-operation (it should be noted that G. R. Porter was not at the Cambridge meeting). Babbage mooted the idea of communicating with friendly societies and 'proprietors of large manufactories'. Nothing more was done until the next day when another meeting was held with Jones in the chair. Jones read a homily to the meeting pointing out that in the narrowest sense statistics would be limited to 'the production and distribution of wealth'. He went on to say, however, that it would be useful to till a wider field so that the section 'would think foreign to the objects of their inquiries no classes of facts relating to communities of men which promise when sufficiently amplified to indicate general laws'.

So far Jones's injunctions were much as might be expected. But he went on to say something which casts a great deal of light on the attitudes behind the upsurge in the statistical movement: 'To repress however to some extent the spirit of premature speculation which is too apt to mingle itself with such researches perhaps it might be prudent to limit as far as possible their reception of such matter to facts capable of being expressed by numbers'.[33] Thus quantification was used because of the desire to avoid the appearance of bringing in what was known as 'party spirit'. The new section had little choice in the matter for the British Association insisted that it confine itself to 'matters of fact, with mere abstractions, and with numerical results' while the 'higher generalizations' of political economy and political philosophy were forbidden.[34] The notion that statistical 'facts' were pure and non-controversial was an unconscionable time dying but by the end of our period the statisticians had done enough to raise serious doubts. Indeed, from the very beginning, the movement was animated by a set of attitudes which owed much to 'higher generalizations'.

After this strange, but necessary, piece of casuistry Jones called for the creation of a more permanent machinery than the Statistical Section could provide. A permanent committee based in London was set up with Babbage as president and Drinkwater as secretary. The committee had the power to add to its number and the hope was expressed that it would grow into a statistical society. An abstract of the proceedings was prepared but not printed by the Association because of the irregularity of the proceedings.[35] However, formal recognition for the future was forthcoming and Sykes and Jones were encouraged to continue their researches.[36]

Jones was to remain active for a little while longer in the movement but the political economists who soon became temporarily involved in the developing statistical society were in a more orthodox mould. Before Quetelet's return to Belgium he went to a dinner in London attended by, among others, Malthus, Nassau Senior, Thomas Tooke (of the Political Economy Club) and Babbage, at which they discussed the issue of child labour in factories and 'roulent generalement sur les questions politiques du jour'.[37] It does not require much insight to guess the tenor of the opinions expressed. Thomas Tooke was chairman of the Royal Commission which was about to deliver itself of the verdict that 'all legislative interference with the disposal of labour extending beyond the age of childhood, properly so called' was out of the question.[38] Nassau Senior was in charge of the Poor Law Commission and was greatly concerned about the parlous state of the poor laws. In a revealing and previously unknown letter to Quetelet in 1833 (here quoted in full) he wrote:

> You appear to have got through your revolution more quietly than could have been hoped – and to have settled down into a quiet government under a sensible King, and with a low taxation very successfully.
>
> We are in the midst of ours. How it will end I know not: I hope as well as yours. If it were not for our dreadful poor law abuses and difficulties I should have no fears – but they have brought us into such a state in which *nec mala nec remedia ferre possumus.*

You will be astonished, when you see our evidence, that society can hold together under such circumstances.[39]

For Nassau Senior it was thus essential that the poor law enquiry should come to the right conclusions. His own attitude to statistics was a curious one since he believed implicitly in the deductive method; he was later to write to Quetelet that 'I do not consider the truths of political economy as founded on Statistical facts, yet its illustrations generally are'.[40] Political economy, or Nassau Senior's version of it, was, therefore, more akin to the godhead than to modern economics. Perhaps this explains why, as Mark Blaug has rightly pointed out, there is in the 1834 Poor Law Report no 'hint of a quantitative view of the problem' of the poor.[41] Senior's own grasp of statistics may be seen in the argument he used to prevent an alteration in the Poor Law Amendment Bill (ironically, one of the very few instances where it can be shown a statistical argument had an important effect on major legislation). Lord Ellenborough wished to make it possible for the authorities to grant relief at their discretion to those over 60. This would, in Nassau Senior's opinion, turn the aged into paupers so he looked up John Rickman's lifetables for Essex in the period 1813–30. They showed that out of those who survived to age 20, nearly half survived to age 60. Hence, concluded Senior, nearly half of the adult population were over 60. At a hurriedly convened conference in the Lord's robing room Senior revealed his dreadful news that, not only the aged, but the whole country would be pauperized by the amendment. Ellenborough then withdrew it.[42]

Clearly with Nassau Senior and statistics it was very much a case of the blind leading the blind. But for the moment nobody was leading anywhere so far as the statistical society was concerned. Jones wrote to Babbage that Thomas Chalmers of Glasgow was keen to activate the Statistical Section next year at Edinburgh but neither Jones nor Babbage expected to be present. However, Jones asked Babbage to 'keep them up to it as far as may be done without unreasonable trouble and keep the section alive at least for Chalmers ... perhaps Drinkwater and you may do more if you are so minded'.[43]

Perhaps. Nothing was done until the end of the year, when the question came up again in Babbage's mail. Francis Place had expressed an interest in helping to form a society.[44] Possibly Babbage was spurred by the need to retain control in the hands of himself and his friends. What is certain is that by late January 1834 enough had been done for G. R. Porter, disillusioned with the possibilities of the Statistical Department of the Board of Trade, to write promising support and stating that Poulett Thomson, J. Deacon

Hume, Charles Knight, and Chadwick had expressed a wish to join.[45]

Babbage and Drinkwater went ahead and began to make more formal arrangements. As secretary, Drinkwater did most of the work but Babbage was left to bring certain people, such as Malthus and Hallam, into the fold.[46] Personal contacts were in fact crucial. Hallam, for example, was responsible for obtaining the adherence of the Marquis of Lansdowne.[47] Others, perhaps not always desired, offered their services.[48] A meeting was held in late February attended by Babbage, Malthus, Jones, Sykes, Drinkwater, G. W. Wood (a Liberal M.P.), William Empson, William Ogilby, William Wolryche Whitmore, and Edward Strutt – all the new members were familiar figures in reforming organizations like the SDUK and Whig or Liberal in politics. It was decided that a statistical society should be formed and a number of people were mentioned as likely members. A public meeting was called for 15 March 1834.[49]

A prospectus was drawn up (by Jones – not Hallam as the centenary history states) and the Marquis of Lansdowne approached to preside at the public meeting. Drinkwater made out a list of some 250 men who might join and they were sent copies of the prospectus.[50] In order to present a non-political face to the public a few prominent Tories were secured. The first motion of the meeting that 'accurate knowledge of the condition and prospects of Society is an object of great national importance not to be obtained without a careful collection and classification of Statistical facts' was moved by a politically balanced team of Henry Goulburn and Francis Jeffery. Babbage and Jones then moved the formation of the Statistical Society and Babbage, Jones, Hallam, and Drinkwater were constituted a provisional committee.[51] Lansdowne promised the assistance of the government and hoped that this would be reciprocated.[52]

With this meeting over it was a matter of drumming up as many names as possible. Desirable Members of Parliament, overwhelmingly Whigs and Liberals, were canvassed for support.[53] E. Carleton Tufnell was obtained as one of the secretaries. Tufnell was another Drinkwater: Assistant Poor Law Commissioner, Factory Commissioner, he had also argued that the factory system was not unhealthy and wanted only the education provisions of the 1833 Factory Bill since by them 'all would be done that human legislation can do'.[54]

Despite this progress all was not ready for the planned first meeting, which was deferred until the beginning of May.[55] When the meeting was held it considered the prospectus originally drawn up by Jones, which had already been amended. The prospectus began with a stern injunction to the society to take as 'the first and most essential rule of its conduct to exclude all *opinions*'. Having crossed that insuperable hurdle with all the ease of an organization which had not yet done anything, the society divided its studies into four groups – 'economical', 'political', 'moral' and intellectual', and 'medical'. Once information on what might usefully be investigated had been obtained from the Statistical Department of the Board of Trade, sub-committees were to draw up schedules of questions, a task that was expected to occupy most of the society's time in the first year. The hope was also expressed that more local societies would spring into being which could then circulate the questionnaires and collect them.[56]

The clause excluding '*opinions*' was repeated when the society chose the emblem of a wheatsheaf with the motto 'Aliis Extenderum', signifying that it collected facts the conclusions from which were to be threshed out elsewhere. This self-denying ordinance was mainly due to Henry Hallam who had 'apprehensions that politics would creep in among us, that we should be engaged in speculations not simply theoretical and philosophical'.[57] Hallam, though a Whig, was a conservative one. He had had strong reservations about the Reform Bill and perhaps, therefore, he was suspicious of the intentions of the more radical men around him. But had the clause been observed, as one leading member noted 20 years later, the society would have been a club for numerate drudges 'accumulating facts idly and unprofitably'.[58]

Yet the clause passed into the rules of the Society and the idea it embodies was long to influence the statistical movement. With the clause approved the meeting could move on to consider the draft constitution prepared by the provisional committee. It was passed with minor amendments. The society was to have a council of 31 members including the president (who could not hold office for more than two years running), four vice-presidents (nominated by the president), a treasurer, and three honorary secretaries. The council had the power to appoint committees. The number of fellows was unlimited but a new fellow could be elected only after nomination by two fellows. The membership fee was two guineas a year which could be compounded for life for 20 guineas. There was also to be a separate category for foreign members (corresponding membership was added later).[59] The organization bears a close resemblance to that suggested by Jeremy Bentham for a 'Statistic Society' in 1831 but it is extremely unlikely that the provisional committee knew of this.[60] There was nothing unusual about the form of the society and Bentham, as elsewhere, was expressing common ideas.

The newly elected council certainly was not Benthamite. Rather it represented an attempt to fit everybody in who had some claim to be there. Surprisingly, those responsible for the creation of the society

The Foundation of the Statistical Society of London 87

did not dominate the offices: Lansdowne was president (starting a long tradition of choosing the president for his name and prestige), Hallam treasurer, and the three secretaries were Tufnell, Charles Hope Maclean, and Woronzow Greig.[61] Maclean was yet another Assistant Poor Law Commissioner and a lawyer. Greig was the son of Mary Somerville by her first marriage and was descended on his father's side from the famous family of Russo-Scottish admirals. He was an old political associate of Babbage's.

Babbage led the rest of the council with Drinkwater, Jones, Sir Charles Lemon, Malthus, Porter, Nassau Senior, Sykes, Thomas Tooke, Whewell, among others.[62] The council soon met with only Whewell absent. Committees were formed according to Jones's plan with the addition of a committee on colonial statistics which was quickly merged with a correspondence committee set up to arrange plans for communicating with provincial societies.[63] All seemed to be going well and the membership soon passed the 300 mark (it was over 200 before the first meeting of the society). Tufnell wrote to the Manchester Statistical Society to inform them that plans were being drawn up for systematic correspondence between the London society and the provincial societies (of which there was actually only one at the time of writing).[64]

All was *not* well. Whewell complained to Quetelet 'we are somewhat embarrassed by the extent of our subject'.[65] Nothing ever came of the scheme for 'systematic' correspondence even when there were societies to correspond with. It was unlikely to while the London society took the view that others were to be little more than its agents. The initial spurt of attendance at the council meetings soon dropped away. Thirty out of 31 attended the first meeting, 18 the second, 13 the third. Average attendance at the next eight meetings before the summer recess was eight, with one meeting failing to reach the quorum of five. Those who had been included for their names and prestige largely ceased attending. The average attendance at the 18 meetings of the council from October to the end of the 1834–5 session was 6.4 with the quorum not reached twice and barely reached on another five occasions. Twelve members failed to attend one of these 18 meetings and another 11 attended one to four times. For its continued existence the society was dependent upon the other eight – Hallam, Greig, Maclean, Drinkwater, Porter, Sykes, Tooke, and Vardon – all of whom attended at least nine times. One foretaste of the future was the fact that Porter headed the list with 17 appearances at the last 18 meetings.

Yet the society kept growing. By the time of the second annual meeting in March 1835 there were 398 fellows, 99 of whom had been added since the previous May. The finances were flourishing and a paid assistant secretary was appointed.⁶⁶ The real difficulty, as council attendances had shown, was getting people to do something beyond pledging their names in a worthy cause. In addition, the early papers read to the society were not of a high standard. Maclean read a report on the 1834 meeting of the Statistical Section of the British Association. Greig gave an impressionistic paper 'On the character and present condition of the Irish labourer' which was full of *'opinions'* but practically devoid of statistics, while the third paper printed in the *Proceedings* was on the accounts and depositors of the Devon and Exeter Savings Bank. Then William Jacob took his 1832 Board of Trade paper off the shelf, Vardon was asked to give a paper on the state of parliamentary representation, while Drinkwater began a series of intensely boring papers based on a book on the statistics of Venice. Porter commented on a work on Spanish statistics, the assistant secretary on a manuscript on the statistics of Odessa. This left Sykes to come somewhere near the heart of the society's business with a rather superficial paper 'On the Increase of Wealth and Expenditure in various Classes of Society, as indicated by Official Returns'.⁶⁷ And that was all. Odessa, Venetia, and the Devon and Exeter Savings Bank no doubt had their place in the society but scarcely as a substitute for serious investigation of the many crucial social and economic issues of the day.

Even an early indication of better times to come was a failure. Porter tried to use the society as a substitute for the Statistical Department by getting it to sponsor a national survey of savings banks. In January 1835 a form of return drawn up by Porter was agreed to by the council.⁶⁸ A month later Drinkwater and Greig were asked to find barristers willing to circulate the forms while they were on the legal circuits.⁶⁹ The 1835–6 session began with an admission that this had not worked and it was resolved to contact the provincial societies while a number of members were to try to distribute these forms in their home areas.⁷⁰ Some three months later it was agreed Porter should send the forms to certain Irish savings banks.⁷¹ Then, as a last expedient, it was decided that the remaining undelivered forms should be handed over to the parliamentary members of the council for franking under parliamentary privilege for circulation.⁷² That was the end of Porter's first venture. Yet it was largely from a group centred on Porter that the revival (or, more accurately, the true foundation) of the society was to come.

That time was not at hand in 1835. The council spent over a year discussing some questionnaires, drafted by Rev. Edward Stanley, designed to elicit local information. There were fears that some of the questions were not purely statistical and it was not until June 1836 that a schedule was approved.⁷³ Two thousand copies were printed but the council could think of nothing better than to approach the factory commissioners and the assistant poor law commissioners to distribute them.[74] Soon after Stanley had presented his draft the council had made what was tantamount to a recognition of its state of creeping paralysis by asking its members to draw up questionnaires on their own special interests. Nothing much appears to have come of this.[75]

However, an optimistic report was submitted by the council in March 1835. Babbage reported to Quetelet 'the Society prospers and continues its labours which you well know are necessarily slow'.[76] Perhaps there was an unwillingness to recognize the symptoms of premature decay for at the first council meeting of the 1835–6 session the committees were cast in the same form as the previous year with very little change in membership.[77] Yet of the committees only one met, the medical statistics committee, which busied itself with the inevitable circulars and the rather more valuable business of obtaining alterations to the Coroners' Bill at that time before Parliament.[78]

Despite some improvement in the standard of the papers read at the ordinary meetings of the society the downward drift as a whole continued. So little had been done that in July 1835 it was decided that no report should be made to the British Association for the Advancement of Science.[79] Attendance at the council meetings was even worse than the previous year. Average attendance at the 24 meetings was 6.1 with a quorum failing to assemble four times and a bare quorum or only one over, ten times. There were never more than nine present. The low point was reached in the winter session of 1835–6. Three times in five meetings up to mid-December the quorum was not reached. Worst of all, at a meeting attended by the hard core of Sykes, Maclean, Porter, Tooke, and Greig, it was found that there were no papers ready for the next meeting.[80] The hat, so to speak, was passed round and Greig dropped in a paper on an Italian book on the geography and statistics of Morocco. Porter also promised a paper on the Danish bills of mortality for 1834.[81] At the next meeting of the council Greig and Porter must have reflected on their generosity for they were the only two to turn up.[82]

Even so a brave face was put forward at the third annual meeting in March 1836. The council were able to report that the total membership had remained roughly stable at 392. It had to confess, however, its failure to establish its claim for accommodation in Somerset House. The lack of achievement in the general affairs of the society was put down to the inevitability of slow progress at first since statistical investigations took time. It all had a faint air of unreality, especially since the report purportedly came from a council of 31 members but was read to an annual general meeting where perhaps no more than 24 people were present.[83]

Despite the self-deception it was the third annual general meeting which almost imperceptibly began a process of reinvigoration which gathered pace later in the 1836–7 session. Drinkwater, too busy with government affairs, had resigned from one of the secretaryships in February 1836. His place was taken by the young and active Rawson Rawson who, on and off, was to be an important figure in the society for the next 50 years. This was a start, but only a start. The committees again went unreconstructed. But in April the council gave evidence of renewed vigour when at a meeting attended by 13 members it was decided to commence a statistical account of London. The aim was to collate and condense existing material and then proceed to the collection of new information. It was also decided to start a record of contemporary statistics.[84]

The thrust was continued when a select committee of Holt Mackenzie, Porter, Rawson, Vardon, Redgrave (of the Home Office), and Greig was set up to supervise the preparation for publication of the statistical account of London. The work was to be aided by a £100 grant to the committee.[85] Both proposals seem to have come from Holt Mackenzie who had a particular interest at the time in the food consumed in London.[86] With the apparent loss of interest by Mackenzie after June the project for a statistical account lapsed.[87]

This setback to the slowly developing renaissance occurred just before the summer recess of 1836 so that the society remained in the doldrums for some months. Then, in December, the necessary process of appraisal of the failures of the previous two and half years began with the creation of a committee on a motion from Porter. It was this act which marks the dividing line between the first and barren phase of the society's existence and its effective reconstitution as an agent for the discussion of social and economic statistics as well as the occasional prosecution of projects of its own. The next few years were by no means ones of uninterrupted success but they contrasted greatly in character, personnel, and achievement with the first three years. Had the renaissance not taken place the London society might have gone the way of all the rest, except Manchester, and disappeared.

[7]
The Statistical Society of London: the improved society

The committee appointed on Porter's motion in December 1836 comprised himself, Rawson and five others. Its function was to consider the existing construction of the committees.¹ Its report was presented to the council in February 1837 and was a sad but realistic appraisal of the society's early history. It pointed out that of the five committees originally created one had never met. Three of the others had ceased to make a quorum after a few meetings and disappeared into a nominal existence. Only one (the medical committee) had continued to operate at all. None of them had reported to the council at the end of the first year. They had, therefore, been given the power to co-opt but still nothing had been presented for approval to the council. One reason was apparent: 'the terms in which the committees were first appointed were too vague and extended.' The society, in other words, had to recognize that it could not mount a full assault on the complete array of statistics. By attempting less it might achieve more. The report recommended that in future five or more fellows who wished to work on a specific topic should be allowed to propose to the council their formation into a committee. In addition, it was proposed to appoint a committee to prepare a digest of the parliamentary papers.²

The process of self-criticism was continued at the annual general meeting the next month. It was re-emphasized that the range of proposed topics in 1834 had been vast. The outcome had been a bar to the understanding of what was possible. Furthermore, the council report argued that there were inherent difficulties in statistical studies, difficulties which had not been fully recognized. The first was the large amount of time and effort required. Nor could that time and effort be devoted to personal aims since all 'speculative matter' had been excluded. It was the council's view that this had deterred many people from personal involvement.³

Underlying the council's report (and the committee's) was a

realization of the limitations of the men responsible for founding the society. We may be more explicit about these than was possible in 1837. The founders were well suited to set up a prestigious society but not to the task of carrying on its work. Babbage was quick to lose his enthusiasm for statistics and became more and more involved in his calculating machine. In 1836 Porter described him as 'overwhelmed with his various pursuits'.[4] Babbage's role became that of an elder statesman. That chance never came Malthus's way, of course, for he died shortly after the society's foundation. Jones's activity in the society was greatly reduced after his appointment to succeed Malthus in 1835. In 1836 he was involved in the passage of the Tithe Commutation Bill and was subsequently made one of the Ecclesiastical Commissioners. Perhaps most significant was what Disraeli called 'his notorious Epicurean habits' which, with his other pursuits, took up all his time, as well as an income of £2000 a year.[5] Drinkwater was also too busy and was never a serious statistical investigator anyway. He played no part in the society after 1835, by which time his career as an official enquirer into social problems had come to an end.[6] Nassau Senior was never interested or concerned enough to do anything and had taken part only at the moment of creation of the society. Tufnell seems to have been completely bound up in his own work as an Assistant Poor Law Commissioner and as a crusader against trade unions. Hallam was willing and interested but not in a position to do a great deal himself as an elderly historian. Tooke was also a regular attender (and was to remain so) but, despite his work on various royal commissions, he did all his private research on monetary issues and did it alone.

Thus, with the exception of Hallam and Tooke, the founders had withdrawn from active involvement by the start of the 1837–8 session. This was recognized at the end of the session when Drinkwater (now known as J. E. D. Bethune), Jones, and Senior were dropped from the council. Babbage remained for another year though he attended only one council meeting in these two years. Thereafter he occasionally served when asked (his interest was briefly rearoused in the early 1850s with the international statistical congress movement). The old guard disappeared almost before they had appeared. The men who now came to prominence in the society were a more professional group, frequently considerably younger, not always as uniformly placed as politically active Whigs or Liberals (though often participating in various reforming organizations and pressure groups). They were led by Porter and Rawson, backed by Maclean. With so many of the founders gone and with his official position as fulcrum, Porter was well placed to exert considerable influence on the society. He must also have been by this time thoroughly disillusioned with the statistical possibilities of the Board of Trade.

Rawson was the perfect foil, adding exceptional energy and industriousness to Porter's experience and influence. He had entered the society in March 1835. Within a few months he was delivering to the fellows a homily on the collection of statistics and the need to attend meetings of sub-committees.[7] Like Porter he was committed in the late 1830s to a national system of education and was at this stage of his career a fervent believer in the ideology of 'improvement' that was the common intellectual ground of the statisticians. In the first number of the *Journal* he made it clear that his hope was that 'statistical investigations may be rendered available to the best of all purposes, that of improving the condition, increasing the health, and diminishing the sufferings and mortality of our countrymen'.[8] Though dogmatic on many points he was, significantly, no slave to even the most sacred of the laws of political economy. At the beginning of 1838 he read a paper on two Belgian charitable institutions which tended to the conclusion that they had been successful in removing indigence.[9] The paper met with unfavourable comment from

> one of our associates famous for his knowledge of Political Economy [who] stated that the system followed in this Establishment must have unfavourable effects on the independent industry of the town. I replied to him that the commission had announced that mendicity had been eradicated, to which he replied that this Establishment could even have caused a large part of this mendicity.[10]

The political economist, who was most likely Tooke, represented the attitudes which had dominated the society at the outset. With men like Rawson taking control the hold of orthodox political economy was weakened.

It must be emphasized that this is not to say that there was not a recognizable set of attitudes which characterized the active members of the society. Porter, for one, was a politically motivated man. Apart from his well-known free-trade views,[11] he was active in the Central Society of Education (as was his wife). He shared the ideology of improvement with Rawson, arguing that the purpose of educating the ignorant was 'to render them wiser and better, and therefore happier beings'.[12] His zeal for education was to lead him into anticlericalism, which he vented in a letter to Quetelet: 'our church is, as you know, enormously wealthy and therefore very powerful – it fears, and with great reason, that if the people were instructed in matters which it imports them to know, the power of the Church would be lessened and its wealth also'.[13] This was the man who had been trying to improve the social statistics collected by the government and who was now to dominate the statistical society. It was Porter who presented to the society a facsimile copy of Magna Carta which was to be framed and hung in the meeting room.[14]

Between them Porter and Rawson greatly influenced the direction the society took between 1837 and 1842. Papers which needed to be vetted were usually referred to them.[15] Even more important was their control of the new venture which was begun in the 1837–8 session, the *Journal*. Since its inception the society had published brief summaries of its meetings under the title of the *Proceedings of the Statistical Society of London*. There had also been an ill-fated attempt to publish a journal containing some of the papers presented at the meetings in full. Volume one, part one of these *Transactions* was published in 1837 as a result of a decision taken the previous March to set up a committee to make a selection of the papers.[16] Various enterprises were considered but it was not until after the election of a new council in March 1838 that a committee was appointed to negotiate with Charles Knight over the proposed formation of the society's own journal.[17] It was quickly decided to publish and Rawson was appointed paid editor at £75 a year, a salary and a post he held in conjunction with his Board of Trade duties.[18]

With Porter and Rawson at its head the society was entering a period of creativity. The fourth annual report, written by Maclean and Rawson, had a most confident tone that had not been heard since the euphoria of the foundation. The council felt that 'a review of the proceedings of the past year affords them much reason to congratulate the Fellows of the Society on its progress, and on its continually improving prospects of usefulness, arising from an evident increase of activity and consequent extension of operations'.[19] The proof was the commencement of a second phase of committee activity which, in contrast with the first, had some solid achievements. In fact, the first of the new committees had been set up before the revival had really gathered momentum, in January 1837. It was on criminal statistics and the core of the committee consisted of Porter, Rawson, and Samuel Redgrave.[20] Despite the strength of the committee it accomplished little. It tried to draw up tabular forms for collecting information concerning criminal offenders, as well as wishing to correspond with the Police Commissioners, but the committee faded away with no publications to its name.[21]

The same could not be said of the second creation of the new phase, the education committee. This was set up in July 1837 on a motion from Sykes. The rest of the committee comprised Porter, B. F. Duppa, Rawson, and Nathaniel Lister, with the power to co-opt a further two members.²² It was thus strongly biased towards the opinions of the Central Society of Education since Porter was a leading member and Duppa was honorary secretary and editor of the Central Society's publications. The committee's function was to digest the reports and supervise the activities of a paid agent who was to do the actual work of the enquiry.²³ Unlike so many earlier committees it got quickly down to business and by the end of 1837 it was able to present an interim report (on the St Martins-in-the-Fields and Strand poor law unions).²⁴ The first report on Westminster was soon completed and 2000 copies were printed.²⁵ Five parishes and 116 schools had been covered.²⁶

The survey was then extended to two other parishes in Westminster, St John's and St Margaret's. The second part of the enquiry was more extensive than the first though it should be noted that it was essentially derivative of the studies carried out by the Manchester Statistical Society in both method and conclusion. The London Society was a latecomer to such surveys and this is apparent in the published second report of its education committee.²⁷ By the end of 1838 a third and final report on Westminster was ready and presented to the society.²⁸

This impressive progress was slowed down by the inevitable problem of finance. The Westminster surveys had cost the society some £95.²⁹ When Rev. Edgell Wyatt Edgell moved for a survey of the schools in either the City or Marylebone he was baulked on the grounds of cost.³⁰ Although the work was resumed the financial question continued to bother the society and at the end of 1840 Rawson moved for a committee to try to obtain a grant from the British Association.³¹ Surveys of the City and Marylebone were in fact carried out but interim reports on them were not issued. It was not until January 1843 that the fourth report of the education committee was read, on the Finsbury survey.³² The committee itself was reformed in April 1843 with somewhat changed membership.³³ The new committee, however, had nothing more to do than to complete the report in hand on part of the Tower Hamlets. A fifth and summary report was prepared which covered the City, Westminster, Marylebone, Finsbury, and St George's-in-the-East.³⁴ The rest of the work on the Tower Hamlets was postponed until the completion of the changes in the parochial boundaries in the area.³⁵ In addition, the committee had been given £25 in the previous session, an amount sufficient only to cover existing debts.³⁶ Consequently, after June 1843 the education committee ceased to meet and the survey of London went uncompleted.

The education committee had been from its foundation very much an instrument of the governing elite of the society. Not all committees came from this nucleus. The third committee founded in the society's renaissance was the committee on the 'statistics of life'. Its creation had been requested by six fellows, led by the eminent vital statistician, T. R. Edmonds.[37] The nature of the committee's immediate interests was revealed when they asked, in February 1838, for circulars to be sent out to all insurance offices.[38] The actuarial activities did not last long for they aroused outside interest. Benjamin Gompertz, a prominent actuarial expert, wrote to Babbage about them[39] and the upshot was the reactivation of a committee of actuaries (outside the society). For the time being actuarial enquiries were left to them.[40] It was not the end of actuarial studies in the society in our period though we may suspect that to some extent the vital statistics committee had been the means to an outside end. The committee's terms of reference enabled new projects to be begun since it had been set up to study all kinds of vital statistics so as to point out defects in existing sources, suggest improved forms and methods, and recommend suitable aims.[41]

With the actuarial work in abeyance the committee concentrated over the next two or three years on the official vital statistics. As with the essays into criminal and educational statistics an important role was played by men in or on the fringes of the government bodies in the field. Very early in its deliberations the committee took up the question of the nature of the 1841 census. A report was presented in June 1838 proposing improvements on the procedures previously adopted and the council, led by Porter, encouraged the committee to further efforts.[42] Another report was prepared in April 1839 which recommended the establishment of a separate committee.[43] Under Porter's prompting this was shortly done.[44] In addition to Porter, Edmonds, and six others it was agreed that the new committee should include Leonard Horner (the chief factory inspector) and William Farr once they had been elected to the council.

Porter sought advice from the Quetelet on the best form for the census.[45] But it was not until April 1840 that the committee presented its report (by which time Farr was on the committee but not Horner).[46] They had gathered together information on the censuses of a number of other countries. They had also spent some time looking at Joseph Fletcher's industrial census of Coventry made for the Royal Commission on Hand-Loom Weavers. With this experience to hand the committee suggested a full census of age, sex, marital status, occupation, place of birth, religion, and health, using the civil registration administrative areas and officers. The report specifically excluded the possibility of taking an educational census, though with regret.[47]

The report was, in effect, the work of the government's own

statisticians plus some of the best men outside the government. The committee's estimate of itself was shown by the fact that the council wanted to get its report printed by the House of Commons.[48] Meanwhile Joseph Fletcher, another government man, and now one of the society's secretaries, prepared a draft census bill which was considered by the committee and then amended by Fletcher. In early June 1840 the council noted that the government had held up its bill to give Fletcher's draft 'due consideration'.[49] When this had been given, the preparations for the census continued with the Registrar-General, T. H. Lister, propounding a scheme to J. E. D. Bethune (Drinkwater) who was responsible for drafting the government bill.[50] The administrative machinery envisaged by Lister followed that suggested by the census committee but Lister's view was that the information sought should be limited to 'a few simple facts' so that 'any sensible man who could read and write' would be able to act as an enumerator. This meant that the scope of the census would be no wider than the names, ages, places of birth, and occupations of the people.[51]

Since it was likely that the use of the civil registration machinery would have occurred without any pressure from the society it was reasonable to conclude that none of its recommendations had greatly influenced the Registrar-General. This came as a shock.[52] Somewhat stung, the council resolved to set up a committee of Sir Charles Lemon, Porter, Fletcher, and Rawson to 'consider the expediency' of preparing an abstract of the committee's report to send to all Members of Parliament.[53] The committee never met since amendments to the government's bill were made in the Commons.[54] The 'attention of other influential members' of the society who were in the Commons had been called to the society's suggestions and credit was claimed for the amendments.[55] While this may have been an exaggeration (and the amendments were minor compared with what the census committee had desired) the pride of achievement lingered on and the experiment was repeated in 1849–50 with a committee, including Farr, which recommended an educational census and sent a deputation to the Home Office.[56] It has become one of the traditional functions of the society to make recommendations on forthcoming censuses.[57]

The consideration of the census had required a separate organization from the vital statistics committee but the latter had not ceased functioning. A rather slim and unenlightening report was drawn up on the sickness and mortality among the metropolitan police force.[58] An unsuccessful attempt was made to influence the Home Office on the forms used in coroners' inquests.[59] Then, paralleling the work of Alexander Tulloch at the War Office, reports were made on the health of British troops in India. Tulloch's enquiries had not yet extended to that area so that when the late president of the Madras Medical Board, James Annesley, offered statistics on the period 1829-38 the committee accepted (persuaded by Porter and Rawson). Annesley supervised the preparation of the abstracts, Tulloch co-operated, and reports were produced which closely follow the pattern of Tulloch's official reports.[60] Apart from this, the committee's major effort was a scheme to collect statistics from the superintendent registrars. Though a promise of aid from the Registrar-General was forthcoming the scheme produced no results.

Nevertheless, the society's interest in vital statistics was strong throughout the 1840s and various other committees came and went. The first was begun by William Farr at the end of 1841 on 'the best means of obtaining periodical enumerations of patients in London hospitals'. It was a very strong committee including, among others, Dr W. A. Guy, Edmonds, Tulloch, Sykes, Fletcher, Clendinning, and Rawson.[61] An enumeration was carried out in January 1842 and a report published which covered the number of patients and their distribution by age, sex, and disease. But the main conclusion was the perennial call for better registers and more information.[62] A second enumeration was carried out the following year and a report published.[63] The committee continued in existence for a further year after the enumeration but once the second report was finished it disappeared.

Farr had also been involved in trying to use the society as a pressure group to push for the extension of civil registration to Scotland and Ireland. The campaign had a number of phases. The first began in late 1840 when Dr W. P. Alison of Edinburgh wrote to state that a committee of the Edinburgh College of Physicians had been formed to consider ways of securing a registration act for Scotland and a government enquiry into the state of the poor in Scotland (Alison was interested in both issues).[64] Rawson therefore moved the appointment of a committee to deliberate on the best means of extending civil registration to Scotland and Ireland. Farr, Fletcher, and Tulloch were also on the committee.[65] Alison's committee sent copies of their petition but the agitation died down without result.[66] It was not raised again in the society until 1845 when the then Registrar-General, Major Graham, wrote a letter to the council.[67] The contents were not specified in the council minutes but the outcome was the appointment of a new registration committee which included Graham and Farr as well as nine other leading Fellows (led by Porter).[68] However, perhaps to Farr's chagrin, Graham asked that the names of Farr and himself be withdrawn so that the society would be 'uninfluenced'.[69] The first report of the committee was not printed but a second report was prepared in 1847 and printed the next year.[70] Despite the impressive backing for the extension of civil registration the campaign failed.

Apart from some very minor enterprises this completes the endeavours of the society (as a body) in vital statistics in the 1840s. But two more committees, apart from those already mentioned, had been set up in the flurry of activity in 1837–8. One of these was as unsuccessful as many of the other committees: the committee on strikes. It had been formed on a motion from Porter and Charles Hope Maclean in January 1838. It hoped to draw up accounts covering the previous fifteen years. For each strike the aim was to include the condition of the workmen at the time of the strike, the terms on which work was resumed, and 'the permanent effects of the several disputes upon the character and condition of the workmen'. The major figures on the committee were the familiar ones of Porter, Sykes, Greig, Maclean, and Rawson.[71] A questionnaire was prepared in which the anti-strike bias nearly universal among the middle and upper-class reformers of the type prominent in the society was evident. The questions led towards the desired conclusion that outside agitators were present and that strikes caused an increase in crime, begging, degrading habits, and decreased attendance, while the workmen contracted debts and lost income permanently, and local trade was damaged.[72] One paper was read on two strikes in the Potteries in 1834 and 1836 which expressed all these opinions, deriving satisfaction only from the fact that the men were forced to resume work after ten weeks, on the employers' terms.[73] That appears to have been the only product of the committee's efforts.

If the strikes committee represented the dominant ideology of the society at its least appealing, as well as the usual lack of results, the committee set up in May 1838 to enquire into the condition of the working classes shows its more productive and charitable side. It had been created on the motion of James Heywood and Porter and, like the education committee, derived from the example of the Manchester Statistical Society (with which Heywood had been associated). Apart from Porter and Heywood the members of the committee were Romilly, J. P. Kay, and R. A. Slaney (as one of the members of the Commons most concerned with the health of towns). The committee received an initial grant of £25 to finance a survey in Westminster.[74] Rawson was later to explain that the purpose of the committee was to afford 'exact data to those active and benevolent members of the legislature who are engaged in endeavours to ameliorate the condition of the working classes'.[75] Two agents were employed for a survey of the parishes of St Margaret's and St John's plus a third for part of the time. Over 16,000 people were included in the survey, the main outcome of which was to provide a well-documented attack on landlords for charging an exorbitant price for sub-standard accommodation. The solution was seen to lie in the foundation of what were later to be called 'model dwellings' companies to provide adequate housing, at a profit, but at a lower rent than those normally charged.[76] That was as far as the committee got, for another £75 had been required to pay off its debts and a moratorium was put on its activities.[77]

The problem of finance had become pressing soon after the society started active enquiries in late 1837. As we have seen, the education committee had required financial assistance from the British Association, from whom help had also been sought for the vital statistics committee. In its annual report in March 1842 the council had to report that it had been decided that no enquiries would be begun until the finances of the society were in a sounder state.[78] The first three years of the society, when nothing had been done, had seen the accumulation of a large amount of stock from subscriptions compounded for life. There was usually a small paper debt at the end of each year which was more than covered by the normally sizeable amount of arrears in annual subscriptions.

With the financing of the new committees, above all the education and working classes committees, the reasonably healthy financial situation abruptly changed. Woronzow Greig, more concerned with financial soundness than statistics, moved a number of motions on the finances in February 1839, pointing out that the society had over-spent the previous year.[79] Rawson, who but two months earlier had been mainly agitated by the fact that the housekeeper appeared to be raiding the stocks of cakes and biscuits,[80] moved for an annual committee of finances.[81] The state of the finances was not too serious at the March 1839 audit, with a good favourable balance once all outstanding debts and assets were allowed for. But the next year was a different matter. In March 1840 there was roughly £60 in hand in cash but debts of over £300. 'Recoverable' arrears were estimated at nearly £160. The society was never in danger of bankruptcy with £870 in stocks, but the rapid deterioration gave good cause for concern.[82] Over the next two years a policy of retrenchment brought outstanding debts down to less than 'recoverable' arrears.[83]

It was clear that a continuous programme of large social surveys was beyond the means of the society. Consequently when a survey of the London poor began in 1844 it was initially funded by a donation from Henry Hallam. It was decided to pick a bad area for the survey as 'it might be more for the good of the labouring class to bring forward some less happily situated district'.[84] A leisurely investigation of St George's-in-the-East over the next two years finally led to the presentation of a report in 1848.[85] The committee's work made clear yet again the commitment of the society, or at least its leaders, to social reform. Indeed, in 1845, the Health of Towns Association was allowed to use the society's rooms.[86] Again, in 1845, a committee was set up to verify the accusations made in the London City Mission's magazine about the sanitary condition of Church Lane, St Giles.[87] The committee's report was an indication of how far the society had come from its early fears of 'opinions'. The area was labelled 'a disgrace to a civilized country' so that even though 'it is not properly within the province of your Committee to make suggestions... they cannot refrain' from suggesting the formation of housing associations.[88] 1500 copies of the report were circulated among those influential 'in removing such deplorable features'.[89]

The more open avowal of the reforming sensibilities of the society dated from the time of the renaissance begun by Porter and Rawson in 1837. From that time until the deaths of Joseph Fletcher and Porter in 1852 there was a considerable continuity and stability in the persons and attitudes dominant with the society. Twenty-eight men attended for at least three years more than one-fifth of the possible council meetings during the years from March 1837 to March 1850. Forty-nine others also served on the council (which throughout these 13 years remained fixed at 31 members). Thus the same names recur again and again in any description of the society's activities. In the late 1830s the society was dominated by Rawson Rawson, Thomas Tooke, C. H. Maclean, Sykes, and Porter with solid backing from Dr Nathaniel Lister, Dr John Clendinning, Holt Mackenzie, William Sturges-Bourne, James Heywood, Henry Hallam, Woronzow Greig, Herman Merivale, Sir John Boileau, Sir Charles Lemon, and Edgell Wyatt Edgell. Of this latter group no information could be found concerning Lister or Clendinning (beyond the fact that the latter was a physician at the Marylebone Infirmary while Lister graduated M.D. from Edinburgh in 1827). Edgell was rector of North Cray in Kent and ran a school there on novel lines.[90] Heywood was one of the founders of the Manchester Statistical Society. Holt Mackenzie was a retired member of the East India Company who had served on the Board of Control. Sturges-Bourne was an old Canningite who had been a secretary of state in 1827 as well as being a member of the central commission of the 1834 poor law enquiry. Boileau was an archaeologist and well-known savant who was prominent in many intellectual circles. Herman Merivale was professor of political economy at Oxford and was later to become a prominent civil servant, succeeding Sir James Stephen at the Colonial Office in 1848.[91]

Changes inevitably took place over the years but more in individuals than in types. Maclean died in 1839 and was replaced by Joseph Fletcher. He was nominated by Porter and Rawson and was very much out of the same stable.[92] He was secretary to the Royal Commission on the Hand-Loom Weavers and was to be secretary to the Royal Commission on Children's Employment. In 1844 he became the official responsible for inspecting the schools of the British and Foreign School Society. In that post he was to find ample scope for his beliefs as, in Richard Johnson's happy phrase, a 'cautious radical'.[93] He was an ardent educationalist and statistician and dominated educational statistics in the second half of the 1840s.

On Rawson's posting to Canada in 1842 Fletcher became editor of the *Journal* and seems to have very much taken over Rawson's place as Porter's trusted confidant and workhorse of the society.[94] By this time other changes had taken place with Greig being succeeded in one of the secretary-ships by Heywood and Clendinning in turn. New men of some importance were William Farr from 1840, Sir Isaac Lyon Goldsmid from 1839, and John Bowring from 1840. Goldsmid was one of the leading British Jews of the time, a utilitarian who had helped to found University College, London. His other main interests were in prison reform and the penal code. Bowring needs little introduction as one of Bentham's faithful disciples. He also acted as a roving commercial reporter for the government as well as serving on various commissions.[95]

Such men as Goldsmid and Bowring were on the outer fringes of the governing circle but one man who rapidly found his way to the centre was William Augustus Guy. He entered the council in 1841 and replaced Clendinning as secretary in 1843. Descended from a long line of medical men he had graduated in 1837, almost immediately becoming professor of forensic medicine at King's College. In 1842 he was made assistant physician to King's College Hospital and was later to help found the Health of Towns Association.[96] He quickly came to associate on the council mainly with Sykes and, from 1846, F. G. P. Neison. Neison was actuary to the Medical, Invalid, and General Life Office and became something of the *enfant terrible* of social statistics in the 1840s. Like Guy he was a professional and viewed with distaste the dogmatism and fact-twisting of men of Chadwick's type. For Chadwick the ends of investigation were more important than the means, whereas Guy and Neison represent perhaps the first example in the society of men who, while still of reforming sympathies (particularly Guy), regarded accurate methodology as at least as important as justifying a preconceived theory.

The other four men who came into varying degrees of prominence in the 1840s were William Drummond Oswald, James Whishaw, John Melville, and William Spence. Of these Spence and Whishaw were the most prominent, Oswald the most active.[97] The leaders of the society in fact fall into a number of groups. The basic division is between the active statisticians who dominated the activities of the society, and the sometimes elderly men of good name and connections. The former included Rawson, Neison, Fletcher, Tooke (in a special sense for he never presented a paper), Guy, Maclean, Sykes, Porter, Farr, Heywood, Greig, and Edgell. Within this group there are occasional hints that there was a slight split between a predominantly governmental group and the non-official statisticians such as Sykes, Guy, and Neison. But the division was one of nuance rather than serious substance. Apart from the active statisticians there were the men of standing, with whom may be included men like Lister and Oswald who played a useful role without being statisticians themselves. The men of standing had one common, though not universal, characteristic: age. By 1840 Hallam was 63, Sturges-Bourne 71, Goldsmid 62, and Spence 57. Most of the others (such as Boileau and Bowring) were in their late forties or fifties. This may not seem to type them as aged but roughly where the notables left off in age the active investigators began. Porter and Sykes were easily the senior two at 50 in 1840. Rawson was still only 30 when he went to Canada in 1842, Fletcher 27 when he joined the council in 1839, Guy 31 (1841), and Farr 33 (1840).

It was the activists who ensured the survival of the society beyond the 1830s. The society remained less rigidly attached to Whig-Liberal orthodox political economy but its base remained narrow. In the 1844 *Journal*, for example, there were reports of Chadwick's paper on vital statistics and the sanitary idea; Neison's critique of Chadwick; two papers by Fletcher on the administration of London; a paper by Porter on railway statistics; a critique of the 1841 Irish census by Hallam; a paper in a series by Guy on occupational health; and a paper on the relationship of lung capacity to health. Of the 72 papers read to the society from 1841 to 1850 (inclusive) exactly half were written by seven of the group of active statisticians plus the assistant secretary in the early 1840s (C. R. Weld).[98] Twenty-eight were on vital and medical statistics; seven on education and crime; three on the condition of the working classes; five on railways (including accidents on the railways); nine were by Fletcher on the 'municipal statistics' of London (largely non-quantitative discussions of the administration of London); and 20 were on a variety of miscellaneous topics. These last, except for a series by J. T. Danson on 'commercial progress', were usually very brief.

The papers read in the 1840s were thus concentrated within a small number of topics and, as will become clearer later, on a small range of questions within those topics. Nevertheless, they were of a much higher standard than those produced in the first three years of the society's existence. It must be recognized, however, that the achievements of the Statistical Society of London in the 'age of enthusiasm' were considerably lower than its aspirations. It had survived, published useful work, and carried out a few surveys. The developing professionalism of some of its leading members was a presage of things to come. But most of its committees had done little or nothing and the rest had quickly run out of funds. Despite its nominal membership of around four hundred the active membership was a mere fraction of that figure. For its continued vigour the society relied on a clique whose number barely reached two figures. But for that clique, the society would most likely have gone the way of the provincial statistical societies. Maclean and Rawson had argued in 1838 that a 'decisive proof of the just estimate which is formed of the value, and of the deep interest which is felt for the result, of Statistical researches is presented in the continual formation of new Societies for the purpose of instituting enquiries of this nature'.[99] Perhaps a 'decisive proof' of just how deep that interest was is the limited success of the London society and the almost complete collapse of the provincial movement.

[8]

The Manchester Statistical Society

The provincial societies lie at the heart of the statistical movement. The Manchester Statistical Society was the first to be founded, far and away the most active, and the only one to survive throughout our period. It was created in September 1833 by a small group of middle-class friends mainly engaged in business in Manchester or the surrounding area. There are three important accounts of the foundation in print. The most recent is contained in two valuable articles by David Elesh. But Elesh draws most of his material for the beginning of the society from T. S. Ashton's centenary history. The latter, as might be expected, is more illuminating than most such works thought it shows some of the faults of the genre as well as an over-sympathetic attitude towards the motives of the founders. A less serious defect is that for his account of the origins of the society Ashton relied on an article written in the 1870s by T. R. Wilkinson.[1]

According to Wilkinson the project was conceived by James Phillips Kay and William Langton, who had been involved in the foundation of the Manchester and Salford District Provident Society in March 1833 and were its secretaries. These two were impressed in the course of their work by the lack of information on education and other subjects. Langton suggested the foundation of a statistical society, a suggestion taken up by Kay with the industrialists Samuel and William Rathbone Greg when he toured Derbyshire with them. On their return another leading member of Manchester's commercial and industrial aristocracy, Benjamin Heywood, was contacted. Rapidly a group of friends and relatives coalesced into a society.[2] The kinship aspect is stressed by Ashton and Elesh but both seem prepared to accept the view that the founders were no more than a collection of local worthies who wished to study the working classes in order to improve their condition.[3]

In fact our knowledge of the sequence of events leading to the foundation of the society may be less reliable than is usually thought.

That knowledge is derived from Wilkinson's account which in its turn was based on his conversations with Langton some 40 years after the event. It is noticeable that this account places its real author in the centre of vision as the prime mover and originator of the society. It is obviously likely that Langton exaggerated his own role: it is also possible that he had only a hazy recollection of events which had occurred so long before. On one point his memory was demonstrably unreliable since the foundation of the Statistical Society of London was ascribed mainly to the efforts of the Earl of Kerry.[4]

Langton may not have played quite the role he is usually seen in though obviously he and Kay were two of the group of founders of the society. Langton was born in Preston in 1803 of a merchant family. He went into commerce and in 1829 became chief cashier of Heywood's bank.[5] Previously, in Liverpool, he had been involved in the Provident Society and so it was not surprising that he founded a similar organization in Manchester in conjunction with James Phillips Kay. Kay was a year younger than Langton, a doctor although his father was a cotton manufacturer in Rochdale. He received his medical training in Edinburgh where he frequently helped W. P. Alison. Kay moved to Manchester and it soon became apparent that the young dispensary worker was an ardent Liberal in politics. The crucial experience of his life was probably the cholera epidemic of 1832, which led him to set down his ideas on the condition of the working classes.[6]

The Moral and Physical Condition of the Working Classes expressed ideas which were to be of great weight in the Manchester Statistical Society.[7] It stressed the value of social self-knowledge to avoid 'physical and moral evils'. Because 'statistics are neglected' self-knowledge was lacking. The development of statistics would in Kay's view convince the public of 'the facts which they proclaim'.[8] The facts were evident. The progress of commerce and industry was to the advantage of all and would '*elevate the physical condition*' of all people. 'Foreign and accidental causes' could hide this trend however. The first was the failure to match urban development with the growth of civic institutions. A more powerful disturbing factor was the continued existence of fetters on demand, notably the corn laws. With these fetters a reduction in the hours of labour would merely mean a reduction in wages. The answer was free trade. Beyond this there was a great need for a general system of education so that the poor would be trained to use their leisure time and inculcated with the realities of 'their political position in society, and the duties that belong to it'.[9] Thus a more moral society would be created in which the evils of long hours, bad sanitation, working-class agitation, improvidence and vice detailed in the early sections of Kay's work would disappear. The middle classes were to lead Britain into this promised land. Their moral and sanitary influence would extend everywhere since 'they acquire by their charity, the right of inquiring into [the people's] arrangements – of instructing them in domestic economy – of recommending sobriety, cleanliness, forethought and method'.[10] Model employers, such as Thomas Ashton, would banish discontent, strikes, and the threat of revolution as they directed society towards a rediscovery of the harmony of interests.[11]

Kay's notions of the functions and preconceptions of social investigations deserve space for they are typical of the provincial statisticians. For all his criticism of the sanitary state of Manchester, even of the long hours worked by the cotton operatives, his was a message with a powerful appeal for the reformist sections of the industrial and commercial bourgeoisie. The 13 men who founded the society on 2 September 1833 were overwhelmingly of this type.[12] The two Greg brothers already mentioned clearly were. Samuel was a paradigm of the 'improving' employers, Liberal in politics, who dominated municipal life. Born in 1804 he was the fourth son of a mill-owner. Like all the Gregs he was educated at Unitarian schools and the University of Edinburgh. He entered business on his own in 1832 and established at his factory a Sunday school, a gymnasium, drawing and singing classes, baths, a library, and an 'order of the silver cross' for good conduct in young women. His brother, William Rathbone Greg, was five years younger though he also entered business in 1832. He was to be a leading figure in the Anti-Corn Law League and it has been noted that one of his distinguishing characteristics was 'to discourage unreasonable expectation from political or even social reform'.[13]

The younger Greg wrote a short volume in 1831 which condemned long hours in factories.[14] It is doubtful whether this work still represented the ideas of the two brothers by late 1833. Their elder brother, R. H. Greg, was a leader of the movement to prove that factory labour was not unhealthy but that urbanization was the culprit. He was to dismiss William's 1831 work as 'written before he had any experience and scarcely any acquaintance with factories'.[15] William's own reaction to a proposed reduction of hours below 12 was to ask, 'Did any nation before ever think of restricting the industry and energies of its people?' The inevitable result would be a reduction in wages and an inability to meet foreign competition.[16] Indeed it may be suggested that the need to provide a coherent justification for the factory system, at least in its more humane forms, was a factor in the founding of the Manchester society. One of the first acts of the society was to constitute Samuel and William Greg a committee to report on the evidence to the 1833 factory commission. Their report, presented in March 1834, argued that the evidence, on the whole, vindicated the factory system. In the Gregs' view the major charges – for example, cruelty and the encouragement of immortality – were proved to be groundless. On the question of unhealthiness the witnesses had split 72 to 17 in favour of the factories. Thus it seemed that 'the weakly children are fatigued by twelve hours' labour, but that healthy ones are not'.[17]

The argument demonstrates an attitude which might have been inferred from an examination of the backgrounds of the other founders. Benjamin Heywood was born in 1793, the son of a banker. As a Dissenter he went to a Scottish university (Glasgow). He served temporarily in Parliament in 1831–2 but ill-health forced his retirement. His major interest was the Mechanics' Institute of which he had been the chief founder in 1824. He had been greatly impressed by Kay's book and was determined to prove that a harmony of interest could exist between a humanitarian employer and an educated work-force. Among the founders he was one of the most genuinely interested in the welfare of the working classes though this interest was still in part due to a desire to save them, and him, from 'the wild schemes of political agitators'. Two of his sons were to marry daughters of William Langton.[18]

Heywood brought with him his two brothers-in-law, Samuel and James Robinson. They were cotton manufacturers, sons of a cotton dealer. Samuel, born in 1794, was an 'improving' employer, founder of the famous Dukinfield village library where he was associated with other Unitarians, notably W. R. Greg, Thomas Ashton, G. W. Wood, and Rev. R. B. Aspland. Like Heywood, he was dismayed at the deep class divisions in the industrial society of Lancashire and wished to prevent social upheaval by a mixture of kindness, inculcation of morality, and an appreciation of the source of the social hierarchy in the laws of the universe.[19] In his view the function of the Manchester Statistical Society was to 'improve the condition of the industrious classes by an accurate investigation of the causes which produce our social evils' thus 'cementing together the different ranks and classes of society'.[20] Apart from being Heywood's brother-in-law he was also a son-in-law of John Kennedy, one of the first two vice-presidents.

Kennedy had been present at Cambridge in June 1833 and had attended the meeting at which the decision to form a statistical section was made.[21] Perhaps, therefore, the idea of a statistical society was present in more minds than William Langton's in Manchester in the summer of 1833. Kennedy was the doyen of the society. Born in 1769 he belonged to an older generation than the others. A self-made man of Scottish birth, he was a prominent cotton-spinner and inventor. One of his daughters married Edwin Chadwick.[22] With him in the new society was another factory owner, Henry McConnell, son of Kennedy's old partner. Also a cotton master was Samuel Dukinfield Darbishire. Henry Newbery came from the banking side of the community (he helped to found the Manchester and Salford Bank in 1836).

The cotton masters were soon augmented by Peter Ewart jr, Henry Houldsworth, and James Murray among others. Family ties helped to increase the membership with Shakespeare Philips and Robert N. Philips, brothers-in-law of R. H. Greg. From a different area of manufacturing came Edward Tootal of silk fame. These men were bound together by class and family ties. They also shared a large common ground intellectually. Of the 28 paid up members in July 1834 13 were members of the Manchester Literary and Philosophical Society in 1848.[23] Many, apart from Langton and Kay, were to hold office in the local provident society.[24] Kennedy, Newbery, Heywood, Shakespeare Philips, and Tootal (with R. H. Greg) had signed a requisition for a reform meeting as early at 1827.[25] Add to this the mechanics' institutes, village libraries, and schools and we have a fair picture of a tightly-knit reforming section of the commercial and industrial aristocracy of Manchester, usually men of the second generation rather than self-made.[26]

As the Gregs showed, they were determined to defend the factory system against what they saw as misinformed criticism, without completely ruling out the possibility of reforms. The twin half of this aspect of their attitudes was an antipathy to the old poor law. Kay gave vent to this antipathy in one of the first papers read to the society. For Kay, relief should not be given where it would not 'encourage industry and virtue'.[27] But there was an obverse side to the often seemingly unfeeling reaction to pauperism. There was an emphasis on moral improvement, on the possibility of the creation of a better world in the middle-class image where the streets would not only be paved and drained but free of crime and drunkenness, full of educated, happy, contented, self-reliant (that is, not dependent on the poor law) work-people. This Utopian vision was manifested in studies of 'moral statistics'. Again it was the Gregs who were to the fore. The first paper read to the society was by W. R. Greg on criminal statistics. What few statistics there were, together with statistics from other countries, were seen to indicate that as education advanced inequality of wealth increased, industry grew, and urbanization intensified so that crimes increased in number but diminished in atrocity.[28] The conclusion seems a little tortuous, probably influenced by the writings of A. M. Guerry (which Greg had obviously read). Guerry had shown a positive correlation between education and crime which Greg had to explain away since it was fundamental to his position that the remedy for crime was education and prosperity. The conclusion, whatever its contradictions, was an interventionist one. The real contradiction in the ideas of men like Kay and Greg was their generally laissez-faire approach to some social issues (such as the poor law and the factory laws) and their highly interventionist beliefs in others (such as education and sanitary reform). This resulted from the tension between moralism and environmentalism in their ideology, a tension between a moralistic attitude of condemnation of laziness, lack of self-reliance, and improvidence, and an environmentalist appreciation of the effects of lack of education and atrocious living conditions.

The Manchester society was formally constituted in September 1833 with 13 members. By mid-October there were 18, a number which grew to 28 at the time of the first annual report in July 1834.[29] A year later there were 40.[30] Manchester men were less fearful of *opinions* than the London society and defined their purpose in rather broader terms. They saw their function as 'the collection of facts illustrative of the condition of Society, and the discussion of subjects of Social and Political Economy; totally excluding Party politics'.[31] Despite the exclusion of 'Party politics' (whatever that meant in what was probably an overwhelmingly Liberal gathering) it is apparent that the society did not expect to leave it to others to thresh out the conclusions from the wheatsheafs of statistics. Such self-denial would scarcely have appealed to Benjamin Heywood, who became president. The two vice-presidents were John Kennedy and Colonel Shaw Kennedy, with Kay as treasurer.[32]

It was decided that the society should try to restrict itself to a small group of intimates; membership was limited to 50. With 12 persons required to vote before a new member could join selectivity was ensured.[33] The society, as we shall see, quickly ran into debt, and a committee was appointed to consider changing the rule. Since the avoidance of the 'sacrifice and disadvantages attending any such extension of the Constitution of the Society as must impair its social character' was desirable it was resolved that they should try to continue with voluntary contributions.[34] They were finally forced to rescind the rule in 1837.[35]

Rules were generally kept to a minimum and the immediate problem facing the society in late 1833 was not finance but where to begin its labours. The Vice-President of the Board of Trade, Poulett

Thomson, was also one of the M.P.s for Manchester and, as outlined in Part I, the society held a conference with him at which it was encouraged to continue its efforts since there was no possibility of wide-ranging government action. Little encouragement was needed – the society's early history was in complete contrast to that of the London society. Where the latter pictured itself in the role of attacking the entire range of statistics, yet could do no more than set up inactive committees, the former chose smaller, more tangible subjects and began work immediately.

We have already noted the small sub-committee of Samuel and W. R. Greg on factory statistics set up at the end of 1833. A sister project was an enquiry into the hand-loom weavers begun by Kay at the same time, though this does not appear to have been one of the society's more successful ventures. It did develop into a survey carried out in one of the poorest areas of Manchester. The survey was financed by Benjamin Heywood who showed the way for amateur societies to complete social surveys by employing an agent to do the fieldwork. The agent was 'an intelligent Irishman, who was himself a hand-loom weaver'. Some 4102 families were covered and the society was sufficiently proud of its work to allow it to be presented to the 1834 meeting of the statistical section of the British Association in its name.[36]

The success of the pilot survey made the society undertake a much more ambitious plan. A committee was formed and over the next seventeen months four agents were employed whose job it was to discover the circumstances of the 'Working Population, or in a word, all those below the rank of shopkeeper'. Geographically the survey eventually encompassed Manchester, Salford, Bury, Ashton, Stalybridge, and Dukinfield. The total cost was £175.[37] The results were first made public at the British Association meeting in September 1837 and were subsequently published. It was a large enquiry indeed – perhaps the largest of its type in our period. Some 64 per cent of the population of Manchester were visited, 74 per cent of Salford, 72 per cent of Bury, 82 per cent of Ashton, 90 per cent of Stalybridge, and 95 per cent of Dukinfield. The last two figures showed the strange social structure of those towns, the first that the survey of Manchester was probably not complete.[38]

The agents had noted the numbers of persons, rooms, and families in each dwelling and the rents paid. They had then noted the occupation, religion, and country of birth of the head of the family and the occupations of the rest. Also taken down was the number of adults in the family earning, the number of children doing likewise, the number of children at day school and Sunday school, and the weekly payments for these schools. This led on to such moral statistics as the number of books in the house, whether or not it was 'comfortably' and well furnished, the length of residence, and whether or not the members of a family belonged to a benefit society. Finally came an enquiry into the number of rooms, the number of sleeping rooms, the number of beds per family, and the state of the water-supply.

The purpose of the inquisition was 'to assist in promoting the progress of the social improvement in the manufacturing population'.[39] Compared with some other surveys the society's was not aggressively moralistic yet the moral concern comes through. Moreover, two questions which were begging for answers went unasked. There were no direct enquiries on income and hours of labour since 'it was feared they could lead to no correct results'. The agents reported that these were the only issues on which there was suspicion of and resistance to their efforts.[40] Nevertheless, it is indicative of the moralistic side of the society's ideology, that it should be thought unworthwhile to press the matter while being much concerned with the numbers of books owned by the working classes.

More obviously committed to ideological needs was the other great success of the society, the education surveys. The members of the society, without seeing the Kerry returns of 1833, do not seem to have trusted the efficiency of the government survey. They appointed their own committee in April 1834 to enquire into the state of education in Manchester. The report was published in 1835, a second edition in 1837. The committee's task had been to examine the day, Sunday, charity, infant, and dame schools in Manchester, the number of children in them, and the 'nature and efficacy' of the instruction. An agent of high ability, John Riddall Wood, was employed, who carried out many other such surveys for the society.

Wood's work led to the satisfying conclusion that, on balance, the Kerry returns had omitted over 8000 schoolchildren. With that proof of more thorough research established it was possible to proceed to the less pleasing results. It was estimated that some two-thirds of the five to 15 age-group were at school, leaving one-third 'receiving no instruction in schools whatever'.[41] While this might be felt to be a misstatement, since it seemed to make unjustifiable assumptions about the nature of school attendance, it should not divert us at this stage from recognizing that the bulk of the report was not statistically based. Whether or not this was due to the still loosely defined nature of 'statistics' is not easy to decide (the society's statement of aims included no reference to numbers). But it is relevant to go beyond quantification for it is in the qualitative parts of the report that the beliefs of the Manchester Statistical Society are most apparent.

The society's main objection to the state of education in Manchester was not to its deficiencies in numbers taught but to its nature. The dame schools could practically be dismissed as educational establishments since they were basically day-care institutions for the children of the working classes. Many of the teachers had other occupations, usually of a menial nature, 'which renders any regular instruction among their scholars absolutely impossible'. The 'schools' were often held in 'very dirty, unwholesome rooms'. The common day schools were a little better but 'still very little fitted to give a very useful education'. Discipline was poor and, most crucial to the Manchester men, 'moral education, real cultivation of mind, and improvement of character are totally neglected'.[42] The other types of schools surveyed were generally superior, though seldom entirely satisfactory. The society concluded that the numbers attending were '*a very imperfect criterion*' of the state of education.[43] On the basis of the Manchester survey, that state was very poor and presented 'a painful and mortifying contrast' to some countries on the Continent (Kay's influence is seen in the paeon of praise to Prussia).[44]

To its credit the society did not rest satisfied with undertaking a survey of its own backyard. With a clarification of the method of arriving at the ages of the children (a direct census of under fives, five to 15s, and over 15s was now taken) the survey was extended to Salford and Bury. The enquiries were modelled on the Manchester one. The conclusions were practically word for word the same. But there was a difference. In the report on Salford the society obviously felt that the trend of public opinion was now running sufficiently strongly in its favour for it to be able to question the advisability of leaving education to the 'sole caprice' of working-class parents.[45]

With the completion of the surveys of Manchester, Salford, and Bury in October 1835 a new committee was formed to survey the state of education in Liverpool. The enquiry took nine months to complete at a cost of £96.[46] Previous surveys had met with occasional obstacles (especially at Salford) but in Liverpool Wood found a great deal of suspicion. It was feared that the survey was a preliminary to government interference and that Wood himself was a government agent. If the schoolteachers did not harbour that suspicion then they were likely to assume that the information was sought by political or religious partisans. The opponents of the society got as far as holding a meeting which excited 'party spirit'. 'Party spirit' was of course a term to use only of the opposition. The society saw itself as merely seeking after truth while its members were 'bound together by no community of political opinions'.[47] The society's protestations should not be taken too seriously since its report recommended the creation of a 'Board of Public Instruction... as the first step in the performance of a duty, which is imperative with every enlightened government'.[48] This was scarcely a non-political statement in 1836.

By this stage the reports on education were falling into a highly predictable pattern in terms of content, format, and conclusions. The report on Bolton deviated in no way.[49] The statistics were becoming more and more subsidiary to the cause of campaigning for a central board of education, state aid, teachers' training schools, and a much higher status for the teaching profession. The reports were used by other educational reformers to back their case.[50] Nevertheless, further surveys were made since it could be argued that so far only the worst type of area – rapidly growing urban centres – had been studied. Consequently, it was decided to look at a quite different type of town and York was chosen. Despite the different environment the society was satisfied that, on the whole, the same conditions prevailed.[51]

There remained three further education surveys. The first was a second survey of part of Salford, the township of Pendleton, in the spring and summer of 1838. The report was briefer than usual and was concerned with the change since the survey of 1835 as well as the reasons for irregular attendance. Except for a massive increase in the number attending Sunday school (from an estimated 9.1 per cent to 14.6 per cent of the population) there was no sign of progress. Indeed, following on two years of bad trade, the reverse was the case (hence at least part of the rise in the Sunday school population).[52] The motives behind the Pendleton survey are obscure – perhaps it was the trial for a complete revision which was never carried out for financial or other reasons. Perhaps the establishment of the Privy Council Committee on Education with Kay as secretary in 1839 ended the need for such work.

The other survey of 1838, that of Rutland, was rather more in the standard pattern. In this instance a rural district was examined to compare with the urban districts already studied. Two major variations from the norm were found in Rutland. Firstly, the 1833 returns were less inaccurate there. Secondly, the quality of the schooling was considerably higher than in the towns.[53] The Rutland survey was followed by the last of the education surveys, that of Kingston-upon-Hull in early 1839.[54] The dating implies that the foundation of the Privy Council Committee was an important factor in bringing an end to the surveys. Both the Rutland and the Hull surveys were accompanied by reports upon the condition of the population (but only of three parishes for Rutland). The usual heads were included plus an enquiry into earnings.[55]

Apart from these major undertakings various smaller projects had been tried. After a paper (not preserved) by Kay on 'The Means Existing for the Religious Instruction of the Working Classes in Large Towns' in January 1835 a committee was appointed to look at the subject further. Printed forms were sent out to Church of England, Roman Catholic, and Dissenting clergy within a few weeks.[56] The response was poor: 11 out of 20 Anglican clergy returned the forms and only five out of 35 Roman Catholics and Dissenters.[57] The other reports of the society were of much less weight than the education and working classes surveys and the projected religious instruction survey. Henry Ashworth, the Bolton industrialist, prepared a report on the number and horsepower of the steam-engines and waterwheels in the Bolton area. James Murray and Richard Birley (both Manchester cotton-masters) did the same for Manchester and Salford. James Meadows undertook a study of the quantity of coal brought into Manchester in 1834 and 1836 and William McConnell of the amount of meat consumed in Manchester in 1836. In addition, a few individual papers were thought worthy of publication, such as Samuel Greg's and Henry Romilly's papers on criminal statistics and Henry Ashworth's on a strike at Preston in 1836–7.[58]

As we have noted, the rush of activity in the first few years of the society's existence was in direct contrast to the lethargy which almost immediately settled on the Statistical Society of London. The contrast may be carried further. Whereas the London society moved out of the doldrums in the late 1830s, the Manchester society began to drift into them. Its membership had reached 46 by the time of the third annual report in October 1836 and was nearing the ceiling laid down in the rules. With the abolition of the limit membership grew to 52 by October 1837 and 60 a year later.[59] Growth then ceased and a reverse movement began so that by 1846 the membership was only 24, less than it had been in July 1834.[60]

Meanwhile, the financial affairs of the society had always been in a precarious position since the surveys cost more than the regular income. At the time of the first audit in October 1835 ordinary subscriptions and the interest on them had brought in £115.8.0. £42 had already been spent on the education enquiry and £88 on the working classes survey. With sundries total expenditure was over £144. Luckily, heavy donations had been made by Kay and others which left a handsome surplus of just over £100. But there were also outstanding bills of £75 which made the financial state less healthy.[61] A year later cash in hand was £52 and outstanding debts £165 (nearly all owed to Wood and another agent for their work, in addition to the large sums already paid).[62] With the reduction in the scale of surveys the society managed to get itself roughly into balance by the end of 1838.[63] It had learnt the lesson London had to learn: statistical surveys were expensive. In 1839, when the total subscription income of the society would have been about £120, J. R. Wood put in a claim for a salary of £200 a year plus one pound a week living away expenses.[64]

In the early days of enthusiasm the society had risked financial ruin to complete surveys. But with the natural waning of enthusiasm the financial realities may have had an impact on the decline which began to set in. In late 1839 W. R. Greg drew up a plan for the future work of the society. Of his 'statistical desiderata' only the survey of the state of education and the condition of the working classes in a purely agricultural district was carried out. Plans for surveys of the state of the working classes in Liverpool and Preston fell through. As late as October 1840 a number of committees were set up but only one – on vital statistics – prepared a report.[65]

Apart from the financial aspect the decline is difficult to explain (though it was small until the 1840s). Part of the reason no doubt lies in the loss of leading figures. Kay went to the Poor Law Commission and then the Privy Council Committee, Stanley to the Bishopric of Norwich, Peter Ewart jr to Bombay, and Colonel Shaw Kennedy to Ireland. New blood of comparable strength was not added. Then again, from 1838 the reforming bourgeoisie had a powerful counter-attraction in the anti-corn law agitation. Ashworth, the McConnells, Darbishire, Thomas Ashton, the Gregs, the Tootals, Henry Romilly, Robert Philips and others were involved in that movement, not to mention Richard Cobden, who had joined the society in 1835. Elesh points out that there was also some division within the society over the means of education with respect to the difficult problem of religious education.[66] However, the most active members seem to have supported the Manchester Society for Promoting National Education.

Despite the losses and distractions the momentum of the 1830s carried the society through to about 1841 or 1842. By then the big surveys were completed and reported on. The rest of the story is difficult to reconstruct for, index itself of decline, the *Appendix to the Minutes* contains no further material after October 1840 (and had been indifferently kept for some time before that date). Rapidly the society declined to the point where its continuation depended on one man, John Roberton. Roberton had been surgeon to the Manchester Lying-in Hospital since 1827. He had given evidence to the 1833 factory commission which had condemned the sanitary condition of Manchester while being generally pro-factory. However, he had called for a 10½ hour day for all workers.[67] In 1840 he delivered a paper to the society in which he called for outdoor relief to widows, arguing that 'there is need at the present moment to watch the measures of these gentlemen [the commissioners and assistant commissioners], lest, in their eagerness to carry into operation certain views as to out-door relief, they unwittingly overlook the claims of humanity'.[68] It is perhaps significant, then, that he did not join the society until 1838 and came to the fore when others had lost interest. By 1842 he dominated the society. According to Ashton eight papers were read in the 1841-2 session, two by Roberton. The next year only two papers were read, one of them by Roberton. Over the next seven sessions he delivered seven out of the 15 papers. In the two sessions 1843-4 and 1844-5 he gave all four papers read.[69] The society was very close to extinction and none of the papers read from 1841 to 1851 have survived. Those that were read were mainly on vital statistics and then frequently on peripheral issues such as the 'Alleged Influence of Climate on Female Puberty in Greece'.

This state of affairs continued to the end of the decade when a revival took place. The proposed dissolution of the society in 1849 spurred one or two men to vigorous activity.[70] In 1850 the council of the Statistical Society of London was able to announce the Manchester society's 'renewed activity on a more popular basis' though the number of papers read shows that it took another year or two for the revival to bear fruit.[71] In the 1853-4 session the published *Transactions* were begun and the society had recovered to a position of stability. By 1857-8 there were 119 members, growing to 144 at the end of the decade.[72] Though it has never approached the prestige and activity of the London society the Manchester Statistical Society has since that time had a continuous existence. But if it had barely survived the 1840s it was alone in that distinction among the provincial societies. The others, which had never reached the heights of Manchester, had long since plunged into oblivion by the end of our period.

[9]

The Other Provincial Societies

Manchester was easily the most important and the most well-known of the provincial statistical societies but short-lived manifestations of the movement appeared in many other towns. By March 1835 the council of the Statistical Society of London had reason to believe that societies had been formed, or were on the point of being formed, in Birmingham, Edinburgh, Glasgow, Hull, Liverpool, and Worcester.[1] Over the next decade organizations were mooted, and sometimes founded, in Aberdeen, Barnsley, Belfast, Bristol, Doncaster, Gateshead, Halifax, Leeds, Leicester, Newcastle, Nottingham, Portsmouth, the Potteries, Sheffield, Tavistock, and Tonbridge.[2] Some of them never got beyond the stage of a statistical gleam in one man's eye. Others, notably in Belfast, Birmingham, Bristol, Glasgow, Leeds, Liverpool, and Newcastle proceeded to a more formal level of existence and produced various surveys.

Apart from Manchester and London the earliest significant statistical society was that set up in Glasgow. Or, more correctly, the *societies* set up in Glasgow. Glasgow was unique in creating two societies, the Statistical Society of Glasgow and the Glasgow and Clydesdale Statistical Society. The former was founded in February 1836 (mainly by Charles R. Baird and Robert Cowan) 'to collect, arrange, and publish, facts illustrative of the condition and prosperity, with a view to the improvement of mankind'. In common with the other provincial societies the 'improving' basis of the society was openly acknowledged. At the time of formation there were 41 members, a number rising over the next two years to 66.[3]

Cowan and Baird, the two founders, were typical figures in the statistical movement. Cowan was a physician at the Glasgow Fever Hospital. In two papers read in 1837 and 1838 he advocated public health reforms, including the introduction of civil registration to Scotland, in order that the 'obstacles to the promotion of social improvement among the lower classes' might be removed.[4] Baird represented more the interests of the reforming industrial bourgeoisie. He had been a lawyer for employers' associations fighting a succession of strikes yet, when exceptionally hard times came in 1837, he was secretary to a committee formed to raise public subscriptions for the poor. Applicants for relief had to state if they were trade unionists on a form to be signed by the Commissioner of Police. Baird wished to go further and use the relief cases as a means of ascertaining the condition of the working classes, though he was overruled.[5] Baird 'was most anxious that the condition of these classes should be enquired into, so as to be improved'.[6] As might be expected in an anti-unionist supporter of the 'improvement' of the lower classes Baird believed that the state was in danger from revolution and upheaval unless the middle classes led the way in sanitary reform and the provision of an English style poor law, savings banks, temperance and friendly societies, recreational facilities and, above all, education to 'improve the moral man'.[7] Baird was secretary to the Statistical Society of Glasgow during its brief existence which probably came to an end some time during the summer of 1838.[8]

The other society in Glasgow, the Glasgow and Clydesdale Statistical Society, had a longer nominal existence but possibly an even briefer actual one. It was formed in April 1836 with James Cleland as president, leading contributor, and dominating influence. Cleland was born in 1770 and had been a businessman involved in the intellectual life of Glasgow before moving into municipal affairs as Superintendent of Public Works in 1814 (a post from which he retired in 1834). As Superintendent Cleland had developed an interest in social statistics which led to a number of works as well as a municipal census in 1819.[9] He conducted the 1831 census of Glasgow which covered a much wider range than the standard census and he was also an early advocate of civil registration in Scotland.[10]

Cleland's statistical interests led him to the 1835 meeting of the British Association in Dublin and perhaps it was his awareness of the growing statistical movement which eventually led to the creation of a society in May 1836. The society was founded in an extraordinary blaze of brilliance with a patron, a president, three vice-presidents, a secretary, a treasurer, and 28 councillors among the 240 fellows plus 116 'honorary and corresponding associates'. Almost every important figure in the Glasgow region was a fellow, including the Principal of the University of Glasgow, the Moderator of the General Assembly, and the chairman of the West India Association. The aims of this assembly of notables were very similar to those of the other Glasgow society: to further 'the knowledge of the present state of a country, with a view to its improvement'. As elsewhere, 'the Society will exclude all opinions from its transactions, and publications, and confine its attention rigorously to facts'.[11]

In fact the baroque edifice of Cleland's society was a sham and a proposed journal finished after one issue containing an article by Cleland and one sent by the Bristol Statistical Society.[12] The end piece of these *Transactions* gave a hint of some of the problems faced by the society, when it appealed for funds to continue publication. Probably more important than lack of money was Cleland's growing ill-health. He had very likely been ill for some time when he withdrew from the Statistical Society of London in April 1839.[13] The Glasgow and Clydeside society may have carried on a nominal existence for in 1847 it was still reputed to have 225 fellows though no other reference is to be found for nearly ten years before that date.[14] Thus it is likely that both the Glasgow societies rapidly disappeared as active bodies without carrying out any social surveys. The reasons for this failure remain unclear as do the reasons for the existence of two separate organizations. One thing is apparent – both societies had an unusually strong Tory connection. The Tory Sheriff of Lanarkshire, Archibald Alison, was president of the Statistical Society of Glasgow while Cleland was a supporter of Sir Robert Peel.[15]

If Glasgow was something of an exceptional case in the statistical movement, Bristol was definitely within the mainstream. It was the first society, though not the last, to be the direct result of proselytizing by the statistical section of the British Association. As with many of the societies Bristol had a central figure, Charles Bowles Fripp. Fripp remains largely unknown though his family was prominent in both the Anglican and Unitarian churches in Gloucestershire.[16] It was Fripp who presented a paper to the Bristol meeting of the British Association in August 1836 on the statistics of education in Bristol. The paper was the result of a private enquiry, formed on the Manchester model, but dependent upon returns from circulars to 'the clergy and other ministers of religion.' Its main conclusions were to stress the inadequacy of the means of education, and the necessity of a statistical society in every large town to enquire into its social conditions.[17]

His audience was receptive to the latter idea. Henry Hallam, whose family influence lay in Gloucestershire, gave encouragement and soon a collection of worthies was gathered. A meeting was held in early September with Hallam in the chair. The standard phrases of the movement were given a west country airing. It was moved that it was 'of great interest and importance, with a view to the future improvement of society, to ascertain with precision and accuracy all such facts as are calculated to illustrate its condition and prospects'. With this self-congratulation on the perception of, if not truth, then the need for truth out of the way, the meeting set up a society to 'collect, arrange and publish the *Local Statistics* of Bristol and its Vicinity, confining its attention to facts, and totally excluding all party politics'.[18]

Apart from Fripp the rest of the founders of the society were prominent figures, usually from a professional background.[19] James Cowles Prichard was a Quaker doctor involved in educational work.[20] His close friend, John Addington Symonds, came from a line of five generations of medical men. Dr Lant Carpenter was perhaps the leading Unitarian divine of the age. He had taught at least some of the Gregs of Manchester and had co-operated with Prichard on educational matters. Charles Pinney was a merchant who had been mayor of Bristol during the 1831 Reform Bill riots and was the first alderman of the reformed corporation. Finally, mention may be made of J. M. Gutch, editor of a pro-Liberal newspaper, and G. B. Jerrard, a well-known mathematician.

These men formed the nucleus of a society which started with 46 members and grew to 54 in 18 months.[21] But an obstacle to progress soon showed itself which must have bothered other societies. The members were willing but not able. They were prominent men of affairs – businessmen, doctors, clergy. They had little time or aptitude for the process of collecting statistics. The first annual report bemoaned the vast field open and argued the need for accurate co-ordinated research. The committee members were not available for 'so arduous and absorbing an employment.' Even if they were it would not be reasonable to expect accuracy, only 'a close approximation.' This would be sufficient 'as affording the basis of a sound municipal economy, and as a guide to the hand of benevolence' which would aid 'the alleviation of distress'.[22]

The attitude is reminiscent of Manchester. It is not the only similarity. J. E. Bromby explained in 1838 that the society had two purposes. The first was to act as a centre for statistical 'zealots'. Secondly, and much more importantly, its function was to study the 'poorer classes' and ascertain their 'means of instruction and improvement' and 'how far they enjoy those comforts and conveniences which every man must enjoy before he is entitled to the epithet of civilized.' The purpose was both an 'amelioration of our statutes' and the extinction of 'Sansculottism'. Bromby further argued that in the industrial world in which Britain now lived the poor were separated from the rich, prevented from actual starvation by the poor law but 'destitute of everything which ennobles life'.

More was required from 'the stewards of unrighteous mammon.' Bromby's last point would perhaps have been phrased a little too strongly for the Manchester men but otherwise they would not have been strongly in disagreement. Where they would have been most wholeheartedly in agreement with Bromby was when he argued 'this, however, is not within the province of the Statistical Society... Their only object is to ascertain, as nearly as possible, what the actual exigencies, and by an accurate exhibition of them, to rouse the community, and eventually the legislature, to take adequate measures to meet them'.[23] Once again we find one of the hallmarks of the movement in the contrast of an ideology stressing the necessity of the wealthy improving the working classes with a disclaimer of *opinions* and 'party politics' and a profession of 'confining their attention strictly to facts.' In Bromby's case the contrast is pointed up by a further example of pressing for state and local action.

There remained the burden of collecting the facts, the 'tedious employment' in Bromby's phrase. As usual recourse was had to an agent who was trained by the Central Society of Education. The first survey, on the condition of the working classes, was based on model schedules from London.[24] An interim report was read to the British Association meeting in Liverpool in 1837 and the final report in the summer of 1839. This first survey, covering over 20,000 people, immediately raised financial problems since it cost £110.[25] Moreover, of the 64 supposed members 49 were in arrears so that the society's cash balance was less than £2. The education survey therefore relied upon aid from the British Association and the London society. The survey, carried out in the first half of 1841, included over 22,000 schoolchildren.[26] But with the completion of the two standard surveys for the provincial societies the Bristol society collapsed. It was presumably wound up because it could think of nothing else to do.

If the enthusiasm of the Bristol society was transitory that of the men of Belfast was similarly so but less productive. The Statistical Society of Ulster centred on the members of the Belfast Natural Historical Society who attended the 1837 meeting of the British Association. In March 1838 a separate Statistical Society was founded with 67 members. The early experience of the society seemed promising. Committees were set up on education, the state of the working classes, the trade between Ireland and Great Britain, the state of agriculture, and the amount of mechanical power in the Belfast area.[27] By May there were 97 members and this figure passed the 100 mark by the time of the first anniversary meeting in

November 1838. By this time the society possessed no less than 14 committees and apparently boundless ambition.[28]

Achievement was another matter. In January 1839 the education committee announced that its sets of questions had gone to the printers. At the next meeting but one the medical committee announced its plans, including a study of 'typhus fever'. But these were still plans. It was not until November that the council could report the completion of the education survey in some parishes. The semblance of activity was illusory: although the society may have dragged on for some years it was later to be remarked that 'it has never been conducted with spirit and is at present somewhat in abeyance'.[29]

The Ulster society was not the only one to arise out of the 1837 Liverpool meeting of the British Association. Viscount Sandon was president of the statistical section and on a number of occasions he urged the formation of a society in Liverpool itself. At the beginning of 1838 the Liverpool society began its life and soon had 85 members. Committees were formed on Anglo-Irish trade, medical statistics and moral and educational statistics, and criminal statistics.[30] The most active figure in the society was William Henry Duncan, an Edinburgh trained man who was physician to the Northern Hospital. In 1840 he wrote the local sanitary report on Liverpool for Edwin Chadwick.[31] The other major influence in the society was John William Harden. A lawyer born in 1809, he was also an Edinburgh graduate. At the time he was a commissioner of bankruptcy, a post suggesting Whig or Liberal connections.[32]

The standard ideology of the movement was most probably in command at Liverpool judging by the subjects of the first three papers read: the condition of the agricultural classes, the causes of crime and the effects of prison discipline, and the building operatives' strike of 1833. Soon it was decided to undertake research into the condition of the working classes. At the annual meeting in October an impression of enterprise was conveyed by the presentation of eight papers.[33] But when the society published an initial number of its *Proceedings* most of the space was given over to bewailing the difficulties of research, in particular its expensiveness and time-consuming nature. Not surprisingly, the society soon ceased to function.

Two more societies had a brief existence in connection with the British Association: Birmingham and Newcastle. At the meeting in Birmingham in 1839 a paper on the educational statistics of Birmingham was read. This was not the first manifestation of the movement in that city. At the end of 1834 a statistical committee of the Philosophical Institution was formed, which wrote to London and Manchester for advice.[34] The committee seems to have disappeared rapidly but the statistical idea surfaced again in early 1838, when the Birmingham Educational Statistical Society was formed. A 'great meeting' was held 'at which a considerable portion of the clergy attended, as well as others not connected with the establishment, and gentlemen around', in the words of a local magistrate, J. Corrie. If Corrie was at all typical then he represented a bluff version of the notion of improvement: 'I have no conception of any other means of forcing civilization downwards in society except education'.[35] The leading member was Francis Clark.[36] There was certainly a Church contingent – for example, William Boultbee of a clerical family. But it was probably untypical since the education survey was to be criticized as unfair to the Anglicans.[37] The medical profession was represented by Corrie's son, John Read Corrie, a Cambridge graduate, and Joseph Hodgson, surgeon at the general hospital and son of a Birmingham merchant.[38] The society appears to have been outside the small-craftsman radical milieu of Birmingham politics.

Intellectually it was closer to Manchester. In fact the education survey was carried out by the regular agent of the Manchester Statistical Society, J. R. Wood, since the Birmingham men were too 'engrossed' in the 1839 riots.[39] The report, too, was his since a sub-committee 'found it impossible to test the accuracy of the statements contained in it, without going over the ground after that gentleman.' The report was therefore sent to the London society as Wood's work. Naturally this report closely followed the format and content of those by the Manchester society but it was a useful body of evidence to add to the growing pressure for 'a general system of education'.[40] It had been intended as the first step in the collection of statistics for the Birmingham meeting of the British Association, which it had been hoped would be held in 1838 but which was deferred to 1839 because of Newcastle's prior claim. On its completion the society could not decide what to do next.[41] Two further reports were completed on commercial and medical statistics. The latter was a forerunner of the local report for Chadwick's sanitary report which was prepared by a committee including J. R. Corrie and Joseph Hodgson.[42]

The Newcastle society was similarly created to collect statistics for the meeting of the British Association in that city in 1838. A committee of the 'Educational Society' was led by William Cargill, David H. Wilson, and Joseph Watson. The three men remain dim figures except that Cargill wrote books on foreign trade and foreign policy in general. The report was more limited in scope than intended because of 'extreme difficulties' of an undefined nature. It contains a short survey of the number of schoolchildren and their literacy. As with other reports the harshest words were reserved for the quality rather than the quantity of education. The report closed with some very facile observations on the state of the working classes, their high wages and yet their wretchedness.[43] The Newcastle committee fits easily into the movement with its mixture of sympathetic environmentalism, antipathetic moralism, and a naive belief in the virtues of education.

Underlying much of the work of the statistical movement lay the belief that the work was properly one for central and local government which had devolved upon private societies and individuals by default. Given this notion, it might be argued that the one city where the movement was completely successful was Leeds, which took municipal action. Yet in Leeds, where a statistical society was formed and where the town council undertook a survey, although the two groups were closely connected the activities of the town council seem to have cut the ground from underneath private endeavour.

The two were roughly contemporaneous. The town council's statistical committee was set up in May 1837, the society a few months later. Since the society was short-lived and abortive it is perhaps easiest to deal with it first. It was formed in January 1838 as an off-shoot of the Literary and Philosophical Society. Its original 15 members stated that their interests were the study of subjects for a statistical account of Leeds, an account of the schools connected with Marshall's works, medical statistics, population, the causes of crime and the effects of punishment on the criminal, the state of the climbing boys, and the history of the union among the Leeds woollen operatives in 1833-4.[44] The rather strange collection of the general and the particular was an obvious reflection of the individual interests of the group. In particular, it is understandable that a prominent member was J. G. Marshall, one of the leading manufacturers of the area, and a man very much of the Benjamin Heywood and Thomas Ashton type. Like them he had been involved at the outset in the mechanics' institute movement.[45] The society appears to have spent much of its time considering what it ought to do, for Samuel Hare, the president, presented a paper in August 1838 to the British Association outlining the 'subjects for statistical inquiries'.[46]

The actual work of statistical research was left to a committee of the town council. The project began in May 1837 when a preliminary committee was set up 'to find out the best method of obtaining statistically the condition of the borough and the expense of carrying out a survey'.[47] The motion had been proposed by Robert Baker, who had also foreshadowed a motion on public health which was not immediately put.[48] From the start, therefore, the town council enquiry was linked with the public health movement. This is not surprising for in aims and character Baker was rather like a Leeds Chadwick. Born in 1803, the son of a druggist, he became a poor law medical officer in Leeds in 1825. He quickly showed his flair for controversy and lack of tact by launching an attack on the state of the local infirmary in 1827. As with Kay the cholera epidemic of 1831–2 was a turning point in his life and caused him to write a brief study of the sanitary inadequacies of Leeds. He became surgeon to two local factories as well as a sub-inspector of factories and the conflict of interest led to charges of his being a 'pluralist placeman' until he was forced to give up his private practice in late 1836.[49] He had also become one of the Liberals on the town council.

Baker was a supporter of the factory system and told the 1833 commission that factory employees were not more 'lanquid, weakly, or debilitated' than other operatives.[50] He also gave tables to J. E. Drinkwater which were to involve the latter in a controversy with M. T. Sadler. The kind of viewpoint subscribed to by Baker and the Leeds statisticians was well put by J. G. Marshall when he stated that it was impossible to tell the effects of long hours of labour on children without

> a careful inquiry into other causes of disease and immorality that in fact produce many of the evils attributed to too long hours of work, and which, if removed, would render any great reduction of the present hours of labour both unnecessary and undesirable. In our opinion, the health of the workpeople in this and other large towns receives very great injury from the filthy and unhealthy state of many of the streets, from want of proper sewerage... The great number of spirit and beer shops, and want of efficient regulation of them, and of police generally, the want of adequate means of education and religious instruction, and of opportunities for healthy recreation.

If Marshall, the improving, humanitarian (to a point) employer, was the Leeds equivalent of the Gregs, Ashton, and Heywoods of Manchester then Baker was his J. P. Kay. Baker was soon to single out Marshall's factory for special praise.[51] But there was a more important politico-medical ally for the Baineses and Marshalls than Baker in 1837. The chairman of the statistical committee was Dr James Williamson, the mayor. He had been appointed a physician to the infirmary some time before Baker as well as becoming physician to the house of recovery and the public dispensary and a lecturer at the medical school. Like Baker he gave evidence to the 1833 commission, defending the factory system and pointing out that even pulmonary consumption in flax mills could be caused by the 'sympathetic irritation... propagated to the lungs' from stomach complaints caused by too much alcohol and poor diet. He wanted 'more opportunity for intellectual, moral, and religious education' and denied that 'any uniform limitation of hours is essential to the physical health of children'.[52] Despite the similarity of their views, both political and medical, the relationship between Williamson and Baker was far from cordial. Their personal conflict came to a head when Chadwick approached Williamson to do the Sanitary Report on Leeds and Baker submitted plans of his own which caused Williamson to resign and Baker to take over.[53]

The clash of personalities did not have an immediate effect on the town council plans. The two men were united in seeing sanitary and educational issues, that is, in a very broad sense, the problems of urbanization, as the root cause of the inadequacies of their society. An alibi for the factory system was to be found by diligent statistical search of the streets, houses, and schools. It was decided to prepare for the survey by writing to the London, Manchester, and Liverpool statistical societies for advice and publications. Before the summer recess a report was drawn up and the council voted £120 to cover the entire cost of the survey.[54] This was to prove a gross underestimate.

After the recess Baker was able to try to take the initiative. At the first meeting there was no quorum with only Baker and one other present. Although in theory nothing was done Baker was directed to present the draft questionnaires he had drawn up. But Williamson soon took charge and the town clerk, Edwin Eddison (another avowed Liberal), was appointed to draw up a report.[55] Eddison's report explained that the survey had not yet begun because of the proposed new valuation of the city which would reduce the work of the statistical committee.[56] The committee lapsed into inactivity while the valuation was carried out. It was not until the committee of the Literary and Philosophical Society jogged it that it came back to life. The statistical committee of the town council adjourned to the society for an 'hour's desultory conversation' then returned and 'separated without doing anything further'.[57] Baker had not been present and without him the committee seemed devoid of initiative. Again the committee left its work to Eddison. He drew up some forms but found competition from Baker.[58] At last, after 18 months without progress, things began to move. A schedule was adopted and Baker succeeded in getting himself in charge of operations. Two agents were to ask the questions and one of the local registrars was to carry out the laborious task of abstraction.[59]

Baker's domination of the survey over the next year was aided, ironically, by a major Tory victory when, at the first meeting of the committee after the November 1838 elections, Liberal absenteeism resulted in Williamson's being deposed as chairman.[60] By this time three agents were being employed and Baker was authorized to employ more as required.[61] Consequently, by the time one of the wards was finished it was apparent that more money would be needed.[62] It was here that the advantages of an official enquiry showed themselves. Another £100 was granted.[63] Interim reports were read and Baker underlined his own motives by recommending that an approach be made to the Improvement Commissioners about the worst street nuisances.[64]

Baker went beyond this, however, and added to the growing antipathy to the survey on the part of some Tories. At one meeting of the committee, where the two Tories present outnumbered the sole Liberal, one of the agents was suspended because he was also employed by the Liberals. Proposed questions on parliamentary and municipal rights and privileges were struck out. Baker had been printing material without the committee's approval. There was more than a suspicion that the survey had been used as a cover for discovering people's politics as well as their condition.[65] Baker had never been the Tories' favourite Liberal and had earlier been singled out for attack for his extravagance over the proposed police force.[66]

Nevertheless, by mid-October 1839 a draft report was ready.[67] With a few revisions it was presented to the town council, who ordered the committee to print, at a cost of not more than £50, the report, or extracts, or an abstract.[68] The reaction to the report is a fair indication of the political alignments behind it. The Tory *Leeds Intelligencer* dismissed it as a political charade. The radical *Leeds Times* gave it a moderately favourable reception.[69] Inevitably, it was the Liberal *Leeds Mercury* that waxed enthusiastic. According to the *Leeds Times* in 1841 the editor of the *Mercury*, Edward Baines jr, had a 'prurient and diseased imagination concerning the working classes'.[70] Baines was an ardent supporter of the large manufacturers and Baker's report provided just the kind of evidence and conclusions needed to clear them.[71]

It was a big report. The chairman of the committee stated that it would take four hours to read, the town clerk six hours if the tables was included.[72] It was also a temporary swan-song for Baker since his unpopularity made him withdraw from the municipal elections the following week. He thus lost his place on the statistical committee and a say in what was going to be published. Acting with dubious propriety, therefore, he sent the report to Rawson Rawson. A long abstract was made of it in the *Journal*.[73] Since this is the paper usually thought of as the official report of the statistical committee it must be emphasized that it was in fact an abstract of Baker's report, published unofficially.

Baker called attention to the insanitary state of the streets, the lack of lavatories, the poor sewage disposal. The houses were small, overcrowded, badly ventilated, and inadequately supplied with water. Baker argued that the moral state of the people showed 'a deplorable laxity of domestic discipline' because of these factors and 'the want of better general regulations'. This was unlikely to be improved without better educational facilities. Finally, he dealt with the physical condition of the population. Mortality was high but Baker cleared the factory system of any blame. Beyond that Baker was less dogmatic in his conclusions but the sanitary state of the town was seen as the prime cause of the deplorable physical condition of the people.

Although Baker's report became known as that of the statistical committee they rejected it for publication. There were obvious inaccuracies – for example, in the tables on church accommodation. Moreover, the size of the original precluded publication and it was decided that an abstract should be prepared.[74] The process of revising and abridging was delegated to Williamson. It took until November 1840, when the proofs were approved and the printing of 1000 copies authorized. It was also recommended that a new committee should be formed to distribute the copies.[75] The council approved. Since it was waging a campaign to obtain an improvement act for Leeds it was natural that the council should ask the committee to look into the best means of improving Leeds.[76] In fact the statistical committee soon found itself responsible for organizing a petition on sewage and ventilation.[77] Furthermore, copies of the abstract and the petition were to be sent to the principal towns of the United Kingdom.[78]

But the abstract had struck trouble. Inaccuracies had been found in several tables, especially those on crime. The committee was becoming weary of the task and speed was essential since the desired bill was before Parliament. It was therefore decided that the report be printed since it still gave a 'fair view'. The committee subsequently faded out of existence. It was suggested that the abstract should be used to support the council's application to Parliament but that plan was dropped.[79] A motion to reappoint the committee was withdrawn in November 1841 and a separate committee on the proposed improvement bill set up instead.[80] By that time Williamson's abstract had been printed.

Copies of it are now rare and it is a little-known document. It was considerably briefer than Baker's published report and was set out in such a fashion as to make its points with clarity and force. The differences of ideas between it and Baker's report were small and not significant. The main differences in the tables are in those of the trades of criminal offenders. Williamson checked the first few figures and found wide discrepancies but time ran out and no further corrections were made after 'clothiers'. Thus the occupations of criminals tables in both abstracts are meaningless. The other major corrections occurred in the tables of religious accommodation since Baker was wrong on the geographical location of the churches.[81]

But it was Baker's inaccurate and unauthorized report which attracted attention. Ever on the alert for ways of spreading the statistical news the London society decided to print 250 copies and send them to the corporations of the major towns and cities with a letter to the mayor explaining the desirability of emulating Leeds.[82] Joseph Fletcher obtained 25 copies for Chadwick to distribute.[83] Little response was forthcoming. Pious hopes were expressed from Gateshead, where action was deferred until after the 1841 census and hence forever.[84] The one solid reply came from Sheffield.

No records of the Sheffield survey appear to have survived. However, we do know that a committee of the town council was set up. The results were sent to Rawson Rawson but publication was deferred until the results of the 1841 census could be incorporated.[85] But there may have been another reason. At the same time that London received the Sheffield report an article was published in the *Leeds Intelligencer* by a Sheffield doctor, George Calvert Holland. It attacked the factory system with a comprehensive set of statistics of earnings, population, crime and mortality.[86] Holland was, therefore, a rare figure in social statistics. Born in 1801, the son of a Sheffield artisan, he was a Unitarian who had graduated in medicine from Edinburgh. After a period in general practice in Manchester he became caught up in a medical controversy of a technical nature. He moved back to Sheffield where he was soon active in the Literary and Philosophical Society, the Mechanics' Library, the Mechanics' Institution, and Liberal politics.[87] Apart from his artisan father his background was typical of the movement. The reversal of the standard ideas on industrialization emphasizes both the unique nature of Sheffield society and Holland's own doubts about the ideology of improvement.

Holland was almost certainly the main figure in the Sheffield survey. In 1841 he gave to the British Association a paper on vital statistics which developed into a book in which he stated that the statistics had been collected at the suggestion of the town council and partly at their expense.[88] In an earlier book he had favoured the factory system for its discipline but had shown his independence of mind by suggesting that education was not as effective as many thought. Holland argued that it was not easy 'to elevate and refine the mass' and that some writings on the subject raised such a utopian vision that the 'imagination riots in the contemplation'.[89]

By 1841 his unorthodoxy had increased to the point where he thought that 'degradation, poverty, and wretchedness' were the inevitable effects of mechanization.[90] He was soon to support protection and trade unionism and earned the enmity of the Sheffield Liberals as a lapsed heretic.[91] His 1843 book was perhaps the most complete statistical onslaught of the period on the ideology of the movement. It was a delicious piece of irony that he should also argue that it was his intention to state facts, not opinions.[92] The 'facts' included the superiority of the working classes of Sheffield to those of other industrial cities where the social hierarchy was more rigid and differentiated. The craft system was better for the people since the 'machine cheapens to the starving point the labour of the industrious mechanic' though Holland still wished to see the craftsmen gathered into disciplined factories.[93] His artisan, like Kay's or Baker's, was to be self-reliant, educated (to a point), and living in a greatly improved sanitary environment but he was also to be a trade unionist and a craftsman, not a passively unorganized machine-tender. As with most such studies the quantification was dwarfed by the social comment. That comment could scarcely have appealed to the Statistical Society of London if it had appeared, as seems likely, in the town council's report. In that sense the 1841 census may have been a useful excuse for excluding an ideologically unpalatable paper.

The Sheffield survey was one of the last manifestations of the independent provincial movement. The Leeds report also aroused interest in Aberdeen where a committee was formed by the burgh council which in the end produced the local sanitary report for Chadwick, a document of meagre attainments.[94] Other ephemera had shown themselves in Halifax and Leicester in the late 1830s. At Barnsley a local mine-owner, Thomas Wilson, had also tried, but failed, to set up a statistical society.[95]

In 1838 Rawson Rawson had stated that the *Journal* had been established partly with the intention of 'uniting the efforts of existing Societies, and of promoting the establishment of others.' The provincial societies were seen as the proof of the vitality of the statistical movement.[96] Eight years later the council was forced to recognize 'how ephemeral is the existence, how transitory the exertion of the local Statistical Societies generally'.[97] As a broadly based interconnected national endeavour the statistical movement had collapsed.

It had left a number of useful reports on education and the condition of the working classes, plus a collection of odds and ends of little value.

Part of the reason for the collapse lies in the amateurism of much of the movement – well-meaning men sitting around having 'an hour's desultory conversation'. A common feature was the discovery that large amounts of time and money were required to complete statistical surveys, time which they could not spare and money which they would not. Nor were there enough professionals to keep up the momentum. Kay was soon siphoned off from Manchester to Chadwick's machine and then to education. Baker was an increasingly busy factory inspector (and personally unsuited to holding together an alliance of local notables). The men of Bristol were always calling on somebody else to do the work. It is useful to remind ourselves that the London society survived because of the enthusiasm of a few – a very few – drawn from the nation at large. Rawson Rawson wrote to Thomas Wilson of Barnsley that he had 'learned by experience to expect little work from any body, and to take the initiative upon myself'.[98]

Amateur groups could sustain activity for a while. But even if they did actually do something then they would, like Bristol, run out of topics and 'finding, as they conceive, that there is nothing more to be done, become virtually extinct'.[99] There was little idea of repeating work, of charting changes. This was natural. The real aims of the societies had seldom been to discover previously unknown facts. The societies were not only 'means to an end', as Ashton rightly notes of Manchester,[100] but means to already perceived ends of a defined nature. The results of the Manchester society's education surveys could have been interpreted to imply that few children were without an appreciable amount of formal education. The possibility was ignored as criticism shifted to a qualitative analysis of the deficiencies of the existing means of instruction. The reports on the working classes were so thoroughly imbued with preconceived notions of the ills of society and their remedies that it is difficult to believe that they led to an expansion of understanding on the part of the investigators. Once, therefore, sufficient propaganda had been assembled there was little point in repeating the proceedings. Moreover, once the debate had been carried to the national level their interest in further local research was hard to sustain. By the early 1840s education and public health appeared (perhaps misleadingly) to have reached this level.

Conclusion: Social Statistics and the Ideology of Improvement in Early Victorian Britain

Whether or not the provincial statisticians were correct in assuming that public health and education were two areas of national politics in which by the end of the 1830s effective action was imminent, there can be no doubt that these two topics formed the hard core of the statistical movement. Throughout the works of the men studied here there is a consensus concerning the problems facing Britain in the early Victorian period and the kinds of solutions required to meet them. Some of that consensus can only be discovered by looking at the statements made by the statisticians outside the framework of the movement proper. It quickly becomes apparent that the statisticians were uniformly committed to policies of economic laissez-faire, if by that term we mean no more than free trade, including the repeal of the corn laws. Equally, they were suspicious of the factory reformers and therefore changed their views on that question reluctantly.[1] They did not look to the factories for the major source of Britain's ills.

Rather than industrialization it was urbanization which dominated the minds of the statisticians. It was the conviction that upon the urban environment 'so much both of the habits and character of the people depends' which made a survey of the condition of the working classes a *sine qua non* for the more active statistical societies.[2] Such enquiries were pioneered by the Manchester society, which to a large extent set the pattern which others were to follow. As we have seen, the Manchester society's work began with the survey of part of Manchester sponsored by Benjamin Heywood, which was expanded to cover a considerable part of urban Lancashire. The published report of the committee responsible for the enquiry is brief and does little more than summarize the tables to be found in the appendix. Yet the beliefs of the Manchester men may be inferred from the indirect evidence of the questions included in the schedules of enquiry.[3]

From these it is apparent that the society's ideal was the fostering of a thrifty and virtuous working class. This ideal was made more apparent in the report of Rutland, where the existence of 'thrifty poverty' was noted with satisfaction. Thus the society's, indeed the movement's, concern was with the moral effects of the physical environment, a concern which could lead at times to a grammatical confusion of the condition of the working classes and the working classes themselves.

In a rural environment the society found to its pleasure that 'the general conduct of the people is marked by sobriety, frugality, and industry'...[4] 'The visitation of the houses of the labouring poor in Rutlandshire, and the observation of their language, manners, and habits, leave a favourable impression with regard to their moral condition'. This could be contrasted with the alarming situation in Hull where dense urban concentrations of insanitary housing led to the moral deterioration of the people. The tension between moralism and environmentalism was particularly apparent when the Hull report dealt with the number of persons per bed. The high ratio was taken as 'not only a signal proof of destitution and discomfort, but a fruitful and certain source of evil'.[5]

The sharing of beds or bedrooms by several people, common among the working classes, was a constant source of dismay to the statisticians because of its destruction of 'delicate feelings'. This and other aspects of the moral argument dominated the reports of the Bristol Statistical Society. The society's first report tabulated the possession of books, the deposits in friendly societies, the number of prints on the walls, the command of the skills of 'domestic economy' (only six women in the 275 families could knit while 79 of the men were stated to be unable to mend their own furniture).[6] In the full report on some 21,000 people indices of this type were taken to prove 'the wretched and barbarous condition in which a mass of our fellow-creatures are living.' However, this was not inevitable since if only 'a reasonable sense of decency and cleanliness could be instilled' there were 'ample means ... to realise most essential improvements.' The culprits were 'improvidence and low sensuality'.[7] The dominance of the moral attitude seems even clearer if it is noted that in the pilot survey enquiries had been made into the physical condition of the people according to whether or not they were 'clean and healthy'. By the time of the final report this had become 'clean and respectable'. Hence 'clean and respectable' and 'in considerable distress' became mutually exclusive categories along with 'dirty and disreputable'.[8]

Yet the society collected much valuable data which, like that in the other statistical surveys, has been all too little used by historians. In the Bristol survey there is information on sub-letting, literacy, the

Conclusion 137

number of severely disabled, the prevalence of various prophylactic measures against smallpox, religious profession, rents, and so on. There are occasional remarkable insights into the details of desperation encompassed in the omnibus term 'poverty': for example, the lack of cupboards and shelves leading to domestic chaos.[9] While the society's reports did not make it entirely clear whether it saw the poor as primarily responsible for their own condition or not, it certainly did not condemn them to remain in their 'wretched' state. Rather the society sent forth a call to action to be 'prosecuted in a becoming spirit, and under a sense of religious duty'.[10] As might have been anticipated from its membership the Bristol Statistical Society saw the working classes as objects of missionary activity. The purpose of its work was to measure the abyss of ignorance and degradation into which the faithful must plunge.

Less heavily evangelical but sometimes as moralistic was a report of a committee of the Statistical Society of London on two parishes in Westminster. It was found that the number of 'theatrical or amatory' pictures exceeded the 'serious' ones.[11] This kind of semi-voyeurist fact-gathering reached its ridiculous limit when the Central Society of Education found that in Marylebone 166 parents were 'able to sing a cheerful song' while 871 could not. The accompanying rural survey found that 197 families cultivated flowers against 244 which did not.[12] In neither survey, supposedly designed to reveal the condition of the working classes, was there any attempt to assess the effects of low wages or unemployment. Indeed, from many of the surveys of the statistical movement it is possible to deduce a better description of the books and pictures of the early Victorian working classes than of their income and expenditure.[13]

The statisticians were often confused and confusing on the direction of causation between poverty and degradation. A committee, comprising many of the leading London statisticians and men like W. P. Alison, could talk of 'the physical evils resulting from moral causes' and yet proceed to a sophisticated analysis in which heavy drinking was seen as both a cause and an effect of destitution. The same committee argued that 'the poorest people have no choice of residence' and that it was the hopelessness of their condition which made them 'blind and callous to consequences.' While this latter statement was linked to an attack upon the futility and dangerousness of trade union activity its tone suggested a more realistic view of the relationship between poverty and degradation.[14] The aim remained the creation of a virtuous and quiescent working class. Humanitarianism, class interest, and statistics made a powerful reforming brew.

Similar motives lay behind the numerous enquiries carried out or sponsored by individuals within the movement. For example, Henry Ashworth of the Manchester Statistical Society painted a picture of black despair with regard to the condition of the working classes during a trade depression in Bolton. The average earnings per family from all sources among 1003 families surveyed was 1s 2d per week.[15] Yet this was no indictment of industrial society but part of a campaign on behalf of limited parliamentary reform and free trade.[16] Less immediately political but more moralistic was a report by William Felkin of Nottingham on a depressed group of Norwich hand-loom weavers. Felkin took a censorious view of their beer drinking and reading of the works of such undesirables as Paine, Carlyle, Voltaire and Volney.[17] Felkin's moral utopia was the well-regulated factory town of Hyde, controlled by Thomas Ashton of the Manchester Statistical Society. There, bibles, musical instruments, pictures, furniture, and 'domestic economy' were the norm, the drink trade was in disarray, and pauperism, crime, and illegitimacy practically non-existent. Ashton had created a society directed towards 'the restraint of vice, the encouragement of virtue, and the promotion of happiness'.[18]

Not surprisingly, the most developed versions of such attitudes were often associated with the London society. A committee of the society produced perhaps the most complete of the early Victorian poverty surveys in 1848. The moralistic argument was weakly represented in the report; both the schedules of questions and the text concentrated on possible environmental factors. Since the mass of material to be included limited the size of the report the comments were largely restricted to summarizing the tables.[19] Yet it is difficult to doubt that the aim of the committee remained, as an 1840 committee report put it, 'the foundation of a superior moral character for the working population'.[20] In fact another report which appeared in 1848 was one of the most ideologically explicit produced by the movement. This was the report on Church Lane, St Giles, by a committee consisting of Sykes, Guy, and Neison. It was similar in many ways to the qualitative sections of Charles Booth's poverty survey. Individual dwellings were described in terse detail based on personal observation. The moral condemnation, the objection made, not to the conditions themselves, but to the associated degeneracy, was entirely offset by ascribing moral failure to those conditions: 'it is physically impossible to preserve the ordinary decencies of life; where all sense of propriety and self respect must be lost, to be replaced only by a recklessness of demeanour which necessarily results from vitiated minds'. The solution was the provision of model dwellings for 'that large class of our labouring population which is prepared to adopt habits of cleanliness and decency'.[21]

Hence by an individual, corporate, and governmental attack on the urban environment the statisticians expected to see the creation of the preconditions for a more moral society. They saw this attack as a necessary but not sufficient condition for that society; without public health measures there was little point in educating at least the very poorest since moral instruction was meaningless in such immoral surroundings:

> with many of the young, brought up in such hot-beds of mental pestilence, the hopeless, but benevolent attempt is making [sic] to implant, by means of general education the seeds of religion, virtue, truth, order, industry, and cleanliness; but which seeds to fructify advantageously, need, it is to be feared, a soil far less rank than can be found in these wretched abodes. Tender minds, once vitiated, present almost insuperable difficulties to reformation; bad habits and depraved feelings gather with the growth and strengthen with the strength.[22]

Public health reforms and education, therefore, were twin aspects of the same problem of moral decay and political unrest among the working classes as far as the statisticians were concerned. Education would ensure the creation of a more moral society. In particular, education was seen as the answer to crime, the most noticeable epiphenomenon of moral degeneracy. To think otherwise was a counsel of despair in the social turmoil of the 15 to 20 years after the Reform Act. But the repeated attempts by the statisticians to prove that education reduced crime can perhaps be understood only in the context of the consternation aroused in 1833 by A. M. Guerry. Guerry, a Frenchman, published in that year a work which was not only heretical but substantiated its heresy by statistical methods.[23] With its shaded maps and histograms it was technically more advanced than any British work to that date but that could not excuse Guerry for arguing that education did not reduce crime.

In general the statisticians became obsessed with Guerry's little book. An indication of how extraordinarily sensitive they were is the treatment of a non-movement statistician at the 1840 British Association meeting. This was Joseph Bentley who, with six agents, had carried out a survey of education and crime in Worcestershire over a period of eight months. He presented his results in a paper but was interrupted by Lord Sandon (the chairman, and past-president of the London society) who told him to stop wasting their time. Rawson said that Bentley's survey could not be reliable since the London society had employed men 'of superior education and talents' and yet even they missed some schools. Bentley managed to continue despite further interjections. His paper was mentioned in the *Athenaeum* which stated he had tried to prove education was not a restraint on crime. Bentley had this corrected and the official report of the meeting summarized his paper without referring to the interruptions. The misunderstanding probably explains the unprecedented behaviour of Sandon and Rawson who had sat through much more dubious papers in the past.[24]

Certainly some of the more prominent statisticians were quick to pounce on Guerry. References to his work, either direct or implied, are common for a number of years after 1833. To gauge the reaction of the mainstream of the statistical movement as well as its own researches we shall confine ourselves to four men: W. R. Greg, G. R. Porter, Rawson Rawson, and Joseph Fletcher. Greg first went into the attack in 1833 and followed with a more rounded paper to the British Association in 1835. In the latter Greg used Quetelet's writings to refute Guerry using the example of the Netherlands. Like Guerry's French data at first sight the statistics showed a direct, not inverse, relationship between the areas of high crime and high education. Greg was forced back to the observation that where there was the greatest quantity of education then crimes of violence were the least. The overall excess of crimes was due to crimes against property and other lesser crimes which were a concomitant of wealthy areas. But this was not to say that it was the educated who were the criminals since it could be 'proved' that 81 per cent of crimes were committed by people with little or no education.[25]

The last part of Greg's argument was developed by Porter who saw property crimes as 'the consequences of civilization'. Unlike Greg, Porter did not adopt Guerry's technique of using shaded maps to indicate the geographical distribution of social variables. But he took Guerry on more directly. Porter stated that Guerry's reliance on the figures for a single year (1831) had misled him. The figures for 1829–33 gave a different impression, particularly for offences against the person. Like Greg he reverted to the level of education of the criminals themselves (for which French statistics were available and provided the model for Porter's own reforms of the British returns). In the four most instructed departments he saw a clear advantage in favour of the educated. In any case Porter, like all the statisticians, thought the index only partially valid since 'education' had such a limited meaning at the time. Much greater improvements could be expected when 'the most numerous class shall be taught to make a proper use of knowledge, by having impressed upon them a right understanding of all their relative and social duties'.[26]

Porter returned to his main themes when the Central Society of Education was in being since it was essential to that society's campaign that Guerry's notions should be crushed. The nature of the dilemma which faced Porter and kindred thinkers of the time if Guerry's theories were allowed to be true was clearly put: 'To what purpose do we charge ourselves with the labour of imparting instruction to the ignorant, if we do not hope by that means to render them wiser and better, and therefore happier beings?' Guerry had to be refuted or the faith of Lancaster and other educational reformers would be nothing more than 'a benevolent dream'.[27] Insofar as Guerry's work suggested any failure of education to stop crime this failure was not one of education *per se* but of existing modes of education. These were not directed, as good education would be, 'to discipline the heart, and to form the character as well as to store the mind'. Taking all the 'facts' into account it was not possible 'to entertain a doubt'.[28]

Not surprisingly Porter's opinions had been echoed by Rawson Rawson in 1840 when he continued the analysis of crime statistics he had begun the previous year.[29] Like Porter, Rawson made great play of the meaning of the term 'education'. This was not 'mere instruction' but 'that moral, combined with intellectual, training, by which the mind is taught to discern, and the heart is led to feel the great object for which man is created, and the duties which he is called upon to fulfil in this stage of his existence'.[30] It followed that the tests of instruction in the criminal returns, accurate though they may have been, were only a very partial test of education (which made it easier to infer more from the figures than they warranted). The criminal tables for 1836 onwards divided those committed for trial into four groups – the illiterate, those who could read and write imperfectly, those who could read and write well, and those with 'superior instruction'. Since 1836 showed an exceptional proportion of the last group Rawson used the figures for 1837-9 – a clear example of excluding inconveniently unfavourable data. Ninety per cent of the convicts fell into the first two classes and could be presumed to have had no education with 'any good influence on their minds'. There was even some doubt whether the third group had had an education 'as would serve to dispel the darkness of ignorance, and enable them to acquire a control over their thoughts and actions'. That left four out of every thousand criminals whom education had failed to deter.[31]

Rawson stated that there must have been a greater number of educated people than this in the population at large. While the poor would always exist at least a population of educated poor would not live in a state which 'debases their minds' and 'destroys their sense of right and wrong'.[32] Rawson was moving into a sermon which though it sounded intensely moralistic was strongly environmentalist. He thought it was a vain hope and a sign of short-sightedness when the law 'expects and claims orderly habits and decent conduct' from people 'bred up in the darkest ignorance, debased by the vilest associations, and exposed to the most bitter trials and temptations'.[33] It followed that the reason for the increase of crime would be 'found in circumstances connected with the social, rather than with the moral, condition of communities'.[34] Here, then, was the complement of sanitary reform, the other answer to the failure to create a moral and peaceful community. 'Improvement' was a Janus figure facing to the sewers and houses in one direction and to the schools in the other.

To the schools in particular for the last and most prolific of our statisticians, Joseph Fletcher. In the late 1840s Fletcher dominated statistical writings on the relation of crime and education with long essays which were included in his official reports as an inspector of schools. He also delivered papers to the British Association and, as editor of the London society's *Journal*, had his major works printed in it to ensure the widest possible audience. Fletcher's first writings, however, were in his capacity as secretary to the hand-loom weavers' commission. He wrote the report on the ribbon-weavers of the Midlands. Fletcher thought that the city weavers were not too morally degraded although they did not realize the value of 'self-cultivation'. Regrettably, many of the more active young men were attracted to 'the strange theoretical confusion of all the relations of civil life, commonly called "*socialism*", with its community of property and exchange of women'.[35] But Fletcher found it difficult to convey the life of debasement and immorality led by the country weavers.[36]

A large part of the remedy was, of course, education. Guerry's 'counter-proposition involved the absurdity that knowledge of truth is the way to error'. Fletcher saw the choice before society as one between good and bad education; it was vital to understand that education should be regarded as the totality of environmental influences at work on the individual, '*industrial, instructional, political*, or *domestic*'. Fletcher wrote a hymn to the possibilities opened up by the Industrial Revolution with a warning of its dangers. In a society no longer composed of 'scattered peasants and walled-up burgesses' it was necessary to have a 'far higher intelligence' disseminated among the masses since this was 'essential to their own welfare and to the peace of society'. In a mass society where the ignorant and depraved could be combined 'political riots are rapidly becoming national instead of local'. It was therefore 'time to substitute sound information' for socialism which was 'the rising political philosophy of the masses'. Proper secular and religious education would achieve two objectives. Firstly, 'the iron-arms of our steam-engines' and 'the iron wings of commerce' would mean that 'the public peace is secured, and our prosperity and advancement will probably be carried beyond all earthly precedent'. Secondly, a society of 'good labourers, good fathers, good subjects'. 'respectable and respected' would emerge.[37] This is the authentic voice of the statistical movement giving full expression to the ideology of improvement.

Despite this early evidence of Fletcher's strong belief in the power of education to create a moral and tranquil society his experience in the government enquiry into the employment of children, particularly in the mines, seems to have aroused some temporary doubts. In 1843 he wrote a paper on crime in Britain in which he argued strongly that criminals were no more ignorant than the population from which they were drawn. That population, the poor, was subject to 'a thousand deteriorating influences, in the places of their abode, their pursuits, their companionship, their want of domestic discipline, and their neglected social position, sufficient to produce far more evil than is usually laid to their want of schooling'. It was these which caused the increase of crime rather than the ever present ignorance of the masses.[38] Fletcher's loss of faith was not long-lived. He became an inspector of schools shortly afterwards and this seems to have restored it.

The restoration was complete by 1847 when he read to the British Association a long paper on the relationship of education to other social parameters (part of which was published in his annual report as an inspector of schools). As this paper is a harbinger of the much more detailed studies he produced two years later we shall limit ourselves to mentioning that Fletcher was satisfied that he had demonstrated that 'greater diffusion of instruction is seen to be the concomitant of every promising figure'.[39] In a paper read to the British Association the following year he covered some of the same ground but also tried to explain the paradox that in some areas the criminal population appeared to be better educated than the population at large. He resolved the paradox, in his own eyes anyway, by arguing that the quality of instruction varied greatly. Therefore, the education index used (the signing of the marriage registers) could not always show a 'careful uprearing of the young ... that is alone blessed to the good end of righteous living in a Christian hope'.[40]

The partial rejection of an index used happily when it satisfies the needs of dogma is not something confined to the social statisticians of the 1830s and 1840s. But it was an especially strong tendency at that time and it is important to understand when and where it took place. Fletcher in the late 1840s was trying to marshal a massive amount of data to prove the social utility of education as the producer of a Christian and stable community dominated by a humanitarian form of the middle-class value system. The culmination of his work was a paper read to the Statistical Society of London in March 1849 at a meeting attended by Prince Albert. With its tables the printed version ran to over 170 pages of the *Journal*.[41] A later version of the paper was published in the Education Committee minutes for 1850. We shall refer to the *Journal* article as the most readily accessible source. In both versions Fletcher presented a number of tables of social indices accompanied by shaded maps showing the variation in each index in England and Wales.

After defending the statistical approach the first part of the paper consisted largely of a description of the indices and a survey of the advance of crime. While the latter was partly seen as a result of economic fluctuations the division into counties suggested to Fletcher that the problem was the by now familiar one of an advance 'in material civilization' unmatched by 'a proportionate moral advancement'. The worst results occurred in a depression 'amidst those classes whose moral ties to the existing framework of society are feeblest and least felt or understood'. The possibility was that the poor would turn to socialism or the like, which denied 'the most cherished axioms of political science, or even the words of Christian truth itself'. Laissez-faire was no answer 'for it is evil that is marching upon us from among them with gigantic strides'. Therefore local action encouraged by the state had to take place in the fields of education, law and order, charity, and sanitary reform. Fletcher's 'us' was made more explicit when he recommended the reform of parts of the judiciary to bring in 'men of middle-class intelligence'.[42]

Fletcher and the other statisticians had disguised propaganda as facts. The purpose of education was revealed as the conversion of one class to the value system of another. Even Chadwick, before he became obsessed with the sanitary idea, had considered education to be of fundamental importance since the pauper children who had been educated were supposed to have become self-reliant while the uneducated 'were continually burthensome and became, drunkards, prostitutes or thieves'.[43] Within this argument on the necessity of education the tension between environmentalism and moralism manifested itself strongly. Chadwick's statement implies an environmentalistic attitude not usually associated with him as early as 1834. The possibilities of slipping into a crude form of moralism were demonstrated by E. C. Tufnell's assertion that 'circumstances are far more dependent on character than character on circumstances'.[44] Still, Tufnell saw an answer in education but clearly the belief could easily dominate that saw poverty solely in terms of moral failure generating no sympathy, and charity only of the most disciplinarian kind. In our period the statisticians managed to preserve the fragile balance.

But poverty was not the main factor in the drive for educational reform. Even crime was only a symptom of a far deeper malaise that the statisticians and like-minded reformers discerned in society. Social discontent was at a peak in the 1830s and 1840s. The world of the middle and upper classes was threatened, in Seymour Tremenheere's phrase, by 'anarchical, Socialist, and infidel forces'.[45] Within the constraints set by their ideological preconceptions the statisticians had to account for the breakdown of social harmony. It could not be due to the factory system: it was axiomatic that that was beneficial even if some aspects, such as child-labour, could be changed. It might be true that much was due to the inferior moral character of the lower classes themselves but that was not very helpful: moral condemnation could not prevent revolution. Means to improve their character had to be found. Means had also to be found to explain to them the unalterable nature of certain social relationships and hierarchies. Otherwise the ignorant would be led into social disruption by agitators.

Hence education. Especially in the sense understood by statisticians and the other educational activists – as a combination of physical, moral, and intellectual instruction. Apart from the schools the agents of such instruction were the town libraries, the 'useful knowledge' purveyors, the town museums, the literary and philosophical institutes, and the botanical gardens.[46] The result James Phillips Kay envisaged as 'the rearing of hardy and intelligent working men, whose character and habits shall afford the largest amount of security to the property and order of the community'.[47] But education was only part of the answer. Equal stress, particularly in the 1840s, was laid by the statisticians on the physically and morally degrading effects of the physical environment. The failure to create a satisfactory urban environment became increasingly apparent. The Chadwickian group carried their case to extremes, as was shown when Lyon Playfair stated that the great extent of ignorance and crime was 'essentially connected with the exposure to bodily disease'.[48] Within the statistical movement education and sanitary reform were more normally seen as complementary parts of the same programme. Surveys of the condition of the working classes and of the state of education went hand in hand. They surveys would reveal 'the circumstances by which [the working classes] are surrounded, and the effects which they are calculated to produce upon them, both morally and physically'.[49]

The statistical societies were formed to prosecute these enquiries. Rawson Rawson specifically acknowledged that 'Benevolent individuals are united in numerous societies for the purpose of inquiring accurately into the state of the poor.'[50] It quickly became a cliché of the movement that the surveys were a necessary preliminary to action. The fourth annual report of the Statistical Society of London welcomed what it thought was the growing recognition that 'statistical data must constitute the *raw material* for all true systems of economy and legislation, local and national'.[51] Yet it was a theory that masked the true intention. Time and again the statisticians embarked upon surveys the major conclusions of which were anticipated and preconceived. It was not really necessary, for example, to know the exact difference between the number of children at dame schools in Manchester and Liverpool before it was possible to legislate for government aid. The real purpose of the enquiries was to reveal to the public by means of 'facts' the condition of the population.

For two reasons these facts were in quantitative form. Partly it was because 'statistics' were understood to mean the study of the actual condition of the population. 'Statistics' also implied some use of quantification. Perhaps more important was the notion that numbers were truly facts, or at least could be presented as if they were. The most significant occurrence in this context was the foundation of the statistical section of the British Association which limited itself to numbers and 'mere abstraction' to avoid the appearance of introducing the 'foul Daemon of disorder'. Moreover, the time seemed ripe for a concerted push for reform backed by a mass of incontrovertible evidence. The passage of the Reform Bill, following close on the removal of some of the disabilities placed upon the Dissenters, opened up the vision of reforming men of 'middle-class intelligence' (in Fletcher's phrase) coming to power. Whether or not this was a realistic appraisal of the post-1832 situation the statisticians were preaching to the wealthier classes and trying to convert them to specific programmes of reform 'to *prevent* misfortune and vice, sickness and improvidence'.[52] Rawson Rawson summed up the aims and methods of the movement in 1838 when he saw the *Journal* as 'an important instrument for developing and diffusing the knowledge of truth, and for detecting and removing error and prejudice'.[53] When they had been removed, from all classes, then that hierarchical society with a working class of 'good labourers, good fathers, and good subjects' which Fletcher foresaw would come into existence on the tide of voluntary and legislative action for the improvement of the lower classes. But above all that society would be a moral one, a society characterized by 'religion, virtue, truth, order, industry, and cleanliness' in the words of the 1848 committee on Church Lane, 'sobriety, cleanliness, forethought and method' in J. P. Kay's version.

Clearly the statisticians did not possess a monopoly of these concepts in early Victorian Britain. Indeed, these concepts formed the dominant value system of the age. It may be suggested that *one* way in which we can approach the political and social conflicts of the period is in terms of a contest over which particular set of reforms was most likely to make Britain actually conform to the ideal. The statisticians wanted to contribute more than voluntary and legislative action in the fields of public health and education: they were also free traders, supporters of the new poor law (if not framers and administrators of it), opposed to trade unions and working class radicals, suspicious of factory acts. In other words, they were part of the new centrist tradition in Britain, represented in politics most of all by Lord John Russell and Sir Robert Peel. The centrists were travelling 'down the road that led by Political Economy to Free Trade'.[54] The statisticians were attempting to dominate that tradition, to mould it to their own particular version of how to create the new moral order. Yet the opponents of the new centrism had their ideas of how to create a not dissimilar moral order of sobriety and industry.[55] The conflict between the centre and an alliance of the extremes over how to achieve this order may have been the main impetus to the growth of government in the early Victorian period.[56]

The statistical movement failed in its particular bid for control of the dominant value system. With the single exception of Manchester the provincial movement collapsed. This indicates that while the ideology of the movement may be regarded as middle class, it was not the ideology of the middle class, which, if it existed at all, can only be described in terms of the value system itself. Moreover, significant reforms in public health and education were prevented, delayed, or sabotaged not by arguments over the principle of them – both the centre and the extremes were in rare agreement that such reforms were desirable – but by a failure to agree on the question of authority. Since all groups saw reforms in public health and, especially, education as a means of social control, who should exercise that control became a matter of crucial concern. Thus the paradoxical fact that more effective intervention was achieved in the highly controversial area of factory reform by 1850 may be explained, since there the issue of authority was far less serious. The statistical movement was defeated by its own argument that it had found the means of creating the new moral order.

Moreover, the long period of mid-Victorian prosperity and comparative tranquility did not favour theories which stressed the urgency of certain kinds of social reforms. If the Great Exhibition marks the transition in society at large from a period of social and economic crisis to one of confidence and stability then the deaths of Porter and Fletcher in 1852 seem to mark the transition in social statistics. This transition led to both a widening and a narrowing of the scope of social statistics, as represented by the Statistical Society of London. A widening in the sense that there was less concentration upon a small number of questions and less dominance by a small clique. If we exclude W. A. Guy, an active survivor of the earlier period, then the seven leading contributors gave one-third of the papers read in the decade 1853–62, compared with one-half in the 1840s. There was a far greater interest in economics than there had been in the 1840s: over 40 per cent of the papers were concerned with economic questions. A number of papers dealt with wages, David Chadwick remarking in 1860 that hitherto the subject had been neglected.[57] There is a discernible growth in the variety of opinions expressed, a process which culminates in the decision in 1873 to begin printing the discussion which followed the papers. Yet there is also a narrowing. To use the fashionable word of our own times, there is less concern for 'relevance'. One quarter of the papers read from 1853 to 1862 were on public health and vital statistics, but they were increasingly concerned with technicalities and with non-controversial descriptions of statistical trends. Moral statistics became of less and less concern with only one-ninth of the papers being on these topics, even if papers on the poor law are included. By 1860 one fellow could (rather prematurely) argue that statistics 'belongs to the domain of Mathematics'.[58] William Farr, arguing in 1864 that statistics would banish error and solve all social problems, sounded distinctly anachronistic, an echo of the era which had seen the foundations of empirical social research in Britain for non-empirical reasons.[59]

The Statistical Society of London in the mid-Victorian period seemed unable to decide if it was primarily concerned with issues or methods. A compromise to preserve some kind of consensus led to a pervading dullness compared with the earlier period.[60] Much of the more important work was carried out instead by the National Association for the Promotion of Social Science, founded in 1857. At times the NAPSS sounded like a weak echo of the early Victorian statistical movement with its avoidance of 'party interest' and yet its visible commitment to particular social and intellectual positions.[61] Many of its leading members were at the same time the leaders of the Statistical Society. The NAPSS collapsed in the mid-1880s at

Conclusion

just the point when empirical social research was undergoing a major revival, led by Charles Booth. Booth's *Life and Labour of the People in London* was arguably the greatest work of social research ever carried out in Britain but it would not be difficult to show that all its main methods and conclusions were foreshadowed by the early Victorian statisticians.[62] It was also one of the last such works which could appear initially within the context of statistics. Statistics and sociology were parting company, a process institutionalized in the foundation of the Sociological Society in 1903.[63] The process of division was scarcely apparent to statisticians in the early Victorian era, for whom the word 'sociology' did not exist. But 'statistics' did. The widespread but short-lived concern with improvement by numbers was a significant movement of the period: its permanent legacy was not so much a new moral order as the indigenous tradition of empirical social research characteristic of British sociology.

Notes to Text

Prelude: Social Statistics in Britain, 1660–1830

1. The most important works on the early history of social statistics are Edwin James Farren, *Historical Essay on the Rise and Early Progress of the Doctrine of Life-Contingencies in England* (London, 1844); D. V. Glass, 'Some Aspects of the Development of Demography', *Jnl Roy. Soc. Arts*, CIV, 1955-6, pp. 854–69; Major Greenwood, *Medical Statistics from Graunt to Farr* (Cambridge, 1948); V. John, *Geschichte der Statistik* (Stuttgart, 1894); John Koren (ed.), *The History of Statistics* (London, 1918); Paul F. Lazarsfeld, 'Notes on the History of Quantification in Sociology – Trends, Sources, and Problems', *Isis*, LII, 1961, pp. 277–333 (also in Harry Woolf (ed.), *Quantification: A History of the Meaning of Measurement in the Natural and Social Sciences* (Indianapolis and New York, 1961); August Meitzen, *History, Theory and Technique of Statistics* (trans. Roland P. Falkner, Philadelphia, 1891); Helen M. Walker, *Studies in the History of Statistical Method* (Baltimore, 1929); Harald Westergaard, *Contributions to the History of Statistics* (London, 1932).
2. The term 'political arithmetic' was invented by Petty and probably first used in a letter to Lord Anglesea dated 17 December 1672. (Charles Henry Hull (ed.), *The Economic Writings of Sir William Petty together with the Observations upon the Bills of Mortality more probably by Captain John Graunt* (2 vols., Cambridge, 1899), I, p. 239n. The Hull collection is hereafter cited as *PEW*.)
3. Richard Foster Jones, *Ancients and Moderns: A Study of the Rise of the Scientific Movement in Seventeeth Century England* (St Louis, Missouri, 1961), esp. pp. 50-1; Margery Purver, *The Royal Society: Concept and Creation* (London, 1967).
4. C. Webster, 'The Origins of the Royal Society', *History of Science*, VI, 1967, p. 125.

5. R. K. Merton, 'Science in Seventeenth Century England', *Osiris*, IV, 1938, pp. 360–632.
6. Lewis S. Feuer, *The Scientific Intellectual: The Psychological and Sociological Origins of Modern Science* (New York, 1963), chapter 1.
7. Lynn Thorndike, 'Newness and Craving for Novelty in Seventeenth Century Science and Medicine', *Jnl. Hist. Ideas*, XII, 1951, pp. 585–98. G. N. Clark, *Science and Social Welfare in the Age of Newton* (Oxford, 1937), pp. 72, 131.
8. The main support for Petty's claims can be found in two works by the Marquis of Lansdowne: *The Petty Papers* (2 vols., London, 1927), II, pp. 273–84 and *The Petty-Southwell Correspondence* (London, 1928), pp. xxiii–xxxii. The list of contemporaries citing Petty as the author has since been added to in P. D. Groenewegen, 'Authorship of the *Natural and Political Observations on the Bills of Mortality*', *Journal of the History of Ideas*, XXVIII, 1967, pp. 601–2. Groenewegen adds John Houghton and Thomas Hale but Major Greenwood had already noted the former (op. cit., p. 37).
9. General agreement on the nature of Graunt's primacy is to be found in the following works: Bernard Benjamin, 'Tercentenary of John Graunt's 'Natural and Political Observations'; The Royal Society Meetings', *Journal of the Institute of Actuaries*, LXXXIX, 1963, pp. 66–70; Benjamin, 'John Graunt's 'Observations', With a foreword', *J. Inst Act.*, XC, 1964, pp. 1–61 (the foreword is at pp. 1–3. This is the only modern reprint of the first edition and is cited hereafter as *Observations*); D. V. Glass, 'Graunt's Life Table', *J. Inst. Act.*, LXXVI, 1950, pp. 61–4; Glass, 'John Graunt and his 'Natural and Political Observations', *Proceedings of the Royal Society* Series B, CLIX, 1964, pp. 2–32 (also in *Notes and Queries*, XIX, 1964, pp. 63–100); Greenwood, op. cit., pp. 36–9; Charles Henry Hull, *Graunt or Petty? The Authorship of the 'Observations upon the Bills of Mortality'* (Boston, 1896) (appeared originally in *Political Science Quarterly*, XI, No. 1, 1896, pp. 105–32); Hull, 'Introduction', *PEW*, I, pp. xxix–liv, Robert Kargon, 'John Graunt, Francis Bacon, and the Royal Society: The Reception of Statistics', *Journal of the History of Medicine*, XVIII, 1963, pp. 337–48; Shichiro Matsukawa; 'The 300th Anniversary of J. Graunt's *Observations* (1662)', *Hitotsubashi Journal of Economics*, III, 1962, pp. 49–60; D. F. Renn, 'John Graunt, Citizen of London', *J. Inst. Act.*, LXXXVIII, 1962, pp. 367–9; Ian Sutherland, 'John Graunt: a Tercentenary Tribute', *JRSS*, Series A, CXXVI, 1963, pp. 537–56.
10. Hull, *Graunt or Petty?*, pp. 130–2; Greenwood, op. cit., pp. 38–9.

11. E.g. see *Petty-Southwell Correspondence*, p. 319.
12. The phrase occurs in *Petty-Southwell Correspondence*, p. 322.
13. Andrew Clark (ed.), *John Aubrey's Brief Lives* (2 vols., Oxford, 1898), II, p. 148.
14. *Petty Papers*, I, p. 262.
15. Ibid., pp. 81–90.
16. There are two biographies of Petty in English: Lord Edmond Fitzmaurice, *The Life of Sir William Petty 1623–1687* (London, 1895) and E. Strauss, *Sir William Petty* (London, 1954). Both are competent but there is need for a study by a specialist in the period making full use of the Bowood papers.
17. See Richard Peters, *Hobbes* (Harmondsworth, Middlesex, 1956), pp. 45–79.
18. For the list see *Petty Papers*, II, p. 5.
19. Lewis S. Feuer, *The Scientific Intellectual*, p. 31; Wilson Lloyd Bevan, 'Sir William Petty', *Publications of the American Economic Association*, IX, 1894, p. 87; Quentin Skinner, 'History and Ideology in the English Revolution', *Historical Journal*, VIII, 1965, p. 171n, 129. Also see Skinner, 'Thomas Hobbes and his Disciples in England and France', *Comparative Studies in Society and History*, VIII, 1965–6, pp. 153–67.
20. Strauss notes the importance of the Down Survey as the model for Petty's later thought (op. cit., p. 196).
21. Richard S. Westfall, *Science and Religion in Seventeenth-Century England* (New Haven, 1958), p. 20.
22. *Observations*, p. 6.
23. The early history of the bills is not known to any high degree of certainty. The evidence suggests that they first appeared in 1519. Until 1603 they were published spasmodically being intended as a means of information in times of high plague-risk. Continuous series were available from 1603 and from 1629 other causes of death than plague were listed.
24. *PEW*, I, pp. lxxv–lxxvii.
25. *Observations*, p. 51.
26. *PEW*, I, pp. 244–5.
27. For an interesting discussion of Petty's use of this phrase see William Letwin, *The Origins of Scientific Economics* (London, 1963), pp. 130–1.
28. Thomas S. Kuhn in *The Structure of Scientific Revolutions* (Chicago, 1964).
29. Walter E. Houghton jr, 'The English Virtuoso in the Seventeenth Century', *Jnl. Hist. Ideas*, III, 1942, pp. 211–19.
30. This has largely been overlooked since the history of social statistics has usually been written by demographers or statisticians. G. N.

Clark argued that the eighteenth century failed to fulfil the promise of the late seventeenth (*Science and Social Welfare*, pp. 142–6).
31. Greenwood, op. cit., pp. 45–7; D. V. Glass, 'Gregory King's Estimate of the Population of England and Wales', *Pop. St.*, III, 1950, pp. 338–75; Peter Laslett, *The World we have lost* (London, 1965), p. 245.
32. 'An Estimate of the Degrees of Mortality of Mankind', *Philosophical Transactions*, XVII, 1696, pp. 596–610.
33. Greenwood, op. cit., p. 41.
34. Marios Raphael, 'The Origins of Public Superannuation Schemes in England' (unpublished Ph.D. thesis, London School of Economics, 1957), pp. 60–87.
35. M. E. Ogborn, *Equitable Assurances* (London, 1962).
36. For the major works see de Moivre, *The Doctrine of Chances* (1724); Richard Hayes, *A New Method for Valuing Annuities upon Lives* (1727); Weyman Lee, *An Essay to Ascertain the Value of Leases and Annuities* (1737); Thomas Simpson, *The Doctrine of Annuities and Reversions* (1742); James Hodgson, *The Valuation of Annuities upon Lives* (1747); Richard Price, *Observations on Reversionary Payments* (1771); William Morgan, *The Doctrine of Annuities and Assurances* (1779); William Dale, *Calculations . . . intended as an introduction to the doctrine of annuities* 1772); Francis Maseres, *The Principle of the Doctrine of Life Annuities* (1783).
37. See his introduction to Morgan, op. cit., pp. xv–xvi as well as *Observations* (5th edn., London, 1792), I, pp. 320–68.
38. Maitland, *History and Survey of London* (3rd edn., London, 1756), pp. 740–2; Short, *Observations on the Bills of Mortality* (London, 1750), pp. vii–xvi.
39. William Heberden (ed.), *A Collection of the Yearly Bills of Mortality* (London, 1759), p. 4.
40. 2nd edn., London, 1781. The first edition had been published the same year.
41. Ibid., p. 195.
42. Ibid., pp. 268–77. Black described a complete administrative machine for the task.
43. William Black, *A Comparative View of the Mortality of the Human Species at all Ages* (London, 1788), pp. xvii–xviii.
44. William Black, *A Dissertation on Insanity* (2nd edn., London, 1811).
45. Andrew Halliday, *Some Remarks on the State of Lunatic Asylums, and on the Number and Condition of the Insane Poor in Scotland* (Edinburgh, 1816).
46. Gilbert Blane, *Observations on the Diseases Incident to Seamen*

(London, 1785); *Select Dissertations on Several Subjects of Medical Science* (2 vols., London, 1833).
47. James Annesley, *Researches into the Causes, Nature, and Treatment of the More Prevalent Diseases of India, and of Warm Climates Generally* (2 vols., London, 1828).
48. Major Greenwood, *Some British Pioneers of Social Medicine* (London, 1948), p. 27.
49. W. H. G. Armytage, 'John Heysham: a Carlisle Bicentenary', *British Medical Journal*, 1953, II, p. 1156.
50. E.g. see *Sketch of a Plan to Exterminate the Casual Small-pox from Great Britain* (London, 1793).
51. J. F. von Bielfeld, *The Elements of Universal Erudition* (trans. by W. Hooper, 3 vols., London, 1770).
52. Ibid., III, p. 269.
53. Ibid., pp. 271–2: F. Bisset Hawkins, *Elements of Medical Statistics* (London, 1829), p. 1; William A Guy, 'On the Original and Acquired Meaning of the term "Statistics"', *JSSL*, XXVIII, 1865, p. 478.
54. Harald Westergaard, *Contributions to the History of Statistics*, pp. 6–8.
55. Ibid., p. 4.
56. Ibid., pp. 11–12.
57. E. A. W. Zimmerman, *Political Survey of Europe* (London, 1787).
58. Thomas B. Clarke, *Statistical View of Germany* (London, 1790).
59. Sir John Sinclair, *The Statistical Account of Scotland*, XX (Edinburgh, 1798), p. xixn.
60. Ibid., p. xviii.
61. *Encyclopaedia Britannica* (3rd edn., Edinburgh, 1797), XII, p. 731.
62. Benjamin Pitts Capper, *A Statistical Account . . . of England and Wales* (London, 1801), esp. pp. xiv, 63–81.
63. Daniel Boileau, *An Essay on the Study of Statistics* (London, 1807), p. 1.
64. Ibid., p. 61.
65. W. T. Brande (ed.), *A Dictionary of Science, Literature, and Art* (London, 1842), p. 1150.
66. *Penny Cyclopaedia* (London, 1833), XXII, p. 456.
67. *Elements of Medical Statistics*, p. 2.
68. H. Gray Funkhouser and Helen M. Walker, 'Playfair and his Charts', *Economic History*, III, 1935, p. 103.
69. William Playfair, *The Commercial and Political Atlas* (London, 1787).
70. William Playfair, *Lineal Arithmetic* (London, 1798).
71. William Playfair, *The Statistical Breviary* (London, 1801), p. 4.

72. H. Gray Funkhouser, 'Historical development of the graphical representation of statistical data', *Osiris*, III, 1937, p. 292.
73. Ibid., p. 294.
74. Charles Ansell, *A Treatise on Friendly Societies* (London, 1835), op. cit., pp. 64, 70.
75. John Rickman, 'Observations on Certain Facts Connected with Human Mortality, Population, and the Comparative Value of Male and Female Life', *London Medical Gazette*, XVI, 1835, pp. 588–9.
76. E.g. see A. J. Taylor, 'The Taking of the Census, 1801–1951', *British Medical Journal*, 1951, I, p. 715.
77. I have to thank Professor Glass for informing me of this reference as well as for sending me a draft of a paper concerned with some of the early censuses. Rickman's paper was reprinted in the *Commercial and Agricultural Magazine*, II, June 1800, pp. 391–9.
78. See Charles, Lord Colchester (ed.), *The Diary and Correspondence of Charles Abbott, Lord Colchester* (3 vols., London, 1860), I, pp. 209–19.
79. Ibid., pp. 209–10.
80. *Hansard's Parliamentary History*, XXXV, coll. 495–6.
81. Ibid., col. 598.
82. 41 Geo III, c.15. Returns of the marriages since 1754 were also made.
83. *Population Bill, Sel. Cttee. Mins. of Ev.*, p. 1; GBPP IV.
84. For the first returns see GBPP 1810 XIV. The returns begin with the figures for 1805.
85. See GBPP 1812 X and GBPP 1833 XXIX.
86. *Cobbett's Parliamentary Debates*, XIV, coll. 713–6.
87. References to the debates over the bills are to be found in the reports for the 1810 session but a fuller account is to be found in *Cobbett's Parliamentary Debates*, XIX (1811), Appendix.
88. *Cobbett's Parliamentary Debates*, XVI, coll. 833–5.
89. *Criminal Commitments and Convictions. Sel. Cttee. Second Rep.*, p. 4; GBPP 1828 VI.
90. *Police of the Metropolis. Sel. Cttee. Rep.*, pp. 6–9; GBPP 1828 VI.
91. Mary Sturt, *The Education of the People* (London, 1967), pp. 47–8.
92. See *Education of the Lower Orders of the Metropolis. Sel. Cttee*; GBPP 1816 IV.
93. See *Children Employed in Manufactories. Sel. Cttee*; GBPP 1816 III.
94. *Education of the Lower Orders. Sel. Cttee. Second Rep.*, p. 3; GBPP 1818 IV.
95. See GBPP 1819 IX, GBPP 1820 XII.
96. Francis Baily, *Doctrine of Life Annuities and Assurances* (2nd

edn., 2 vols., London, 1813). See particularly the appendix to the second volume.
97. Joshua Milne, *A Treatise on the Valuation of Annuities and Assurances on Lives and Survivorships* (2 vols., London, 1815).
98. *Laws Respecting Friendly Societies Sel. Cttee. Mins. of Ev.*, p. 91; GBPP 1825 IV.
99. Ibid., *Rep.*, p. 17.
100. *Laws Respecting Friendly Societies. Sel. Cttee. Rep.*, p. 11; GBPP 1826-7 III.
101. Francis Corbaux, *The Doctrine of Compound Interest* (London, 1825), p. 105.
102. *Elements of Medical Statistics*, pp. 10-11.
103. *Population Bill. Sel. Cttee. Mins. of Ev.*, p. 2; GBPP 1830 IV. The thesis that the growth of Dissent was responsible for a decline in registration efficiency has recently suffered powerful opposition – see P. E. Razzell, 'The Evaluation of Baptism as a Form of Birth Registration through Cross-Matching Census and Parish Register Data', *Pop. St.*, XXVI, 1972, p. 128.
104. For a lengthier discussion of the making of the Registration Act of 1836 see my article in the *Journal of Ecclesiastical History*, XXIV, October 1973.

1 The Statistical Department of the Board of Trade

1. Lucy Brown, *The Board of Trade and the Free Trade Movement, 1830-42* (Oxford, 1958), pp. 77-8. Dr Brown describes the work of the Department at pp. 76-93.
2. Charles Badham, *The Life of James Deacon Hume: Secretary of the Board of Trade* (London, 1859), pp. 131-2.
3. For brief sketches of Hume and Jacob see Brown, op. cit., pp. 23-5.
4. William Jacob, 'Observations and Suggestions Respecting the Collation, Concentration, and Diffusion of Statistical Knowledge Regarding the State of the United Kingdom', *Transactions of the Statistical Society of London*, I, pt. i, p. 1. That it is Jacob's original paper is shown by the advocacy of a Statistical Department which in a footnote is stated to have since been formed (ibid., p. 2). Dr Brown does not appear to have been aware of the existence of the paper, which is understandable, for the only copy of the *Transactions* I know of is in the library of the Royal Statistical Society.
5. Ibid.
6. Public Record Office, B.T.5/40, f. 489 (*Minutes*, 30 March 1832).
7. B.T.3/23, ff. 226-33 and B.T.24/1, ff. 1-3 (Thomas Lack to Treasury, 31 March 1832).
8. B.T.3/25, f. 21 (*In-letters*, 13 April 1832).

9. B.T.5/40, ff. 506-7.
10. For a biography of Knight see Althea C. Cherry, 'A Life of Charles Knight (1791-1837), with special reference to his political and educational activities' (unpublished M.A. thesis, London, 1942).
11. Brown, op. cit., p. 27. Monica C. Grobel, 'The Society for the Diffusion of Useful Knowledge' (unpublished M.A. thesis, London, 1933), p. 354.
12. Brown, op. cit., p. 28.
13. G. R. Porter, *On the Nature and Properties of the Sugar-Cane* (London, 1830), esp. pp. vi, 193-9 and 288-9.
14. Brown, op. cit., p. 28.
15. Quoted in Robert Blake, *Disraeli* (London, 1969), p. 323.
16. *DNB*.
17. *Public Documents. Sel. Cttee. First Rep.*; GBPP 1833 XII.
18. Ibid. *Second Rep.*, p. 3; GBPP 1833 XII.
19. Brown, op. cit., p. 28.
20. John Marshall, *A digest of all the accounts relating to the population, production, revenues ... of ... Great Britain and Ireland* (London, 1833).
21. *Statistical Illustrations of the territorial extent and population, commerce, taxation, consumption, insolvency, pauperism and crime of the British Empire* (London, 1825). For Marshall's authorship see Marshall, *An Analysis and Compendium of all the Returns made to Parliament* (London, 1835), 'Conclusions', p. vi.
22. Brown, op. cit., pp. 28-9. B.T.5/41, ff. 543-4 (*Minutes*, 31 January 1834).
23. For his father, Sir William Rawson, see *DNB*.
24. *JRSS*, LXII, 1899, pp. 677-9. Strangely, Rawson was not entered in *DNB*.
25. B.T.24/1, ff. 57-8 (letter to Hon. G. Lamb, 11 November 1833).
26. B.T.5/41, f. 569 (*Minutes, 25 February 1834*). B.T.3/24, f. 484 (*Out-letters*, 27 February 1834).
27. *Quetelet Papers*, Porter to Quetelet, 28 May 1835. The Quetelet collection is in the possession of the Belgian Royal Academy of Sciences, to whom I am indebted for photocopying a large number of letters. A catalogue to this rich and previously unexplored source is Liliane Wellens-de-Donder, 'Inventaire de la correspondance d'Adolphe Quetelet', *Mémoires de l'Académie royale de Belgique, Classes des Sciences*, t. XXXVII, f. 2, 1966.
28. B.T.24/1, f. 86 (Porter to Lord John Russell, 15 May 1835).
29. B.T.24/1, ff. 4-5 (7 June to 28 June 1832). Dr Brown states that the letter-book covers the period September 1832 to April 1834 (op. cit., p. 83 n. 2). In fact it runs from March 1832 to August 1838.
30. Ibid., ff. 9-11 (30 August 1832).

31. *Tables of the Revenue, Population, Commerce ... of the United Kingdom and its Dependencies. Part I. From 1820 to 1831, both inclusive*; GBPP 1833 XLI. B.T.24/1, f. 36 (13 May 1833).
32. Ibid., ff. 17-19 (19, 22 and 23 November 1832).
33. Ibid., ff. 21-2 (21 December 1832) and ff. 23-4 (5 January 1833).
34. For example see *Tables ... Part III. 1820–1833*, pp. 411-12, GBPP 1835 XLIX.
35. B.T.24/1, ff. 27, 34 (7 February and 19 April 1833).
36. *Tables ... Part III*, pp. 412-23.
37. Ibid., pp. 401-4.
38. B.T.24/1, ff. 39-40 (18 July 1833).
39. Ibid., ff. 52-3 (26 August 1833).
40. Ibid., ff. 53, 60 (2 September 1833 and 1 January 1834).
41. *Public Documents. Sel. Cttee. Second Rep.*, p. 27; GBPP 1833 XII.
42. 'Agricultural Returns', *JSSL*, I, June 1838, pp. 89-96. G. R. Porter, 'Suggestions in favour of the Systematic Collection of the Statistics of Agriculture', *JSSL*, II, October 1839, pp. 291-6.
43. *Tables ... Part IX. 1839*; GBPP 1841 XXIV.
44. *Tables ... Part XV, Section B. 1845*; GBPP 1847 LXV.
45. Edward Barrington de Fonblanque, *The Life of Albany Fonblanque* (London, 1874), p. 45.
46. Quoted in Blake, op. cit., p. 323.
47. Brown, op. cit., p. 88.
48. Dr Brown discusses in some detail the example of the working out of import values, ibid., pp. 88-92.
49. *Official Salaries. Sel. Cttee. Mins. of Ev.*, p. 85; GBPP 1850 XV.
50. *Public Offices. R. Comm. Rep.*, pp. 147-8; GBPP 1854 XXVII.
51. G. R. Porter, *Progress of the Nation* (3 vols., London, 1836).
52. In 1830 the permanent staff of the Board of Trade consisted of two joint assistant-secretaries, a comptroller of corn returns, and about a dozen clerks (Brown, op. cit., p. 20).
53. J. P. Kay, 'Results of a Conference with Mr. Thomson concerning the Objects towards which the Society should direct its attention', *Appendix to the Minutes of the Manchester Statistical Society*, f. 4. This volume is housed in the Manchester Central Library. Kay's paper is in manuscript form. Also see T. S. Ashton, *Economic and Social Investigations in Manchester, 1833–1933* (London, 1934), p. 14. Ashton refers to the *Appendix to the Minutes* as the *Guard Book*.
54. E.g. see Norman McCord, *The Anti-Corn Law League* (2nd edn., London, 1968), p. 186.

2 The Work of the General Register Office

1. 6 and 7 Gul. IV, c. 86.
2. The administration of civil registration was tied to that of the new poor law. For the difficulties caused by opposition to the latter see N. C. Edsall, *The Anti-Poor Law Movement, 1834–1844* (Manchester, 1971), pp. 67–8, 76–7.
3. *Chadwick Papers*, Chadwick to Dr T. Laycock, 13 April 1844. These papers are housed in University College, London.
4. *Registrar-General of Births, etc. Office*, pp. 4–6; GBPP 1847 XXXIV. Graham was appointed in June 1842 though Nassau Senior had recommended Chadwick for the job (*Chadwick Papers*, copy of letter from Nassau Senior to Sir James Graham, 6 June 1842).
5. *Registrar-General of Births, etc. Office*, pp. 6–7.
6. See below.
7. *Chadwick Papers*, Chadwick to 'My Lord', 8 January 1841.
8. *The Times*, 7 January 1839.
9. P.R.O. 30/22/2C, ff. 176–7, Lister to Lord John Russell, 22 September 1836; ff. 278–9, Lister to Russell, 15 October 1836. *First Annual Report of the Registrar-General. App. (A) to (F), esp. App. (D)*; GBPP 1839 XVI. The annual reports will hereafter be referred to as *First Report, Second Report*, etc.
10. *Hand-Loom Weavers: R. Comm. Reps.*, Pt. V, p. 425; GBPP 1840 XXIV.
11. *Leeds Intelligencer*, 24 June 1837.
12. *Sixth Report*, pp. ix–xi; GBPP 1840 XIX.
13. At Leeds, for example, the vicar tried to persuade Anglicans to ignore the Registration Act (*Leeds Mercury*, 1 July 1837). For cases involving refusal of information, sometimes incited by clergy, see P.R.O. H.O.39/4.
14. *First Report*, pp. 13–17.
15. *Third Report*, p. 17; GBPP 1841–2 Sess. 2 VI.
16. *Fourth Report*, p. 9; GBPP 1842 XIX.
17. *Sixth Report*, p. xxiii.
18. Ibid., pp. xix–xxiv.
19. Ibid., pp. xxxii–xxxiii.
20. D. V. Glass, 'A Note on the Under-Registration of Births in Britain in the Nineteenth Century', *Pop. St.*, V, 1951–2, pp. 70–88, esp. p. 85.
21. Ibid., pp. 84–6.
22. A crude birth rate of 36·3 is a little higher than estimates for the 1860s but the fertility rate of 152 per thousand is marginally lower (Glass, op. cit., p. 85).

23. Professor Glass calculates the under-registration for these two periods as 6·0 per cent and 4·9 per cent respectively. On 8 February 1844 Major Graham wrote to Chadwick, 'I calculate that out of 10 births at present at least 1 escapes Registration' (*Chadwick Papers*). In 1865 Farr estimated under-registration at 5·4 per cent: 'On Infant Mortality and the Alleged Inaccuracies of the English Census', *JSSL*, XXVIII, 1865, p. 134.
24. *First Report*, pp. 12–13.
25. Ibid. *App. (M)*.
26. E.g. see *Lancet*, 1836–7, II, pp. 345–6, 348–9.
27. *Seventh Report*, pp. xviii–xxi; GBPP 1846 XIX.
28. *Medical Times*, XII, 1845, p. 436. Also see *Lancet*, 1845, II, pp. 270–2.
29. *The Times*, 3 September 1845. Also see 2 November 1846.
30. *First Report, App. (P)*.
31. *Fourth Report, App.*, pp. 91–105.
32. *London Medical Gazette*, XXXI, 1843, pp. 788–92.
33. *Seventh Report*, pp. xviii–xxii.
34. Ibid., p. vi.
35. M. A. Heasman and L. Lipworth, 'Accuracy of Certification of Cause of Death', *General Register Office. Studies on Medical and Population Subjects*, No. 20, 1966, pp. 51–2. Chadwick often criticized the registration of the causes of death (see his letters to G. C. Holland, C. R. Pemberton, and W. Payne in his papers).
36. This account of Farr's early life is based upon four sources: some notes for a biography by Joseph Whittall in *Farr papers*, X, ff. 2–3; Major Greenwood, *The Medical Dictator and Other Biographical Studies* (London, 1936), pp. 91–120; some long obituaries and a typewritten survey of bibliographical and biographical materials in *Farr papers*, IX; finally, see N. A. Humphreys (ed.) *Vital Statistics: a Memorial Volume of Selections from the Writings of William Farr* (London, 1885), pp. vii–xxiv. The Farr papers are held in the British Library of Political and Economic Science (L.S.E.). For Farr's enrolment at University College, London, in 1831–2 see H. Hale Bellot, *University College, London, 1826–1926* (London, 1929), p. 186. Farr remarried in 1841.
37. N. A. Humphreys (ed.), op. cit., p. xix.
38. *Farr papers*, II, f. 41.
39. *First Report, App. (P)*, p. 65.
40. *Second Report, App.*, pp. 9–12.
41. *Fifth Report*, pp. xxxiii–xxxiv.
42. *Eighth Report*, p. xxv.
43. *Ninth Report*, p. xvii; GBPP 1847–8 XXXV.
44. *Second Report*, p. 11.

45. *First Report, App.* (P), pp. 64-5.
46. Ibid., pp. 78-9.
47. *Second Report. App.*, pp. 9-12.
48. Ibid., p. 12.
49. *Third Report*, pp. 9-10.
50. Ibid. *App.*, pp. 5-15.
51. Ibid., pp. 15-19.
52. *Fourth Report*, pp. 85-90.
53. Ibid., pp. 6-9.
54. See General Register Office, CZ1. 1.
55. *Fifth Report*, pp. vi-vii.
56. Ibid., p. ix.
57. Ibid., pp. xii-xv.
58. Ibid., pp. xviii-xxiii.
59. Ibid., p. xvi.
60. Ibid., p. xxxiii.
61. Ibid., p. xxvii.
62. Ibid., pp. xxxvi-xxxvii. The graphs were discussed at pp. xxiii-xxvi.
63. Ibid., pp. 32-59; pp. 60-159.
64. Ibid., p. xxviii.
65. Ibid., *App.* pp. 161-78.
66. Ibid., pp. 186-7. In true Farr fashion there was a footnote on the derivation of 'midwife' from 'medewyf' meaning a woman of mede or merit, deserving recompense.
67. Ibid., pp. 197-209.
68. Ibid., pp. 211-4.
69. Ibid., pp. 214-5.
70. Ibid., pp. 246-324.
71. *Eighth Report*, pp. 289-325.
72. *Seventh Report*, pp. xii-xiii.
73. *Eighth Report*, pp. ix-xxvi. *Ninth Report*, pp. vi-xvii.
74. *Seventh Report*, p. v. The phraseology is ambiguous and could mean an annual census.
75. Ibid., p. xii.
76. Ibid., p. xvii.
77. Ibid., *App.*; GBPP 1846 XIX.
78. *Ninth Report. App.*; GBPP 1849 XXI.
79. *Tenth Report*; GBPP 1849 XXI. The reports were separately republished in a smaller format and when the tenth report was published, three years later in 1852, it included much fuller tables including ones on the cause of death.

3 The Health of the Armed Forces

1. Sir Andrew Halliday, *A Letter to the Right Honble. the Secretary at War, on Sickness and Mortality in the West Indies; Being a Review of Captain Tulloch's Statistical Report* (London, 1839), pp. 3-4.
2. *Statistical Report on the Sickness, Mortality, and Invaliding among the Troops in the West Indies*, p. iii; GBPP 1837-8 XL. Hereafter referred to as *West Indies (1)*.
3. *Barracks (Bahamas, etc.)*, p. 3; GBPP 1840 XXXIV.
4. Ibid., p. 53.
5. *West Indies (1)*, p. iii.
6. John Brown, *Horae Subsecivae* (Edinburgh, 1858), p. 246. More generally, see pp. 246-68.
7. Marshall, 'On the Mortality of the Infantry of the French Army', *Edin. Med. Surg. Jnl.*, XLII, 1835, p. 49.
8. *DNB*.
9. There is no question of Tulloch's authorship. An editorial note later acknowledged it (1838, Pt. III, p. 235n) and some of the copies in the University of Edinburgh Library contain Tulloch's signature.
10. Tulloch, 'Observations on Military Pensions', *United Service Journal*, 1835, Pt. I, p. 166.
11. Tulloch, 'On the Mortality of Officers in the Army', *Un. Serv. Jnl.*, 1835, Pt. II, pp. 145-72.
12. Ibid., p. 172.
13. Tulloch later became a major-general and was responsible for the damning enquiry into the deficiencies of the commissariat in the Crimea.
14. For Balfour see *Modern English Biography, Supplement*.
15. The Tulloch papers are held at the County Record Office, Newport, Monmouthshire. They include papers on the Crimean commission and papers of General Alexander Bruce Tulloch, who served in various colonial conflicts later in the century. The papers were discovered a few years ago and are not well known. Their over-all condition is excellent and they are catalogued.
16. *Quetelet papers*, Tulloch to Quetelet, October 1837.
17. Ibid., Tulloch to Quetelet, 15 January 1838.
18. *Barracks (Bahamas, etc.)*, pp. 58-62; GBPP 1840 XXXIV.
19. Ibid., pp. 74-5.
20. *West Indies (1)*, p. iv.
21. Henry Marshall, 'Mortality of the French Infantry', *British Annals of Medicine, Pharmacy, Vital Statistics, and General Science*, I, 1837, p. 597.
22. *West Indies (1)*, pp. 79-81.

23. Ibid., pp. 82-3.
24. Ibid., pp. 84-6.
25. Ibid., pp. 88-9.
26. Ibid., p. 95.
27. 'Mortality of British Troops in the West Indies', *British Annals of Medicine, Pharmacy, Vital Statistics, and General Science*, I, April 1837, pp. 475-6.
28. *West Indies (1)*, pp. 97-103.
29. J. W. C. Lever, 'On the Sickness and Mortality among the Troops in the United Kingdom. Abstract of the Report of Major Tulloch', *JSSL*, II, July 1839, pp. 250-60. 'Report of a Committee of the Statistical Society of London, appointed to collect and inquire into Vital Statistics, upon the Sickness and Mortality among the European and Native Troops serving in the Madras Presidency, from the year 1793 to 1838', *JSSL*, III, July 1840, pp. 113-43. 'Second Report', *JSSL*, IV, July 1841, pp. 137-55.
30. *Statistical Report on...the Troops in the United Kingdom*, pp. 5-6; GBPP 1839 XVI.
31. *Statistical Report on...the Troops in the Mediterranean*, pp. 64a-65a; GBPP 1839 XVI.
32. *Statistical Report on...the Troops on the Western Coast of Africa*, pp. 9, 26; GBPP 1840 XXX.
33. See the reports on the Cape of Good Hope and Mauritius in the same paper as the West Africa report and the report on Ceylon, Burma, and the Tenasserim Provinces; GBBP 1842 XXVII.
34. *Statistical Report on...the Troops in the United Kingdom, the Mediterranean, and British America*; GBPP 1852-3 LIX.
35. E.g. see Tulloch, 'Comparison of the Sickness, Mortality and Prevailing Diseases among Seamen and Soldiers, as shown by the Naval and Military Statistical Reports', *JSSL*, IV, April 1841, pp. 1-16 and T. Graham Balfour, 'Comparison of the Sickness, Mortality, and Prevailing Diseases among Seamen and Soldiers, as shown by the Naval and Military Statistical Reports', *JSSL*, VIII, March 1845, pp. 77-86.
36. P.R.O. Adm. 105/71, ff. 92-6 (28 June 1836).
37. Ibid., ff. 97-102.
38. *Statistical Reports on the Health of the Navy*, Pt. I, p. iii; GBPP 1840 XXX.
39. *Modern English Biography, Supplement*.
40. John Wilson, *Memoirs of West Indian Fever* (London, 1827), p. 123.
41. *Reports, Pt I*, pp. vi-x.
42. P.R.O. Adm. 1/3532 (*In-letters*, 29 January 1839).
43. *Reports, Pt. I*, pp. x-xx. The libraries were started in August 1838.

44. *Statistical Reports on the Health of the Navy for the Years 1830 to 1836, Pt. II*, p. iv; GBPP 1841 Sess. 2 VI.
45. Ibid.
46. Ibid., p. x.
47. Ibid., p. vi.
48. Ibid., p. viii.
49. *DNB*.
50. Philip D. Curtin, *The Image of Africa: British Ideas and Actions* (London, 1965), pp. 346–7, 354–5.
51. *Statistical Reports on the Health of the Navy for the Years 1837 to 1843, Pt. I*; GBPP 1849 XXXII.
52. Ibid., *Pt. II*; GBPP 1852–3 LXI.
53. Ibid., p. vi.
54. Ibid., pp. 87–94.
55. Ibid., p. 89.
56. Ibid., *Pt. III*, GBPP 1854 LXVIII.

4 Edwin Chadwick and Sanitary Statistics

1. R. A. Lewis, *Edwin Chadwick and the Public Health Movement, 1832–1854* (London, 1952). S. E. Finer, *The Life and Times of Edwin Chadwick* (London, 1952).
2. Lewis, op. cit., pp. 8–10, 33. Finer, op. cit., pp. 12–27, 29. [Edwin Chadwick], 'Life Assurances', *Westminster Review*, IX, 1828, pp. 384–421.
3. For a more detailed exposition of this theory see my article in the *Journal of Ecclesiastical History*, XXIV, 1973.
4. *Chadwick papers*, Chadwick to Dr T. Laycock, 13 April 1844.
5. Ibid.
6. *Fourth Annual Report of the Poor Law Commissioners. App. (A), No. 1*, p. 63; GBPP 1837–8 XXVIII.
7. Ibid., p. 68.
8. Ibid., pp. 83–6.
9. M. W. Flinn, introduction to Edwin Chadwick, *Sanitary Report on the Condition of the Labouring Population of Great Britain* (Edinburgh, 1965), p. 45. The introduction will hereafter be cited as 'Flinn', the report as 'Chadwick'.
10. For Chadwick's tenuous position at Somerset House see Finer, op. cit., pp. 154–207.
11. Flinn, p. 45.
12. *Health of Towns. Sel. Cttee. Mins. of Ev.*, p. 1; GBPP 1840 XI.
13. See Flinn, pp. 45–6, for Chadwick's reaction.
14. Ibid.
15. Finer, op. cit., pp. 210–11.

16. *Report*, pp. xv–xxii.
17. Finer, op. cit., p. 212.
18. Chadwick, pp. 423–4.
19. Ibid., pp. 80–99.
20. Ibid., pp. 99–166.
21. G. A. Walker, *Gatherings from Grave Yards* (London, 1839), p. 13.
22. Chadwick, p. 97.
23. Ibid., p. 189.
24. William Pulteney Alison, *Observations on the Management of the Poor in Scotland and its Effects on the Health of Great Towns* (Edinburgh, 1840).
25. *Local Reports on the Sanitary Condition of the Labouring Population of Scotland* (London, 1842), pp. 13–22.
26. Ibid., pp. 1–12, 34–9.
27. Arnott was taken as the authority for conditions in Edinburgh. It might also be mentioned that there was only one direct reference to William Farr (Chadwick, p. 231).
28. Chadwick, p. 114.
29. Ibid., p. 115.
30. Ibid., pp. 167–219.
31. Ibid., p. 176.
32. Ibid., pp. 219–20.
33. See Dr William Baker on Derby, *Local Reports ... England and Wales* (London, 1842), p. 181.
34. Chadwick, p. 220.
35. Ibid., pp. 224–5.
36. Calculated from the tables at pp. 228–30. The figures are somewhat approximate because Chadwick's figures for the proportions occurring at each decennial interval of ages above twenty are loosely expressed as '1 in 15', '1 in 1', and so on.
37. Ibid., pp. 241–54.
38. Flinn, p. 66.
39. See Chadwick, p. 265.
40. Ibid., pp. 285–7.
41. Edwin Chadwick, 'On the best Modes of representing accurately, by Statistical Returns, the Duration of Life, and the Pressure and Progress of the Causes of Mortality amongst different Classes of the Community, and amongst the Populations of different Districts and Countries', *JSSL*, VII, April 1844, p. 5. The paper was read in December 1843.
42. Ibid., pp. 1–6.
43. Ibid., p. 7.
44. Ibid.
45. Ibid., p. 9.

46. F. G. P. Neison, 'On a Method recently proposed for conducting Inquiries into the Comparative Sanatory Condition of various Districts, with Illustrations, derived from numerous places in Great Britain at the period of the last Census', *JSSL*, VII, April 1844, pp. 40–68. Read January 1844.
47. Ibid., pp. 41–6.
48. Ibid., p. 51.
49. Ibid., pp. 52–3.
50. Flinn. p. 71.
51. *State of Large Towns and Populous Districts. R. Comm. First Rep.*, p. v; GBPP 1844 XVII. There was one further large-scale government enquiry in the 1840's: the Metropolitan Sanitary Commission of 1847. Chadwick, Southwood Smith and Richard Jones were three of the five commissioners. Some statistical evidence was given based upon the registration data but it was of a familiar type. The strength of the commission's reports lay more in their detailed analysis of possible sewerage systems for London (see GBPP 1847–8 XXXII). The Health of London Association also produced a survey of the sanitary state of London in 1847 but this added nothing of particular note. The Health of Towns Association did not produce any new surveys.
52. *Mins. of Ev.*, pp. 69–86.
53. Ibid., pp. 343–9.
54. *Appendix*, pp. 12–13.
55. Ibid., p. 14.
56. Ibid., p. 16.
57. Ibid., pp. 19–21.
58. Ibid., pp. 25–8.
59. Ibid., p. 30.
60. *Second Report, App., Pt. II*, pp. 106–16; GBPP 1845 XVIII.
61. Ibid., pp. 47–61.
62. Ibid., pp. 67–72.
63. Ibid., p. 69.
64. Ibid., p. 70.
65. *Health of Towns. Sel. Cttee. Mins. of Ev. (G. A. Walker)*, p. 188.
66. For Fletcher's career see below.
67. *Health of Towns Sel. Cttee. Mins. of Ev.*, p. 73.
68. Ibid., p. xiv.
69. Chadwick, p. 190. More generally see pp. 167–204.
70. Ibid., p. 205.
71. Ibid., p. 279.
72. Ibid., pp. 205–6.

5 The Government and Moral Statistics

1. *Abstract of Answers. Education*, I, p. 3; GBPP 1835 XLI.
2. Quoted in M. Drake, 'The census, 1801–1891' in E. A. Wrigley (ed.), *Nineteenth-century society: Essays in the use of quantitative methods for the study of social data* (Cambridge, 1972), p. 11. I was unable to consult Dr Drake's article before writing the prelude, which still gives a more complete account of the origins of the 1801 census.
3. *Abstract of Answers. Education*, I, p. 3.
4. *Education. Sel. Cttee. Mins. of Ev.*, p. 18; GBPP 1834 IX.
5. By combining the Kerry returns and the local surveys Dr E. G. West has tried to argue that as large a proportion of national income was being spent on education in the early 1830s as in the 1920s (see 'Resource Allocation and Growth in Early Nineteenth Century British Education', EcHR, 2nd ser., XXIII, 1970, pp. 68–95). For criticisms of his arguments see my thesis, 'Social Statistics in Britain, 1830–1852' (Edinburgh, 1971), pp. 363–79 and J. S. Hurt, Professor West on Early Nineteenth-Century Education', EcHR, 2nd ser., XXIV, 1971, pp. 624–32 (for West's reply see pp. 633–42).
6. *JSSL*, XIII, August 1850, p. 269.
7. Ibid., III, April 1840, p. 98.
8. 13 and 14 Vict., c. 53.
9. *1851 Education Census*, p. ix.
10. Ibid., p. xiii.
11. *Hansard*, 3rd ser., CXIV, coll. 1305–8 (14 March 1851).
12. Ibid., CXV, col. 630 (27 March 1851).
13. *1851 Education Census*, p. xi.
14. Ibid., pp. cii–civ.
15. Ibid.
16. Ibid., pp. cv–cvii.
17. Ibid., p. xiii. There were 30,610 local enumerators.
18. Ibid., p. xiv.
19. Ibid., pp. xxi–xxvi.
20. Ibid., pp. xxix–xxx.
21. Ibid., p. xxxi.
22. Ibid., pp. xxxi–xxxvi.
23. Ibid., pp. xxxix–xl.
24. Ibid., pp. xl–xli.
25. Ibid., pp. xli–xliii.
26. Ibid., pp. xliv–lxxix.
27. Ibid., p. lxxx.
28. Ibid., pp. lxxxiii–lxxxiv.
29. Ibid., pp. lxxxiv–lxxxviii.

30. Ibid., p. lxxxix.
31. Ibid., pp. lxxxix–xc.
32. J. R. B. Johnson, 'The Education Department 1839-1864: A Study in Social Policy and the Growth of Government' (unpublished Ph.D. thesis, Cambridge, 1968), pp. 359-60. Also see his article 'Educational Policy and Social Control in Early Victorian England', *Past and Present*, no. 49, 1970, pp. 96-119 wherein he finds in the environmental-moral tension a clue to some of the social theories of the period.
32. B. I. Coleman ('The incidence of education in mid-century' in E. A. Wrigley (ed.), op. cit., pp. 397-410) argues that the census occupation data for students is more useful than the education census. It may be doubted, however, whether it is more accurate.
34. K. S. Inglis, 'Patterns of Religious Worship in 1851', *Jnl. of Ecclesiastical History*, XI, 1960, pp. 74-86. David M. Thompson, 'The 1851 Religious Census: Problems and Possibilities', *Victorian Studies*, XI, 1967, pp. 87-97. W. S. F. Pickering, 'The 1851 Religious Census – a useless experiment?', *British Jnl. of Sociology*, XVIII, 1967, pp. 382-407.
35. Inglis, op. cit., p. 74.
36. William Collins, *Statistics of the Church Accommodation of Glasgow, Barony, and Gorbals* (Glasgow, 1836).
37. See *JSSL*, I, October 1838, p. 379.
38. Edgell, 'Moral Statistics of the Parishes of St. James, St. George, and St. Anne Soho, in the City of Westminster', *JSSL*, I, December 1938, pp. 479-81. Weight, 'Statistics of the Parish of St. George the Martyr, Southwark', *JSSL*, III, April 1840, pp. 60-1.
39. *JSSL*, III, April 1840, p. 98.
40. See *JSSL*, XIII, August 1850, pp. 267-9.
41. Inglis, op. cit., p. 75. R. A. Soloway, *Prelates and People: Ecclesiastical Social Thought in England, 1783-1852* (London, 1969), p. 436.
42. Inglis, p. 76.
43. Horace Mann, 'On the Statistical Position of Religious Bodies in England and Wales', *JSSL*, XVIII, 1855, p. 146.
44. Thompson, op. cit., pp. 88-90.
45. *Census of Great Britain, 1851. Religious Worship. England and Wales*, p. clii; GBPP 1852-3 LXXXIX.
46. Thompson, op. cit., pp. 91-6.
47. Ibid., p. 92.
48. *1851 Religious Census*, pp. xi–xxx.
49. Ibid., p. xxxi.
50. Ibid., pp. c–ci.
51. Ibid., pp. xxxii–cxviii.

52. Ibid., p. viii.
53. Ibid., p. clviii.
54. Ibid., p. clix.
55. Ibid., pp. clix–clx.
56. Ibid., p. clx.
57. Ibid.
58. Ibid., pp. clxi–clxii.
59. Ibid., p. clxviii.
60. For a general survey of nineteenth-century criminal statistics see V. A. C. Gatrell and T. B. Hadden, 'Criminal statistics and their interpretation' in E. A. Wrigley (ed.), op. cit., pp. 336–96.
61. See *Criminal Offenders (England and Wales). 1834*; GBPP 1835 XLV.
62. See *Criminal Offenders (England and Wales). 1835*; GBPP 1836 XLI.
63. J. J. Tobias, *Crime and Industrial Society in the Nineteenth Century* (London, 1967), pp. 14–21, 256–67.
64. Gatrell and Hadden, op. cit., p. 361.
65. *Appendix to the Minutes of the Manchester Statistical Society* (Manchester Central Library), f. 104. Hereafter referred to as *App. Mins.*
66. 'Remarks on the Classification of Offences', *Collection of Miscellaneous Reports and Papers of the Manchester Statistical Society* (London, 1838), pp. 15–23.
67. 'On the erroneous principle, and defective classification of the Official Statistical Tables of crime', *Proceedings of the Statistical Society of London*, I, pp. 193–208.
68. *DNB*.
69. Gatrell and Hadden, op. cit., p. 343.
70. *Criminal Offenders (England and Wales). 1845*, p. 5; GBPP 1846 XXXIV.

6 *The Foundation of the Statistical Society of London*

1. A royal charter was granted in 1886. There is an official centenary history of the society: James Bonar and Henry W. Macrosty, *Annals of the Royal Statistical Society, 1834–1934* (London, 1934). This is of value as one of the few accurate accounts in print but does not utilize all available sources and is otherwise unsatisfactory from a historian's point of view.
2. *Babbage papers*, B.M. Add. Mss. 37185, ff. 481–2, D. Brewster (of the Philosophical Society of York) to Charles Babbage, 4 February 1831. Brewster mentioned backing from the Royal Society, the Royal Society of Edinburgh, and the Royal Irish Academy. For a

useful though limited account of the foundation see O. J. R. Howarth, *The British Association for the Advancement of Science: A Retrospect, 1831–1921* (London, 1922), pp. 1–27.
3. B.M. Add. Mss. 37186, f. 43, Brewster to Babbage, 14 August 1831. Ibid., ff. 136–8, William Vernon Harcourt to Babbage, 27 August 1831.
4. See Charles Babbage, *On the Economy of Manufactures* (London, 1832).
5. B.M. Add. Mss. 37186, ff. 97–8, draft of a letter from Babbage to Brougham, 23 September 1831.
6. 'Proceedings of the Second Meeting of the British Association for the Advancement of Science', *Trans. BAAS*, I, 1831–2, p. 107.
7. *Passages from the Life of a Philosopher* (London, 1864), p. 432. Also see Babbage, *The Exposition of 1851* (2nd edn., London, 1851), p. 16.
8. 'Note sur l'origine de la Société de Statistique de Londres, par M. Babbage'. This note is in the Quetelet papers in Brussels and was written in September 1853 when Babbage was in Brussels for the first statistical congress. It is in French.
9. See *Passages*, p. 432. In the note for Quetelet Babbage stated 'these lacked a section'.
10. *Quetelet papers*, W. Whewell to Quetelet, 2 April 1833. The best biography of Quetelet in English is Frank H. Hankins, 'Adolphe Quetelet as Statistician', *Columbia University Studies in History, Economics, and Public Law*, XXX, no. 4, 1908. For further references see Liliane Wellens-de Donder, op. cit.
11. *Literary Gazette and Journal of Belles Lettres*, 1833, p. 437.
12. There are three accounts by Babbage of what happened: *Passages*, p. 433; *The Exposition of 1851*, pp. 16–17; and the note in *Quetelet papers*.
13. Note in *Quetelet papers*.
14. Ibid.
15. *Lithographed signatures of the members who met at Cambridge ... 1833. With a report of the proceedings ... and ... list of members* (Cambridge, 1833), pp. xxviii–xxix.
16. A recent biography of Babbage is Maboth Moseley, *Irascible Genius: A Life of Charles Babbage, Inventor* (London, 1964). However, there is still no full-scale biography of Babbage which utilizes all the available material. Moseley's biography concentrates on Babbage and his calculating machine.
17. There are a number of letters in B.M. Add. Mss. 37184 on this.
18. See B.M. Add. Mss. 37186 and 37187 for relevant correspondence.
19. B.M. Add. Mss. 37187, ff. 540–1, Richard Miller to Babbage, 20 May 1833.

20. For Babbage's own account see *Passages*, chap. XXI.
21. Details of Drinkwater's early life are taken from his father's manuscript autobiography, National Library of Scotland Ms. 1835.
22. B.M. Add. Mss. 37183, f. 144, Whewell to Babbage, 29 December 1824.
23. For the last see B.M. Add. Mss. 37186, ff. 463-4, W. H. Ord to Babbage, 13 June 1832. There is a need for a good study of the S.D.U.K. to supersede Muriel C. Grobel's massive disorganized thesis 'The Society for the Diffusion of Useful Knowledge, 1826-46' (unpublished M.A. thesis, London, 1933).
24. See *Employment of Children in Factories. R. Comm. First Rep., C.1*; GBPP 1833 XX. The report was dated 7 June. Drinkwater had got involved in a pamphlet war with M. T. Sadler over the effects of factory labour on mortality. Drinkwater was backed by Brougham in his career (see two letters to Brougham in *Brougham papers*, University College London, dated 15 August 1831 and 13 August 1835).
25. James Sykes, *Biographical Notices of Colonel William Henry Sykes, with Manuscript Appendix* (1857). This volume is in the British Museum.
26. See *Proceedings of the Statistical Society of London*, I, p. 71.
27. William Whewell (ed.), *Literary Remains, consisting of Lectures and Tracts on Political Economy of the late Rev. Richard Jones* (London, 1859), p. xxi. Jones was born in 1790.
28. Marion Bowley, *Nassau Senior and Classical Economics* (London, 1967), p. 40.
29. 'An Introductory Lecture on Political Economy, delivered at King's College, London, on February 27, 1833' in Whewell (ed.), *Literary Remains*, p. 571.
30. *Quetelet papers*, Malthus to Quetelet, 2 July 1833. Also see Quetelet, *Physique Sociale* (2 vols., Brussels, 1869), II, p. 451. I owe the latter reference to Professor D. V. Glass.
31. B.M. Add. Mss. 37188, f. 371, Malthus to Babbage, 10 June 1834.
32. This account is based on a diary kept by Drinkwater which covers the affairs of the organizing committees from 27 June 1833 to 15 March 1834 (hereafter referred to as *Diary*). It is in the keeping of the Royal Statistical Society, to whom I am indebted for permission to use their records.
33. *Diary*.
34. *Lithographed signatures of the members who met at Cambridge*, p. 90.
35. *Diary*.
36. *Trans. BAAS*, II, 1833, p. 483.
37. Quetelet, 'Notes Extraites d'un voyage en Angleterre aux mois de

juin et de juillet 1833', *Correspondance mathématique et physique*, VIII, 1835, pp. 14–15.
38. *Employment of Children in Factories. R. Comm. Second Rep.*, pp. 5–6; GBPP 1833 XXI. The report was dated 13 July 1833.
39. *Quetelet papers*, Nassau Senior to Quetelet, 12 March 1833. Senior wrote about thirty letters to Quetelet over the period 1831–51 which have survived. One expresses his views on the Irish famine.
40. Ibid., Nassau Senior to Quetelet, September 1841. On a number of occasions he confessed himself unable to understand Quetelet's works.
41. 'The Myth of the Old Poor Law and the Making of the New', *Journal of Economic History*, XXIII, 1963, p. 177.
42. Nassau Senior, 'An Account of the Conferences on the Poor Law Amendment Act', University of London Ms. 173, ff. 214–8.
43. B.M. Add. Mss. 37188, ff. 4–5, Jones to Babbage, 3 July 1833.
44. Ibid., ff. 98–100, Charles Toplis to Babbage, 4 December 1833.
45. Ibid., ff. 175–6, G. R. Porter to Babbage, 22 January 1834. It should be noted that Porter felt it necessary to explain that Chadwick was one of the poor law commisioners. Chadwick played no part in the formation of the society and did not join until June 1834.
46. Ibid., ff. 218–9, Drinkwater to Babage 8 February 1834.
47. Ibid., ff. 126–7, Hallam to Babbage, n.d.
48. Ibid., ff. 214–5, Howard Elphinstone to Sykes, 6 February 1834. Ibid., f. 259, Joseph Hume to Babbage, 17 March 1834. Babbage's friend and patron, the Duke of Somerset, wrote: 'I hope they will not admit objectionable characters, that drive away quiet people. Men who are always endeavouring to push their way into what they call good society, who are to be seen everywhere, who know the world, but never try to know anything else' (ibid., ff. 266–7).
49. *Diary. Minutes of the Statistical Society of London*, I, f. 1 (hereafter *MSSL*).
50. The list is in the *Diary*.
51. *MSSL*, I, ff. 2–3.
52. *Gentleman's Magazine*, 2nd ser., I, April 1834, p. 422. *Literary Gazette*, 22 March 1834.
53. B.M. Add. Mss. 37188, ff. 274–5, Drinkwater to Babbage, 21 March 1834, for a list W. W. Whitmore was to take down to the Commons.
54. *Employment of Children in Factories. R. Comm. Supp. Rep. Pt. I*, p. 227; GBPP 1834 XIX.
55. *MSSL*, I, f. 3.
56. Ibid., ff. 4–8. The division of statistics followed the plan put forward by Jones at Cambridge.

57. See remarks by Sir Charles Lemon in 'Report of the Seventeenth Annual Meeting', *JSSL*, XIV, 1851, p. 104.
58. Ditto Lord Overstone, ibid., p. 103.
59. *MSSL*, I, ff. 8–14.
60. See *Bentham papers*, CXLIX, ff. 237–53. The papers are in University College London.
61. *MSSL*, I, f. 16.
62. The other members of the council were William Burge, Rev. George D'Oyley, Howard Elphinstone (who had asked to be on and had to be let on because of his connections), Earl Fitzwilliam, Henry Goulburn, Joseph Henry Green (the surgeon), Edmund Halswell, Francis Bisset Hawkins, Francis Jeffery, John Lefevre, the Bishop of London, Samuel Jones Loyd (later Lord Overstone), Lord Sandon, Poulett Scrope, John Sims (M.D.), and Thomas Vardon (the clerk of the House of Commons).
63. *Minutes of the Council of the Statistical Society of London*, I, ff. 1, 3 (hereafter *MCSSL*).
64. *App. Mins.*, f. 10. The letter was dated 27 May 1834.
65. *Quetelet papers*, Whewell to Quetelet, 4 August 1834.
66. *MSSL*, I, ff. 17–19.
67. For summaries of these papers see *Proceedings of the Statistical Society of London*, I. The *Proceedings* pre-date the more well-known *Journal*.
68. *MCSSL*, I, f. 21 (14 January 1835). It was about this time that Porter's assistant at the Board of Trade, Rawson Rawson, joined the society.
69. Ibid., f. 28.
70. Ibid., f. 40.
71. Ibid., f. 53.
72. Ibid., f. 58.
73. Ibid., f. 100. Stanley had first submitted his proposals in January 1835.
74. Ibid., f. 105.
75. Ibid., f. 26 (28 January 1835). Nassau Senior put himself down for the condition of the labouring classes, Jones for rent, Whewell education and literature, Porter crime, savings banks, and agriculture, Drinkwater machinery and manufactures, Samuel Jones Loyd currency, and Sykes 'a selection from Mr. Stanley's paper'.
76. *Quetelet papers* (27 April 1835).
77. *MCSSL*, I, f. 38. The changes were mainly those required to allow for the changed membership of the council.
78. Ibid., f. 56.
79. Ibid., f. 61.
80. Ibid., f. 71 (27 November 1835).

81. See *Proc. SSL*, I.
82. *MCSSL*, I, f. 71.
83. The minutes of the society record that at this meeting each member of the new council received 23 votes except for a 22 to one split for two nominations. Allowing for the chairman this would suggest 24 fellows present (*MSSL*, I, f. 37).
84. *MCSSL*, f. 94.
85. Ibid., f. 97a.
86. He gave a paper on the subject in June.
87. He attended eight of the first ten meetings of the council but then failed to attend another in the 1836-7 session.

7 The Statistical Society of London: the improved society

1. *MCSSL*, I, f. 117.
2. Ibid., ff. 129-30.
3. *MSSL*, I, ff. 38-47.
4. *Quetelet papers*, Porter to Quetelet, 20 December 1836. Also see Babbage to Quetelet, 12 August 1838: 'I have been so heavily employed on the great Calculating Engine that I have neglected my best friends'.
5. Robert Blake, *Disraeli*, p. 325. Disraeli described him as a 'warm adherent' of the Liberals and refused him a pension when the commission ended.
6. He later went to India.
7. Rawson Rawson, 'On the Collection of Statistics', *Proc. SSL.* I, pp. 41-3. The paper was read in June 1835.
8. *JSSL*, I, 1839, p. 444.
9. 'An Acccount of the Atelier de Charité, a Charitable Institution for employing Indigent Persons, at Ghent, and of a similar establishment at Petegem in Belgium: with a statement of the present condition of the prisons in Ghent and of Gaols in Ireland, with reference to the Penitentiary System', *Proc. SSL*, II, pp. 26-30.
10. *Quetelet papers*, Rawson to Quetelet, 22 January 1838. The above is a translation from the original French.
11. See Lucy Brown, op. cit., *passim*.
12. 'Statistics of Crime and Education in France', *First Publication of the Central Society of Education*, 1837, p. 317. On a number of occasions Porter got permission for the Central Society of Education to use the society's rooms.
13. *Quetelet papers*, Porter to Quetelet, 4 June 1839.
14. *MCSSL*, I, f. 172.
15. For example, papers by William Felkin in 1837, James Heywood in 1838, and Alexander M. Tulloch in 1838. When Joseph Hume

suggested accounts of the trade of the major cities Porter and Rawson were constituted a committee to consider the question.
16. *MCSSL*, I, f. 48.
17. Ibid., f. 186.
18. Ibid., f. 226.
19. *JSSL*, I, May 1838, p. 5.
20. *MCSSL*, I, f. 123.
21. *JSSL*, I, May 1838, pp. 6-7.
22. *MCSSL*, I, f. 156.
23. Ibid.
24. Ibid., f. 168.
25. Ibid., f. 176.
26. 'Report of the Committee Appointed by the Council of the Society to inquire into the State of Education in the Parishes of London', *Proc. SSL*, II, pp. 21-3.
27. See *JSSL*, I, August 1838, pp. 193-204, 298-315.
28. Ibid., December 1838, pp. 449-77.
29. Ibid., II, April 1839, p. 130.
30. *MCSSL*, I, f. 212.
31. Ibid., f. 291.
32. See *JSSL*, VI February 1843, pp. 28-43. The survey was completed in April 1842.
33. *MCSSL*, I, f. 371.
34. See *JSSL*, VI, August 1843, pp. 211-18.
35. Ibid., p. 211.
36. Ibid., May 1843, p. 90.
37. *MCSSL*, I, f. 171.
38. Ibid., f. 176.
39. B.M. Add. Mss. 37190, f. 391, Benjamin Gompertz to Babbage, 7 March 1838.
40. *JSSL*, II, April 1839, p. 130.
41. *Proc. SSL*, II, p. 31. *JSSL*, I, April 1838, p. 6.
42. *MCSSL*, I, f. 196. The report was drawn up in March.
43. Ibid., f. 224.
44. Ibid., f. 228.
45. *Quetelet papers*, Porter to Quetelet, 4 June 1839. Rawson later wrote an official letter asking for information under certain heads (20 December 1839).
46. Horner never, in fact, joined the council.
47. See *JSSL*, III, April 1840, pp. 72-102.
48. *MCSSL*, I, f. 268.
49. Ibid., ff. 275-6, 277 (29 May and 12 June 1840).
50. For the official history see *History of the Census of 1841*. This manuscript has been in the possession of the General Register Office

(where it was written some time in the mid-1840s) but is due to go to the Public Record Office. I do not know if T. H. Lister and Nathaniel Lister were related.
51. T. H. Lister to J. E. D. Bethune, 27 June 1840, reproduced in *History of the Census of 1841*, pp. 1–6. The census of age was more detailed than before.
52. MCSSL, I, f. 279 (26 June 1840). It should be noted that the council's reaction pre-dated Lister's letter by a day. Lister's letter confirmed a conversation held a few days previously. Clearly the council kept itself very well informed.
53. Ibid., f. 280.
54. Ibid., f. 282.
55. *JSSL*, IV, April 1841, pp. 69–70. Also *Quetelet papers*, Rawson to Quetelet, 28 August 1840.
56. See *JSSL*, XIII, August 1850, pp. 267–8.
57. Bernard Benjamin, 'The 1971 Population Census and after', *JRSS*, Series A, CXXXIII, 1970, p. 240.
58. See *JSSL*, II, July 1839, pp. 193–7.
59. Ibid., April 1839, p. 130.
60. Ibid., III, July 1840, pp. 113–43 and IV, July 1841, pp. 137–55.
61. MCSSL, I, f. 319.
62. See *JSSL*, V, July 1842, pp. 168–76.
63. Ibid., VII, September 1844, pp. 214–31.
64. MCSSL, I, f. 286.
65. Ibid., f. 290.
66. Ibid., f. 306.
67. Ibid., f. 423. The letter was dated 28 February 1845.
68. Ibid., f. 425.
69. Ibid., f. 427.
70. See *JSSL*, XI, August 1848, pp. 282–7.
71. MCSSL, I, f. 174.
72. *JSSL*, I, May 1838, pp. 11–13.
73. John Boyle, 'An Account of Strikes in the Potteries, in the Years 1834 and 1836', *JSSL*, I, May 1838, pp. 37–45. William Felkin had given a paper at the 1837 British Association meeting on the strike of the silkweavers in Derby in 1833–4 (see *Proc. SSL*, II, pp. 11–16).
74. MCSSL, I, f. 194.
75. *JSSL*, III, April 1840, p. 11.
76. Ibid., pp. 14–24.
77. MCSSL, I, f. 235.
78. *JSSL*, V, April 1842, p. 86.
79. MCSSL, I, ff. 214–15.
80. Ibid., f. 208a.
81. Ibid., f. 216.

82. *JSSL*, III, April 1840, pp. 12-13.
83. Ibid., VI, May 1843, p. 93.
84. *MCSSL*, I, ff. 398-9.
85. See *JSSL*, XI, August 1848, pp. 193-249. The published report claims that an average area, not one of the 'lowest sinks', had been studied.
86. *MCSSL*, I, ff. 435-6.
87. Ibid., II, ff. 20-1.
88. *JSSL*, XI, March 1848, pp. 1-19.
89. Ibid., p. 98.
90. For a report on his school by Joseph Fletcher see *Children's Employment. R. Comm. Second Rep. Trades and Manufactures*, App. Pt. II, pp. 112-18; GBPP 1843 XV.
91. Information on Holt Mackenzie, Sturges-Bourne, Boileau, and Merivale comes from *DNB*.
92. *MCSSL*, I, f. 240.
93. J. R. B. Johnson, op. cit., p. 407.
94. He continued to hold the posts of secretary and editor after becoming a schools inspector.
95. *DNB*.
96. Ibid.
97. Oswald and Melville are somewhat grey figures, the former being one of the secretaries from 1843 until his death in 1847. Whishaw was a Liberal lawyer who became a charity commissioner. Spence was an entomologist, a pillar of the Entomological and Royal Societies.
98. The seven were Farr, Fletcher, Porter, Rawson, Sykes, Guy, and Neison. Fletcher led with 13 papers. A further four papers came from committees including these men. The dominance would be more marked if volume were taken as the guide.
99. *JSSL*, I, May 1838, p. 8.

8 The Manchester Statistical Society

1. David Elesh, 'The Manchester Statistical Society: A Case Study of a Discontinuity in the History of Empirical Social Research', *Jnl. Hist. Behavioural Sciences*, VIII, 1972, pp. 280-301, 407-17. T. S. Ashton, *Economic and Social Investigations in Manchester, 1833-1933* (London, 1934). Thomas Read Wilkinson, 'On the Origin and History of the Manchester Statistical Society', *Trans. Manchester Stat. Soc.*, 1875-6, pp. 9-24.
2. Wilkinson, op. cit., pp. 12-13.
3. Ashton, op. cit., pp. 11-12; Elesh, op. cit., pp. 282-6.
4. Wilkinson, op. cit., p. 16.

5. *DNB.*
6. Frank Smith, *The Life and Work of Sir James Kay Shuttleworth* (London, 1923).
7. Manchester, 1832. Dr Johnson has pointed out that the first edition was more 'voluntarist' in its approach to social questions than the second ('The Education Department', p. 36). All subsequent references are to the second edition reprinted in *Four Periods of Public Education* (London, 1862).
8. *Moral and Physical Condition*, pp. 3-5.
9. Ibid., pp. 49-63.
10. Ibid., pp. 64-5.
11. Ibid., pp. 71-4.
12. *App. Mins.*, f. 8.
13. *DNB.*
14. *An Enquiry into the State of the Manufacturing Population, and the Causes and Cures of the Evils therein Existing* (London, 1831).
15. See *Employment of Children in Factories. R. Comm. Supp. Rep., Pt. I*, p. 303; GBPP 1834 XIX. Ibid., *First Rep., D.2*, pp. 30-9; GBPP 1833 XX. Ibid., *Mins. of Ev., E*, p. 27; GBPP 1833 XX. R. H. Greg, *The Factory Question* (1837), quoted in J. T. Ward, *The Factory Movement*, p. 169.
16. *Employment of Children in Factories. R. Comm. Supp. Rep., Pt. II*, pp. 146-7; GBPP 1834 XX.
17. *Analysis of the Evidence taken before the Factory Commissioners* (Manchester, 1834).
18. Thomas Heywood, *A Memoir of Sir Benjamin Heywood* (Manchester, 1888), *passim*. Mabel Tylecote, *The Mechanics' Institutes of Lancashire and Yorkshire before 1851* (Manchester, 1957), pp. 120-1. Elesh, op. cit., p. 285 (Elesh fails to note that the relationship of Langton and Heywood could not have existed in 1833 when Langton was 30).
19. Tylecote, op. cit., p. 121.
20. Ibid., p. 122.
21. Drinkwater's *Diary*, 27 June 1833. Also present was Dr Lant Carpenter who had taught some of the Gregs.
22. *DNB.*
23. See *Memoirs of the Manchester Literary and Philosophical Society*, 2nd ser., VIII, pp. 2-8.
24. Ashton, op. cit., p. 11.
25. Archibald Prentice, *Historical Sketches and Personal Recollections of Manchester* (London, 1851), p. 305.
26. For a full study of a similar network of organizations in Leeds see R. J. Morris, 'The Organization and Attitudes of the Principal

Secular Voluntary Societies of the Leeds' Middle Class, 1830–51' (unpublished D.Phil. thesis, Oxford, 1971).
27. J. P. Kay, 'Defects in the Constitution of Dispensaries', *App. Mins.*, f. 6. Read November 1833.
28. 'Brief Memoir on the Present State of Criminal Statistics', *App. Mins.*, f. 1.
29. *App. Mins.*, f. 8.
30. Ibid., f. 37.
31. Ibid., frontispiece.
32. No secretaries were appointed in the first year. James Shaw Kennedy was born in Ayrshire in 1788, a nephew of Macadam. He had a distinguished war record and was stationed in Manchester from 1825 to 1836 (when he became Inspector-general of the Irish constabulary).
33. *App. Mins.*, frontispiece.
34. Ibid., f. 12.
35. Ibid., f. 98.
36. See *Trans. BAAS*, III, 1834, p. 690.
37. *Report of a Committee of the Manchester Statistical Society on the Condition of the Working Classes, in an extensive Manufacturing District, in 1834, 1835, and 1836* (London, 1838).
38. Ibid., p. 6.
39. *App. Mins.*, f. 8.
40. *Report*, p. 5.
41. *Report on the State of Education in Manchester in 1834* (2nd edn., London, 1837), p. 3.
42. Ibid., pp. 5–10.
43. Ibid., p. 15.
44. Ibid., p. 17.
45. *Report on the State of Education in Salford in 1835* (London, 1836), p. 21.
46. *Report on the State of Education in Liverpool in 1835–1836* (London, 1836), p. 1.
47. Ibid., pp. 3–5.
48. Ibid., p. 43.
49. *Report on the State of Education in Bolton in 1836* (London, 1837).
50. E.g., see B. F. Duppa, 'Analysis of the Reports of the Manchester Statistical Society on the State of Education in the Boroughs of Manchester, Liverpool, Salford, and Bury', *First Publication of the Central Society of Education*, 1837, pp. 292–304.
51. *Report on the State of Education in York in 1837* (London, 1837).
52. 'Report on the State of Education in the Township of Pendleton, 1838', *JSSL*, II, March 1839, pp. 65–83.
53. 'Report on the State of Education in the County of Rutland in the year 1838', *JSSL*, II, October 1839, pp. 303–15.

54. 'Report on the State of Education in the Borough of Kingston-upon-Hull' *JSSL*, IV, July 1841, pp. 156-75.
55. 'Report on the Condition of the Population in three Parishes in Rutlandshire in March 1839', *JSSL*, II, October 1839, pp. 297-302. 'Report on the Condition of the Working Classes in the Town of Kingston-upon-Hull', *JSSL*, V, July 1842, pp. 212-21.
56. *App. Mins.*, f. 23.
57. Ibid., f. 57.
58. All these papers are to be found in *Collection of Miscellaneous Reports and Papers of the Manchester Statistical Society* (London, 1838). A copy of this volume is in the Manchester Central Library.
59. *App. Mins.*, ff. 98, 107.
60. Ashton, op. cit., p. 131.
61. *App. Mins.*, f. 43.
62. Ibid., f. 80.
63. Ibid., f. 108.
64. Ibid., f. 111.
65. Ashton, op. cit., p. 34.
66. See Archibald Prentice, *History of the Anti-Corn Law League* (2 vols., London, 1853) for mention of all these names. Cf. Ashton, op. cit., p. 130. Elesh, op. cit., pp. 408-9 (also see pp. 409-12 for other organizations members were involved in).
67. *Employment of Children in Factories. R. Comm. Supp. Rep.*, Pt. I, pp. 229-54; GBPP 1834 XIX.
68. *On a Recent Proposal of the Poor Law Commissioners to Refuse Out-door Relief to Widows with Families* [?Manchester, 1840?], p. 3. The only copy of this paper I know of is in the Earl Grey papers, Durham.
69. Ashton, op. cit., pp. 144-5. Ashton gives no source for his knowledge of these papers (there is no official record).
70. Ibid., p. 130.
71. *JSSL*, XIII, May 1850, p. 98.
72. Ashton, op. cit., p. 140.

9 The Other Provincial Societies

1. *MSSL*, I, f. 18.
2. Evidence for the plans for most of these comes from letters recorded in the council minutes of the Statistical Society of London.
3. *JSSL*, I, June 1838, p. 115.
4. Robert Cowan, *Vital Statistics of Glasgow* (Glasgow, 1838), esp. pp. 14, 45.
5. C. R. Baird, 'Observations upon the Poorest Class of Operatives in Glasgow in 1837', *JSSL*, I, July 1838, pp. 167-8. *Local Reports on*

the *Sanitary Condition of the Labouring Population of Scotland* (London, 1842), pp. 159, 162.
6. *Local Reports ... Scotland*, p. 159.
7. Ibid., pp. 193-5.
8. The last letter from the society to London was dated April 1838 (*MCSSL*, I, f. 186).
9. George MacGregor, *The History of Glasgow* (Glasgow, 1881), pp. 418-19. James Cleland, *Annals of Glasgow* (2 vols., Glasgow, 1816), II, p. 121. Robert Renwick (ed.), *Extracts from the Records of the Burgh of Glasgow* (Glasgow, 1915), X, pp. 485-6.
10. James Cleland, *Enumeration of the Inhabitants of the City of Glasgow and County of Lanark* (Glasgow, 1832). *Letter to His Grace the Duke of Hamilton and Brandon Respecting the Parochial Registers of Scotland* (Glasgow, 1834).
11. *Constitution and Regulations of the Glasgow and Clydesdale Statistical Society* (Glasgow, 1836), pp. 3-15.
12. *Transactions of the Glasgow and Clydesdale Statistical Society*, I, 1837.
13. *MCSSL*, I, f. 225.
14. Rev. A. Hume, *The Learned Societies and Printing Clubs of the United Kingdom* (London, 1847), pp. 190-1.
15. James Cleland, *Description of the Banquet given in Honour of the Right Hon. Sir Robert Peel* (Glasgow, 1837).
16. *Alumni Cantabrigienses*, *Alumni Oxonienses* (under Tripp), *DNB* (under Lant Carpenter).
17. Charles Bowles Fripp, *Statistics of Popular Education in Bristol* (Bristol, 1837). This was the paper reprinted in the *Transactions of the Glasgow and Clydesdale Statistical Society*.
18. *Proceedings of the Bristol Statistical Society, 1836-41*, a volume in Bristol Central Library. The meeting is described in an unidentified newspaper cutting. The volume includes the annual reports.
19. Eight members of the provisional council are mentioned in *DNB*.
20. John Addington Symonds, *Some Account of the Life, Writings, and Character of the late James Cowles Prichard* (Bristol, 1849), pp. 6-8.
21. *JSSL*, I, May 1838, p. 49.
22. *First Annual Report* (1837), p. 7.
23. *JSSL*, I, January 1839, p. 550.
24. *First Annual Report*, pp. 7-9.
25. C. B. Fripp, 'Report of an Inquiry into the Condition of the Working Classes in the City of Bristol', *Third Annual Report*, p. 10 and *JSSL*, II, October 1839, p. 369.
26. 'Report on the Statistics of Education in Bristol', *JSSL*, IV, October 1841, pp. 250-1.

27. *JSSL*, I, May 1838, p. 50.
28. Ibid., January 1839, pp. 553-4. Ibid., II, April 1839, pp. 187-8.
29. Ibid., January 1840, p. 461. Rev. A. Hume, op. cit., p. 215.
30. Ibid., I, May 1838, p. 49.
31. *Local Reports ... England*, pp. 282-94.
32. *Modern English Biography*.
33. *JSSL*, I, May 1838, p. 52. Ibid., June 1838, p. 118. Ibid., January 1839, pp. 552-3.
34. *MCSSL*, I, ff. 19, 67. *App. Mins.*, f. 41.
35. *Education of the Poorer Classes in England and Wales. Sel. Cttee. Mins. of Ev.*, pp. 92, 94; GBPP 1837-8 VII.
36. No information was found concerning Clark except that he may have been the son of a doctor.
37. *Children's Employment. R. Comm. Second Rep. App. Pt. I*, p. f. 185; GBPP 1843 XIV.
38. For Hodgson see *DNB* otherwise *Alumni Oxonienses*.
39. *Athenaeum*, 31 August 1839, p. 648.
40. *JSSL*, III, April 1840, pp. 25-49.
41. *Education of the Poorer Classes in England and Wales. Sel. Cttee. Mins. of Ev.* (J. R. Wood), p. 126; GBPP 1837-8 VII.
42. For the other report see *JSSL*, II, January 1840, pp. 434-41.
43. William Cargill *et al.*, 'Educational, Criminal and Society Statistics of Newcastle-upon-Tyne', *JSSL*, I, October 1838, pp. 355-61. *Second Report of the Committee of the Educational Society on the State of Education in Newcastle-upon-Tyne* (1839).
44. *JSSL*, I, June 1838, p. 116.
45. Mabel Tylecote, op. cit., p. 57.
46. *JSSL*, I, November 1838, pp. 426-7.
47. *Minutes of the Leeds Town Council*, IV, f. 205.
48. Ibid., f. 194.
49. F. Beckwith, 'Robert Baker', *University of Leeds Review*, VII, 1960-1, pp. 40-2. W. R. Lee, 'Robert Baker: The First Doctor in the Factory Department. Part I, 1803-1858', *British Journal of Industrial Medicine*, XXI, 1964, pp. 84-5. *Employment of Children in Factories. R. Comm. Medical Rep. C. 3*; p. 14; GBPP 1833 XXI.
50. Ibid., *Supp. Rep. Pt. II*, p. 79; GBPP 1834 XX.
51. *Factories Act. Educational Provisions. Rep. by R. J. Saunders, App. 5*, pp. 61-2; GBPP 1839 XLII.
52. *Employment of Children in Factories. R. Comm. Medical Rep. C. 3*, pp. 8-10; GBPP 1833 XXI.
53. Flinn, pp. 50-1.
54. *Minutes of the Leeds Town Council Statistical Committee*, ff. 2-4. This volume is to be found on shelf 36 of the committee's strong-

room of the Leeds Town Council Record Office (the minutes are hereafter cited as *MLSC*). Also see *MCSSL*, I, f. 148 for the letter to London.
55. Ibid., ff. 4-6. For Eddison's appointment as town clerk see Derek Fraser, 'Politics in Leeds, 1830-1852' (unpublished Ph.D. thesis, Leeds, 1969) p. 180.
56. *Minutes of the Leeds Town Council*, IV, ff. 286-7.
57. *MLSC*, ff. 7-8.
58. Ibid., f. 9 (October 1838). Baker was sometimes occupied elsewhere as a factory inspector.
59. Ibid., ff. 10-11.
60. Ibid., f. 12.
61. Ibid., f. 14.
62. Ibid., f. 16 (February 1839).
63. *Minutes of the Leeds Town Council*, IV, f. 520.
64. *MLSC*, ff. 16-20.
65. Ibid., ff. 22-3. *Leeds Intelligencer*, 2 November 1839.
66. Fraser, op. cit., p. 199. *Leeds Intelligencer*, 6 May 1837.
67. *MLSC*, f. 23.
68. *Minutes of the Leeds Town Council*, IV, f. 525.
69. *Leeds Times*, 2 November 1839.
70. Quoted in Alexander Tyrell, 'Class Consciousness in Early Victorian Britain: Samuel Smiles, Leeds Politics, and the Self-Help Creed', *Journal of British Studies*, IX, 1970, p. 112.
71. *Leeds Mercury*, 2 November 1839.
72. *Leeds Intelligencer*, 2 November 1839.
73. *JSSL*, II, January 1840, pp. 397-424.
74. *MLSC*, f. 29.
75. Ibid., f. 31.
76. *Minutes of the Leeds Town Council*, V, ff. 218-9.
77. Ibid., ff. 242-5.
78. *MLSC*, ff. 35-6.
79. *Minutes of the Leeds Town Council*, V, f. 349.
80. Ibid., f. 432. *Leeds Intelligencer*, 13 November 1841.
81. *Abstract of the Report of the Statistical Committee (For 1838, 39, 40) of the Town Council of the Borough of Leeds* (Leeds, 1841).
82. *MCSSL*, I, f. 247 (January 1840).
83. Ibid., f. 257.
84. Ibid., ff. 267, 270.
85. *JSSL*, V, April 1842, p. 89.
86. *Leeds Intelligencer*, 8 May 1841.
87. *DNB*.
88. George Calvert Holland, *The Vital Statistics of Sheffield* (London, 1843), p. v.

89. Holland, *An Inquiry into the Moral, Social, and Intellectual Condition of the Industrious Classes of Sheffield, Part I: The Abuses and Evils of Charity, Especially of Medical Charitable Institutions* (London, 1839), esp. pp. 10–12, 19–20.
90. *Leeds Intelligencer*, 8 May 1841.
91. E. R. Wickham, *Church and People in an Industrial City* (London, 1957), p. 91.
92. *Vital Statistics*, p. 3.
93. Ibid., p. 11.
94. *JSSL*, IV, January 1842; p. 358. *MCSSL*, I, ff. 318, 332. *Local Reports ... Scotland*, pp. 286–300.
95. For Barnsley see the Wilson papers in Leeds Central Library, DB 178/28.
96. *JSSL*, I, May 1838, pp. 5, 8.
97. *JSSL*, IX, June 1846, p. 99.
98. *Wilson papers*, Rawson to Wilson, 10 July 1839.
99. *JSSL*, VII, June 1845, p. 100.
100. Ashton, op. cit., p. 11.

Conclusion: Social Statistics and the Ideology of Improvement in Early Victorian Britain

1. For a valuable discussion of the changing nature of laissez-faire ideology with respect to factory reform see Ann P. W. Robson, 'The Factory Controversy 1830–53' (unpublished Ph.D. thesis, London, 1958).
2. 'Report of the Statistical Society of Manchester on the Condition of the Working Classes in the Town of Kingston-upon-Hull', *JSSL*, V, July 1842, p. 213.
3. See above, pp. 111–12.
4. 'Report of the Manchester Statistical Society on the Condition of the Population in Three Parishes in Rutlandshire, in March, 1839', *JSSL*, II, October 1839, pp. 297–9.
5. *JSSL*, V, July 1842, pp. 213–5.
6. *First Report of the Bristol Stat. Soc.*, pp. 13–15. Also see *JSSL*, I, June 1838, pp. 86–8.
7. *Third Report of the Bristol Stat. Soc.*, pp. 7–9.
8. Cf. *First Report* and *Third Report* (also see *JSSL*, I, June 1838, p. 87 and II, October 1839, p. 372).
9. *First Report*, also *JSSL*, I, June 1838, p. 87.
10. *Third Report*, p. 9.
11. For the full report see *JSSL*, III, April 1840, pp. 14–24.
12. *First Publication of the Central Society of Education*, 1837, pp. 338–59.

13. Though there are some notable exceptions, especially William Neild, 'Comparative Statement of the Income and Expenditure of certain Families of the Working Class in Manchester and Dukinfield, in the Years 1836 and 1841', *JSSL*, IV, January 1842, pp. 320-34.
14. 'Report of a Committee of the B.A.A.S. on the Vital Statistics of Large Towns in Scotland', *JSSL*, VI, May 1843, pp. 149-65.
15. 'Statistics of the present Depression of Trade at Bolton', *JSSL*, V, April 1842, pp. 74-81.
16. Archibald Prentice, *History of the Anti-Corn Law League*, I, pp. 185-6.
17. *JSSL*, I, January 1839, pp. 540-1. Presumably he meant Carlile.
18. Ibid., November 1838, pp. 416-20.
19. Ibid., XI, August 1848, pp. 193-249.
20. 'Report of a Committee, on the State of the Working Classes in the Parishes of St. Margaret and St. John, Westminster', *JSSL*, III, April 1840, p. 18.
21. *JSSL*, XI, March 1848, pp. 1-18.
22. Ibid., p. 17.
23. *Essai sur la Statistique Morale de la France* (Paris, 1833).
24. Joseph Bentley, *State of Education, Crime* ... (London, 1842), pp. 29-49. *Athenaeum*, 10 and 17 October 1840. *Trans. BAAS*, 1840, p. 184.
25. W. R. Greg, *Social Statistics of the Netherlands* (Manchester, 1835).
26. Porter, 'On the Connexion between Crime and Ignorance, as Exhibited in Criminal Calendars', *Trans. SSL*, I, pp. 97-103, Read December 1835.
27. Porter, 'Statistics of Crime and Education in France', *First Publication of the Central Society of Education*, 1837, p. 317.
28. Ibid., pp. 323, 325.
29. Rawson, 'An Enquiry into the Condition of Criminal Offenders in England and Wales, with respect to Education; or, Statistics of Education among the Criminal and General Population of England and other Countries', *JSSL*, III, January 1841, pp. 331-52.
30. Ibid., p. 331.
31. Ibid., pp. 333-4.
32. Ibid., pp. 334-6.
33. Ibid., p. 351.
34. Ibid., p. 352.
35. *Hand-Loom Weavers. R. Comm. Reps.*, Pt. IV, p. 74; GBPP 1840 XXIV.
36. Ibid., pp. 75-82. Fletcher provides, of course, an interesting counter-example to the supposed superiority of rural morals but this does not seem to have affected his general conclusion.
37. Ibid., pp. 170-84.

38. Fletcher, 'Progress of Crime in the United Kingdom', *JSSL*, VI, August 1843, pp. 233–6.
39. Fletcher, 'Moral and Educational Statistics of England and Wales', *JSSL*, X, September 1847, p. 211.
40. Fletcher, 'Moral and Educational Statistics of England and Wales', *JSSL*, XI, November 1848, p. 346.
41. Fletcher, 'Moral and Educational Statistics of England and Wales', *JSSL*, XII, 1849, pp. 151–76, 188–335.
42. Ibid., pp. 171–2. Fletcher did not imply a rejection of economic laissez-faire by this argument.
43. *Drunkenness. Sel. Cttee. Mins. of Ev.*, p. 34; GBPP 1834 VIII.
44. *Local Reports . . . England and Wales*, p. 56.
45. *Report on Mining Districts*, p. 28; GBPP 1850 XXIII.
46. Thomas Wyse, *Education Reform: or, the Necessity of a National System of Education* (London, 1836), pp. 326–30.
47. Kay, 'On the Establishment of Pauper Schools, Part I', *JSSL*, I, May 1838, p. 23.
48. *State of Large Towns and Populous Districts. R. Comm. Second Rep. App. Pt. II*, p. 71; GBPP 1845 XVIII.
49. G. S. Kenrick, 'Statistics of Merthyr Tydfil', *JSSL*, IX, March 1846, p. 14.
50. 'Second Publication of the Central Society of Education', *JSSL*, I, May 1838, p. 45.
51. *JSSL*, I, May 1838, p. 8.
52. G. R. Porter, 'Results of an Enquiry into the Condition of the Labouring Classes in the Five Parishes in the County of Norfolk', *Third Publication of the Central Society of Education*, 1839, p. 370.
53. *JSSL*, I, May 1838, pp. 1–2.
54. The phrase is Professor Kitson Clark's in 'The Repeal of the Corn Laws and the Politics of the Forties', *EcHR*, 2nd ser., IV, 1951, p. 9.
55. For the moral preoccupations of many radicals in the early 1830s see Patricia Hollis, *The Pauper Press* (Oxford, 1970).
56. In this view the much over-discussed Benthamites were but one group of the centrists. Some Benthamites were statisticians, a very few statisticians were Benthamites. Chadwick was Chadwick. It might be remarked that it is time that historians stopped calling any middle-class intellectual with a coherent social ideology a Benthamite. Apparently for no better reason than this a large number of the prominent social statisticians of the period have at various times been labelled Benthamites.
57. David Chadwick, 'On the Rate of Wages in Manchester and Salford, and the Manufacturing Districts of Lancashire, 1839–59', *JSSL*, XXIII, 1860, pp. 1–36.

58. J. J. Fox in *JSSL*, XXIII, 1860, p. 331.
59. See his address as president of Section F of the B.A.A.S. in *JSSL*, XXVII, 1864.
60. Cf. Philip Abrams, *The Origins of British Sociology, 1834–1914*.
61. Lawrence Ritt, 'The Victorian Conscience in Action: The National Association for the Promotion of Social Science, 1857–1886' (unpublished Ph.D. thesis, Columbia, 1959), pp. 126–48.
62. This is not to ignore the claims of Henry Mayhew whose importance has recently been exaggerated.
63. For a brief but illuminating discussion of this see Abrams, op. cit.

Bibliography of Primary Sources

A. *MANUSCRIPT*

a. *Official*

In the General Register Office:
  History of the Census of 1841 (due to be transferred to the Public Record Office).
In the Leeds Town Clerk's Record Office, Committees' Strongroom:
  Minute Book of the Town Council, vols. IV, V.
  Minute Book of the Town Council Statistical Committee, 1837-41.
In the Public Record Office:
  Adm.1/3531. In-letters from the Physician-General, 1835-9.
  Adm.105/70, 71, 72. Reports, etc., of the Physician-General, 1832-9.
  Adm.133/4, 5 (IND 7729, 7730). Digest and index of letters received, 1835-7.
  B.T.2/23. Out-letters, 1832-3.
  B.T.5/40, 41. Minutes, 1831-4.
  B.T.2411. Out-letters of the Statistical Department, 1832-8.
  H.O.39/4. Letters from the General Register Office.
  H.O.44/29. Miscellaneous correspondence, 1836.
  H.O.44/49. Miscellaneous correspondence, 1831-7.
  M.H.71. Minutes of the Health of Towns Commission, 1843-5.

b. *Collections of papers, etc.*

In the Belgian National Centre for the History of the Sciences (Royal Library of Belgium, Brussels):
  Quetelet papers.
In the British Library of Political and Economic Science:
  Farr papers.
In the British Museum:
  Babbage papers. Add. Mss. 37182-37201.
In the Leeds Central Library:
  Thomas Wilson papers, Mss. DB 178/22, 23, 28.
In the Manchester Central Library:
  Appendix to the Minutes of the Manchester Statistical Society.

In the Monmouthshire County Record Office, Newport:
  Tulloch papers, Box D.460.
In the National Library of Scotland:
  Autobiography of John Drinkwater Bethune, Ms. 1835.
In the Royal Statistical Society Library:
  Diary of John Elliot Drinkwater, 1833-4 (minutes of the Statistical Section of the British Association).
  Minutes of the Statistical Society of London, 1834-52.
  Minutes of the Council of the Statistical Society of London, 1834-52.
  Reports of the Council of the Statistical Society of London, 1834-52.
In the Library of University College, London:
  Bentham papers.
  Chadwick papers.
In the Library of the University of London:
  Nassau William Senior's account of the conferences on the Poor Law Amendment Act of 1834. Ms. 173.

B. PUBLISHED

a. *Official*

ADMINISTRATION, ETC.

Official Salaries. Sel. Cttee.; GBPP 1850 XV.
Official Statistics. Sel. Cttee.; GBPP 1881 XXX.
Public Documents. Sel. Cttee.; GBPP 1833 XII.
Public Offices. R. Comms.; GBPP 1854 XXVII.
Return of the Number and Description of the Existing Commissions of Inquiry; GBPP 1834 XLI.
Return of all Commissions issued since 1830; GBPP 1837-8 XXXVI.
Return of all Commissions issued or appointed since 1st May 1838, and of the Number and Titles of the former Commissions now in operation; GBPP 1842 XXVI.
Return of the Commissions issued or appointed since 1842; GBPP 1846 XXV.

AGRICULTURE AND INDUSTRY

Agriculture. Sel. Cttee.; GBPP 1833 V.
Children Employed in Manufactories. Sel. Cttee.; GBPP 1816 III.
Children's Employment. R. Comm. First Rep. Mines; GBPP 1842 XV, XVI, XVII.
Children's Employment. R. Comm. Second Rep. Trades and Manufactures; GBPP 1843 XIII, XIV, XV.
Cotton and Woollen Factories. Return; GBPP 1836 XLV.
Employment of Children in Factories. R. Comm. First Rep.; GBPP 1833 XX.
——. *Second Rep.*; GBPP 1833 XXI.
——. *Supp. Rep. Pt. I*; GBPP 1834 XIX.
——. *Supp. Rep. Pt. II*; GBPP 1834 XX.

Employment in Manufacturing Districts. Sel. Cttee.; GBPP 1830 X.
Factories Bill. Sel. Cttee.; GBPP 1831–2 XV.
Factories. Inspectors' Reports, 1834–50.
Factories. A Return of the Total Number of Persons Employed, etc.; GBPP 1847 XLVI.
Factories. Returns; GBPP 1839 XLII.
Factories. Returns. Numbers visited by Inspectors, etc.; GBPP 1839 XLII.
Factories. Returns of the Numbers, etc.; GBPP 1850 XLII.
Factories Act. Educational Provisions. Returns; GBPP 1839 XLII.
Factories. Children. Returns; GBPP 1836 XLV.
Factories. Power Looms. Returns; GBPP 1836 XLV.
Factory Children. Heights, etc. Returns; GBPP 1837 L.
Mills and Factories. Sel. Cttee.; GBPP 1840 X.
Reports of Special Assistant Poor Law Commissioners on the Employment of Women and Children in Agriculture; GBPP 1843 XII.
Special Reports by the Inspectors of Factories on Accidents; GBPP 1841 X.

ARMY AND NAVY

Barracks (Bahamas, etc.); GBPP 1840 XXXIV.
Mortality in the Army; GBPP 1850 XXXV.
Statistical Reports on the Health of the Navy for the Years 1830 to 1836. Pt. I; GBPP 1840 XXX.
——. Pt. II; GBPP 1841 Sess. 2 VI.
Statistical Reports on the Health of the Navy for the Years 1837 to 1843. Pt. I; GBPP 1849 XXXII.
——. Pt. II; GBPP 1852–3 LXI.
——. Pt. III; GBPP 1854 LXVIII.
Statistical Report on the Sickness, Mortality, and Invaliding among the Troops in the West Indies; GBPP 1837–8 XL.
—— *in the United Kingdom, the Mediterranean, and British America*; GBPP 1839 XVI.
—— *in Western Africa, St. Helena, The Cape of Good Hope, and the Mauritius*; GBPP 1840 XXX.
—— *in Ceylon, the Tenasserim Provinces, and the Burmese Empire*; GBPP 1842 XXVII.

CIVIL REGISTRATION

Annual Reports of the Registrar-General of Births, Deaths, and Marriages in England and Wales, 1838–51.
Medical Poor Relief. Sel. Cttee.; GBPP 1844 IX.
Parliamentary Proceedings Relating to the Marriage and Registration Acts, 1836. Collection of reports and bills in the General Register Office.
Parochial Registration. Sel. Cttee.; GBPP 1833 XIV.
Press Clippings. Collection in the General Register Office (CZ1.1).
Registrar-General of Births, etc., Office; GBPP 1847 XXXIV.

Regulations for the Duties of Registrars of Births and Deaths and Deputy Registrars, January 1838. In the General Register Office (M.11.2(1)).

Regulations for the Duties of Superintendent Registrars, January 1838. In the General Register Office (M.92.10 and M.11.2(1)).

CRIME, ETC.

Criminal Commitments and Convictions in England and Wales. Sel. Cttee. First Rep.; GBPP 1826–7 VI.

——. Second Rep.; GBPP 1828 VI.

Criminal Offenders (England and Wales). Annual Tables, 1834–51.

Criminal Offenders (Scotland). Annual Tables, 1835–51.

Drunkenness. Sel. Cttee.; GBPP 1834 III.

Police of the Metropolis. Sel. Cttee.; GBPP 1828 VI.

EDUCATION

Abstract of the Answers and Returns Relative to the State of Education in England and Wales; GBPP 1835 XLI, XLII, XLIII.

Education. Sel. Cttee.; GBPP 1834 IX.

Education (England). Sel. Cttee.; GBPP 1835 VII.

Education of the Lower Orders of the Metropolis. Sel. Cttee.; GBPP 1816 IV.

——. GBPP 1817 III.

Education of the Lower Orders. Sel. Cttee.; GBPP 1818 IV.

Education of the Poorer Classes in England and Wales. Sel. Cttee.; GBPP 1837–8 VII.

Education (Manchester and Salford). Sel. Cttee.; GBPP 1852–3 XXIV.

Education. Papers; GBPP 1839 XLI.

Minutes of the Privy Council Committee on Education, 1839–51.

HEALTH OF TOWNS AND CONDITION OF THE WORKING CLASSES

Annual Reports of the Poor Law Commissioners for England and Wales, 1834–47.

Condition of the Poorer Classes. R. Comm.; GBPP 1835 XXXII.

Doctrine of Contagion in the Plague. Sel. Cttee.; GBPP 1819 II.

Hand-Loom Weavers. R. Comm. Copy of Instructions to Assistant Commissioners; GBPP 1837–8 XLV.

Hand-Loom Weavers. R. Comm. Reps. Pt. I; GBPP 1839 XLII.

——. Pt. II; GBPP 1840 XXIII.

——. Pt. III; GBPP 1840 XXIV.

Health of Towns. Sel. Cttee.; GBPP 1840 XI.

Improvement of the Health of the Metropolis. R. Comm.; GBPP 1847–8 XXXII.

Improvement of the Health of Towns. Sel. Cttee.; GBPP 1842 X.

Local Reports on the Sanitary Condition of the Labouring Population of England (London, 1842).

Local Reports on the Sanitary Condition of the Labouring Population of Scotland (London, 1842).

State of Large Towns and Populous Districts. R. Comm. First Rep.;
   GBPP 1844 XVII.
——. *Second Rep.*; GBPP 1845 XVIII.
State of the Population in the Mining Districts. Annual Reports of the Commissioner, 1843–50.

VITAL STATISTICS

Bill for Taking an Account of the Population of Great Britain. Sel. Cttee.; GBPP 1830 IV.
Emigration, Scotland. Sel. Cttee.; GBPP 1841 VI.
Population. Census of 1801. Abstract; GBPP 1801–2 VI.
——. *Parish Registers*; GBPP 1801–2 VII.
Population. Census of 1811. Abstract; GBPP 1812 XI.
Population. Census of 1821. Abstract; GBPP 1822 XV.
Population. Census of 1831. Abstract; GBPP 1833 XXXVI, XXXVII, XXXVIII.
Population. Census of 1841; GBPP 1843 XXII, XIII.
——; GBPP 1844 XXVIII.
Population. Census of 1851. Tables; GBPP 1851 XLIII.
——. *Forms and Instructions*; GBPP 1851 XLIII.
——; GBPP 1852–3 LXXXVI–XC.
——; GBPP 1854 LIX.
Census of England and Wales. Returns of expenses, etc., for 1841–61; GBPP 1863 XXIX.

MISCELLANEOUS

Annual Tables of the Revenue, Population, Commerce, etc., of the United Kingdom and its Dependencies, 1833–51.

b. *Newspapers, periodicals, etc.*

Athenaeum.
Bristol Statistical Society, *Proceedings, 1836–41*.
British Almanac and Companion to the Almanac.
British Annals of Medicine, Pharmacy, Vital Statistics, and General Science.
British Association for the Advancement of Science, *Reports* and *Transactions.*
Central Society of Education, *First, Second, and Third Publications.*
Correspondence Mathématique et Physique.
Edinburgh Medical and Surgical Journal.
Gentleman's Magazine.
Glasgow and Clydesdale Statistical Society, *Transactions.*
Hansard.
Lancet.
Leeds Intelligencer.
Leeds Mercury.
Leeds Times.
Literary Gazette and Journal of Belles Lettres.
London Medical Gazette.

Manchester Statistical Society, *Miscellaneous Papers, 1837-61*.
Medical Times.
Mirror of Parliament.
Monthly Review.
Pamphleteer.
Parliamentary Review, and Family Magazine.
Penny Cyclopaedia.
Provincial Medical and Surgical Association, *Transactions*.
Quarterly Journal of Education.
Statistical Society of London, *Journal, Proceedings, Transactions*.
United Service Journal.
Westminster Review.

c. *Individual Works*

Adam, William. *First Report on the State of Education in Bengal* (Calcutta, 1835).
——. *Second Report* . . . (Calcutta, 1836).
——. *Third Report* . . . (Calcutta, 1838).
Aitken, George A. *The Life and Works of John Arbuthnot* (Oxford, 1892).
Alison, William Pulteney. *Observations on the Management of the Poor in Scotland and its Effects on the Health of the Great Towns* (Edinburgh, 1840).
Annesley, James. *Researches into the Causes, Nature, and Treatment of the More Prevalent Diseases of India, and of Warm Climates Generally* (2 vols., London, 1828).
Ansell, Charles. *A Treatise on Friendly Societies* (London, 1835).
Aspland, Sydney. *A Treatise on the Act for Marriages in England, and the Act for Registering Births, Deaths, and Marriages, in England* (London, 1836).
Babbage, Charles. *A Comparative View of the Various Institutions for the Assurance of Lives* (London, 1826).
——. *On the Economy of Machinery and Manufactures* (London, 1832).
——. *The Exposition of 1851; or, Views of the Industry, the Science, and the Government of England* (2nd edn., London, 1851).
——. *Passages from the Life of a Philosopher* (London, 1864).
Baily, Francis. *The Doctrine of Life Annuities and Assurances* (2 vols., London, 1813).
Baines, Edward jr. *The Social, Educational, and Religious State of the Manufacturing Districts* (London, 1843).
Baly, William. *On the Mortality in Prisons and the diseases most frequently fatal to prisoners* (London, 1845).
Baly, William and Gull, William W. *Reports on Epidemic Cholera* (London, 1854).
Bateman, Thomas. *Reports on the Diseases of London* (London, 1819).
Bell, John. *London's Remembrancer* (London, 1665).
Benjamin, Bernard. 'John Graunt's "Observations". With a foreword', *Journal of the Institute of Actuaries*, XC, 1964, pp. 1-61.

Bentley, Joseph. *The State of Education, Contrasted with the State of Crime, at a Glance, in England and Wales* (Manchester, 1838).
——. *State of Education, Crime, . . .* (London, 1842).
Bielfeld, J. F. von. *The Elements of Universal Erudition* (trans. W. Hooper, London, 1770).
Bigland, Ralph. *Observations on Marriages, Baptisms, and Burials, as Preserved in Parochial Registers* (London, 1764).
Black, William. *Observations, Medical and Political on the Small-pox* (2nd edn., London, 1781).
——. *A Comparative View of the Mortality of the Human Species at all ages* (London, 1788).
——. *A Dissertation on Insanity. Illustrated with Tables, and Extracted from between Two and Three Thousand Cases in Bedlam* (2nd edn., London, 1811).
Blane, Gilbert. *Observations on the Diseases Incident to Seamen* (London, 1785).
——. *Select Dissertations on Several Subjects of Medical Science* (2 vols., London, 1833).
Boetticher, J. G. *Statistical Tables; Exhibiting a View of All the States of Europe* (trans. William Playfair, London, 1800).
Boileau, Daniel. *An Essay on the Study of Statistics* (London, 1807).
Boone, Rev. James Shergold. *The Educational Economy of England, Part I* (London, 1838).
British Association for the Advancement of Science. *Lithographed Signatures of the Members who met at Cambridge, June 1833, With a Report of the Proceedings at the Public Meetings during the Week; and an Alphabetical List of the Members* (Cambridge, 1833).
Burn, John Southerden. *The History of Parish Registers in England* (London, 1829).
Burrington, George. *An Answer to Dr. William Brakenridge's Letter concerning the Number of Inhabitants within the London Bills of Mortality* (London, 1757).
Burrows, George Man. *Commentaries on the Causes, Forms, Symptoms, and Treatment Moral and Medical, of Insanity* (London, 1828).
——. *Observations on the Comparative Mortality of Paris and London* (London, 1815).
Capper, Benjamin Pitts. *A Statistical Account of the Population and Cultivation, Produce and Consumption, of England and Wales* (London, 1801).
Chadwick, Edwin. *An Essay on the Means of Insurance against the Casualties of Sickness, Decrepitude, and Mortality* (2nd edn., London, 1836).
——. *Sanitary Report on the Condition of the Labouring Population of Great Britain* (ed. with an introduction by M. W. Flinn, Edinburgh, 1965).
Chalmers, Thomas. *The Christian and Civic Economy of Large Towns* (3 vols., Glasgow, 1821-6).

——. *On Political Economy in Connexion with the Moral State and Moral Prospects of Society* (Glasgow, 1832).
Clark, John. *Observations on Fevers* (London, 1780).
Clarke, Thomas B. *A Statistical View of Germany* (London, 1790).
——. *Publicistical Survey of the Different Forms of Government of all States and Communities in the World* (London, 1791).
Cleland, James. *Annals of Glasgow* (Glasgow, 1816).
——. *Enumeration of the Inhabitants of Scotland* (Glasgow, 1823).
——. *Statistical Tables Relative to the City of Glasgow* (3rd edn., Glasgow 1823).
——. *The Rise and Progress of the City of Glasgow* (Glasgow, 1829).
——. *Enumeration of the Inhabitants of the City of Glasgow and the County of Lanark* (Glasgow, 1832).
——. *Letter to His Grace the Duke of Hamilton and Brandon Respecting the Parochial Registers of Scotland* (Glasgow, 1834).
——. *Glasgow Bridewell, or House of Correction* (Glasgow, 1835).
——. *A Historical Account of the Bills of Mortality, and the Probability of Human Life, in Glasgow and Other Large Towns* (Glasgow, 1836).
——. *Description of the Banquet given in Honour of the Right Hon.* (Glasgow, 1837).
——. *Statistical Facts Descriptive of the Former and Present State of Sir Robert Peel* (Glasgow, 1837).
Collins, Robert. *A Practical Treatise on Midwifery, Containing the Result of Sixteen Thousand Six Hundred and Fifty-four Births Occurring in the Dublin Lying-in Hospital* (London, 1835).
Collins, William. *Statistics of the Church Accommodation in Glasgow, Barony, and Gorbals* (Glasgow, 1836).
Cooke, Layton. *A Series of Statistical Charts* (London, 1827).
Corbaux, Francis. *The Doctrine of Compound Interest* (London, 1825).
——. *On the Natural and Mathematical Laws Concerning Population, Vitality, and Mortality* (London, 1833).
Cowan, Robert. *Vital Statistics of Glasgow* (Glasgow, 1838).
Dale, William. *Calculations ... intended as an introduction to the study of the doctrine of annuities* (London, 1772).
Davenant, Charles. *Discourses on the Publick Revenue, and on the Trade of England, Parts I and II* (London, 1698).
——. *An Essay upon the Probable Methods of making a People Gainers in the Ballance of Trade* (London, 1699).
——. *A Discourse upon Grants and Resumptions* (London, 1700).
——. *Essays* (London, 1701).
——. *Essays upon Peace at Home and War Abroad, Part I* (London, 1704).
Davies, Griffith. *Tables of Life Contingencies* (London, 1825).
Dod, R. P. *Parliamentary Pocket Companion, for 1833; including a Compendious Peerage* (London, 1833).
Drinkwater, John Elliott. *Letter to Michael Thomas Sadler* (Leeds, 1833).

Drinkwater, John Elliot and Power, Alfred. *Replies to Mr. M. T. Sadler's Protest Against the Factory Commission* (Leeds, 1833).
Duppa, Baldwin Francis. *The Education of the Peasantry in England* (London, 1834).
Edmonds, T. R. *Life Tables* (London, 1832).
——. *An Enquiry into the Principles of Population, Exhibiting a System of Regulations for the Poor* (London, 1832).
Farren, Edwin James. *Historical Essays on the Rise and Early Progress of the Doctrine of Life-Contingencies in England* (London, 1844).
Felkin, William. *History of the Machine-Wrought Hosiery and Lace Manufacturers* (reprinted with an introduction by Stanley D. Chapman, Newton Abbot, 1967).
Fripp, C. Bowles. *Statistics of Popular Education in Bristol* (Bristol, 1837).
Grant, James. *Random Recollections of the House of Commons, from the Year 1830 to the Close of 1835* (London, 1836).
Graunt, John. See above under Benjamin, Bernard.
Greg, William Rathbone. *Essays on Political and Social Science* (2 vols., London, 1853).
——. *An Enquiry into the State of the Manufacturing Population, and the Causes and Cures of the Evils therein Existing* (London, 1831).
——. *Social Statistics of the Netherlands* (Manchester, 1835).
Guerry, A. M. *Essai sur la Statistique Morale de la France* (Paris, 1833).
Halliday, Andrew. *Some Remarks on the State of Lunatic Asylums, and on the Number and Condition of the Insane Poor in Scotland* (Edinburgh, 1816).
——. *A Letter to the Right Honble. the Secretary at War, on Sickness and Mortality in the West Indies; Being a Review of Captain Tulloch's Report* (London, 1839).
Hanway, Jonas. *Letters on the Importance of the Rising Generation of the labouring part of our fellow-subjects* (2 vols., London, 1767).
Hare, Samuel. *Statistical Report of 190 Cases of Insanity, Admitted into the Retreat, Near Leeds, During Ten Years, from 1830 to 1840* (London, 1844).
Hawkins, Francis Bisset. *Elements of Medical Statistics* (London, 1829).
Hayes, Richard. *A New Method of Valuing Annuities upon Lives* (London, 1727).
——. *An Estimate of Places for Life* (London, 1728).
Haygarth, John. *Sketch of a Plan to Exterminate the Casual Small-Pox from Great Britain; and to Introduce General Inoculation* (London, 1793).
Heberden, William (ed.). *A Collection of the Yearly Bills of Mortality from 1657 to 1758 inclusive* (London, 1759).
Heberden, William jr. *Observations on the Increase and Decrease of Different Diseases, and Particularly of the Plague* (London, 1801).
Heysham, John. *Observations on the Bills of Mortality for the Year 1779* (Carlisle, 1780). Six similar works cover the years 1779–88.

———. *An Account of the Jail Fever, or Typhus Carcerum: As it Appeared at Carlisle in the Year 1781* (Carlisle, 1783).
Hill, Frederic. *Crime: Its Account, Causes, and Remedies* (London, 1853).
———. *National Education: Its Present State and Prospects* (2 vols., London, 1836).
Hodgson, James. *The Valuation of Annuities upon Lives; Deduced from the London Bills of Mortality* (London, 1747).
Holland, G. Calvert. *An Inquiry into the Moral, Social, and Intellectual Conditions of the Industrious Classes of Sheffield, Part I: The Abuses and Evils of Charity, Especially of Medical Charitable Institutions* (London, 1839).
———. *The Vital Statistics of Sheffield* (London, 1843).
Howlett, Rev. John. *An Examination of Dr. Price's Essay on the Population of England and Wales; and the Doctrine of an Increased Population in this Kingdom, Established by Facts* (Maidstone, 1781).
Hull, Charles Henry (ed.). *The Economic Writings of Sir William Petty together with the Observations upon the Bills of Mortality more probably by Captain John Graunt* (Cambridge, 1899).
Hume, Rev. A. *The Learned Societies and Printing Clubs of the United Kingdom* (London, 1847).
———. *Remarks on the Census of Religious Worship for England and Wales, with Suggestions for an Improved Census in 1861* (London, 1860).
Hutcheon, William (ed.). *Whigs and Whiggism: Political Writings by Benjamin Disraeli* (London, 1913).
Jones, Rev. Richard. *An Essay on the Distribution of Wealth, and on the sources of Taxation* (London, 1831).
Jurin, James. *A Letter to the Learned Caleb Cotesworth, M.D. Containing a Comparison between the Mortality of the Natural Small Pox, and that given by Inoculation* (London, 1723).
———. *An Account of the Success of Inoculating the Small Pox in Great Britain. With a Comparison between the Miscarriages in that Practice, and the Mortality of the Natural Small-Pox* (London, 1724).
Kay-Shuttleworth, James Phillips. *Four Periods of Public Education as Reviewed in 1832–1839–1846–1852* (London, 1862).
King, Gregory. *Two Tracts* (ed. with an introduction by George E. Barnet, Baltimore, 1936).
Lansdowne, Marquis of (ed.). *The Petty – Southwell Correspondence, 1676–1687* (London, 1928).
———. *The Petty Papers: some unpublished writings of Sir William Petty, Edited from the Bowood Papers* (2 vols., London, 1927).
Lee, Weyman. *An Essay to ascertain the Value of Leases and Annuities upon Lives, and to Estimate the Chances of the Duration of Lives* (London, 1737).
Leeds Town Council. *Abstract of the Report of the Statistical Committee for 1838, 39, 40* (Leeds, 1841).

McCulloch, J. R. *A Statistical Account of the British Empire* (2 vols., London, 1837).
——. *The Principles of Political Economy* (Edinburgh, 1825).
——. 'Statistics' in W. T. Brande (ed.), *A Dictionary of Science, Literature, and Art* (London, 1842).
Marshall, John. *Statistical Illustrations of the territorial extent and population, commerce, taxation, consumption, insolvency, pauperism, and crime of the British Empire* (London, 1825).
——. *A digest of all the accounts relating to the population, production, revenues ... of ... Great Britain and Ireland* (London, 1833).
——. *An Analysis and Compendium of all the Returns made to Parliament* (London, 1835).
Maseres, Francis. *The Principles of the Doctrine of Life Annuities* (London, 1783).
Miller, H. *Papers Relative to the State of Crime in the City of Glasgow, with Observations of a Remedial Nature* (Glasgow, 1840).
Milne, Joshua. *A Treatise on the Valuation of Annuities and Assurances on Lives and Survivorships* (2 vols., London, 1815).
Moivre, Abraham de. *The Doctrine of Chances: or, a Method of Calculating the Probabilities of Events in Play* (3rd edn., London, 1756).
Morgan, William. *The Doctrine of Annuities and Assurances on Lives and Survivorships, Stated and Explained* (London, 1779).
Partridge, Rev. S. *Remarks Upon, and Proposed Improvements of, the Bill for Parish-Registers* (Boston, 1812).
Percival, Thomas. *Tables showing the Number of Deaths occasioned by the Small-Pox ...* (Manchester, 1775).
Pett, Sir Peter. *The Happy Future State of England* (London, 1688).
Petty, Sir William. 'The Advice of W.P. to Mr. Samuel Hartlib, for the Advancement of some particular Parts of Learning' (1648), *Harleian Miscellany*, VI, 1745, pp. 1–13.
——. *The History of the Survey of Ireland, commonly called the Down Survey* (ed. by T. A. Larcom, Dublin, 1851).
Playfair, William. *The Commercial and Political Atlas* (2nd edn., London, 1787 and 3rd edn., London, 1801).
——. *Lineal Arithmetic: Applied to Shew the Progress of the Commerce and Revenue of England During the Present Century* (London, 1798).
——. *The Statistical Breviary* (London, 1801).
Porter, George Richardson. *The Nature and Properties of Sugar-Cane* (London, 1830).
——. *Progress of the Nation* (3 vols., London, 1836–43).
Prentice, Archibald. *Historical Sketches and Personal Recollections of Manchester* (London, 1851).
——. *History of the Anti-Corn Law League* (2 vols., London, 1853).
Price, Richard. *Observations on the Expectations of Lives, the Increase of Mankind, the Influence of Great Towns on Population, and particularly the State of London, with respect to Healthfulness and Number of Inhabitants* (London, 1796).

——. *Observations on Revisionary Payments: on Schemes for providing Annuities for Widows, and for Persons in Old Age* (London, 1769).
Roberton, John. *Observations on the Mortality and Physical Management of Children* (London, 1827).
——. *On a Recent Proposal of the Poor Law Commissioners to Refuse Out-door Relief to Widows with Families* [?Manchester, 1840?]
Sadler, Michael Thomas. *The Law of Population* (London, 1830).
——. *Factory Statistics* (London, 1836).
Short, Thomas. *A Comparative History of the Increase and Decrease of Mankind in England, and Several Countries Abroad* (London, 1767).
——. *New Observations, Natural, Moral, Civil, Political, and Medical, on City, Town, and Country Bills of Mortality* (London, 1750).
Simpson, Thomas. *The Nature and Laws of Chance* (London, 1762).
——. *The Doctrine of Annuities and Reversions, deduced from General and Evident Principles* (London, 1742).
——. *Select Exercises for Young Proficients in the Mathematicks* (London, 1752).
Sinclair, Sir John. *The Statistical Account of Scotland* (21 vols., Edinburgh, 1791-9).
Smith, Thomas Southwood. *A Treatise on Fever* (London, 1830).
——. *The Philosophy of Health* (2 vols., London, 1835-7).
Templeman, Thomas. *A New Survey of the Globe* (London, 1729).
Vaughan, Robert. *Thoughts on the Past and Present State of Religion in England* (London, 1838).
Wales, William. *An Inquiry into the Present State of Population in England and Wales; and the Proportion which the present Number of Inhabitants bears to the Number at former Periods* (London, 1781).
Walker, G. A. *Gatherings from Grave Yards* (London, 1839).
Watt, Alexander. *The Glasgow Bills of Mortality for 1841 and 1842* (Glasgow, 1844).
Whewell, William (ed.). *Literary Remains, Consisting of Lectures and Tracts on Political Economy, of the late Rev. Richard Jones* (London, 1859).
Wyse, Thomas. *Education Reform: or, the necessity of a National System of Education* (London, 1836).
Young, Arthur. *Proposals to the Legislature for Numbering the People* (London, 1771).
——. *Political Arithmetic* (London, 1774).
——. *Political Arithmetic, Part II* (London, 1779).
Zimmerman, E. A. W. *A Political Survey of the Present State of Europe, in Sixteen Tables* (London, 1787).
Author Unknown. *A Letter to a Member of Parliament, on the Registering and Numbering the People of Great Britain* (London, 1753).

Index

Abbott, Charles, 12–13
Achenwall, Gottfried, 10
Admiralty, 16, 50
Alison, Sir Archibald, 121
Alison, William P., 56–7, 98, 106, 137
Annesley, James, 9, 98
Ansell, Charles, 12
Anti-Corn Law League, 107, 116
Armed forces, health of, 9, 45–52, 97–8
Arnott, Neil, 54, 55, 57
Ashton, Thomas, 107, 108, 116, 138
Ashworth, Henry, 115, 116, 138
Aspland, Rev. R. B., 108
Aubrey, John, 2, 3
Auckland, Lord, 21

Babbage, Charles, 77–85 *passim*, 89, 92, 96, 171
Bailey, Francis, 15
Baines, Edward jr., 129
Baird, Charles, 119–20
Baker, Robert, 65, 126–31, 133
Balfour, Thomas Graham, 47, 50, 52
Bentham, Jeremy, 53, 86, 102
Benthamism, 82, 187
Bentley, Joseph, 139–40
Bethune, J. E. D., *see* Drinkwater, John Elliot
Bielfeld, J. F. von, 10
Birley, Richard, 115

Birmingham Educational Statistical Society, 124–5
Births, civil registration of, 29, 31–33, 39
Black, William, 8–9
Blane, Gilbert, 9
Blomfield, Charles, Bishop of London, 54
Board of Trade, 16, 19–27, 84, 86, 93, 94, 110
Boileau, Daniel, 11
Boileau, John, 101, 103
Booth, Charles, 22, 41, 138, 149
Bowring, John, 102, 103
Bristol Statistical Society, 121–3, 133, 136–7
British and Foreign School Society, 23, 102
British Association for the Advancement of Science, 24, 70, 77–83, 88, 89, 100, 111, 120, 121, 123, 124, 125, 126, 131, 142, 143, 170–171
Bromby, J. E., 122–3
Brougham, Henry, 13, 21, 78
Bryson, Alexander, 52
Burnet, William, 50

Capper, Benjamin, 11
Cargill, William, 125
Carpenter, Lant, 122
Cavendish, William, 79
Censuses, 3, 9, 12–13, 30, 38, 42, 60, 66–72, 96–7, 120, 131

Index

Central Society of Education, 16, 93, 95, 123, 140, 175
Chadwick, David, 148
Chadwick, Edwin, 29, 30, 35, 36, 37, 40, 41, 53-64, 85, 102, 103, 109, 124, 128, 131, 133, 144, 165
Chalmers, George, 7
Chalmers, Thomas, 84
Chandos, second Marquis of, 21
Clark, Francis, 125
Clark, Sir James, 35
Clay, Rev. John, 62
Cleland, James, 23, 24, 120-1
Clendinning, John, 98, 101, 102
Cobden, Richard, 116
Conring, Hermann, 10
Corbaux, Francis, 15
Corrie, J., 125
Corrie, J. R., 125
Cowan, Robert, 119
Cromwell, Henry, 3, 4
Cullen, William, 33, 52

Danson, J. T., 103
Darbishire, S. D., 109, 116
Davenant, Charles, 7
Deaths, civil registration of, 29, 33-34, 39, 40, 53, 58
Disputes, industrial, 99, 115, 120, 124
Disraeli, Benjamin, 21, 92
Dissenters, Protestant, 8, 15, 70-1, 146
D'Oyley, Rev. George, 79
Drinkwater, Col. John, 80
Drinkwater, John Elliot, 79-92 *passim*, 97, 127
Duncan, W. H., 61, 124
Duppa, B. F., 94-5

Eddison, Edwin, 128
Edgell, Rev. Edgell, 70, 101, 193
Edmonds, T. R., 96, 98
Education, effects and purpose of, 68-9, 106-7, 113, 114, 139, 144, 145; *see also* Statistics, education
Ellenborough, Lord, 53, 84
Empson, William, 85

Evelyn, John, 2
Ewart, Peter jr., 109, 116

Farr, William, 15, 27, 29-33 *passim*, 34-43, 47, 52, 54, 59, 61, 66, 96, 97, 98, 102, 103, 148, 161
Felkin, William, 138
Finlaison, John, 15
Fitzwilliam, third Earl, 82
Fletcher, Joseph, 63, 96-103 *passim*, 131, 142-4, 146, 148
Fonblanque, Albany, 25
Free Trade, 21, 93, 107, 116, 135, 147
Fripp, C. B., 121-2

General Register Office, 15, 27, 29-43, 45, 66
Glasgow, Statistical Society of, 119-20, 121
Glasgow and Clydesdale Statistical Society, 119, 120-1
Goldsmid, I. L., 102, 103
Gompertz, Benjamin, 96
Gott, Benjamin, 24
Goulburn, Henry, 85
Graham, Maj. George, 29-30, 31, 35, 38, 40, 66, 98
Graphical methods, 11-12, 39, 155-156
Graunt, John, 1, 2, 3, 7, 152
Greg, R. H., 107, 109, 116
Greg, Samuel, 73, 105, 107-8, 111, 115, 116
Greg, W. R., 105, 107-8, 109-10, 111, 116, 140
Greig, Woronzow, 79, 87, 88, 89, 99-103 *passim*
Guerry, A. M., 109, 139-41
Gutch, J. M., 122
Guy, William A., 61, 98, 102, 103, 138, 148

Hallam, Henry, 82, 85, 86, 87, 92, 101, 103, 121
Halley, Edmund, 7
Halliday, Sir Andrew, 9, 45, 49
Harden, J. W., 124

Index

Hare, Samuel, 126
Harrington, John, 3
Hawkins, F. Bisset, 11, 15
Haygarth, John, 9
Health of Towns Association, 16, 60, 101, 102
Heberden, William, 8
Heysham, John, 9, 15
Heywood, Benjamin, 105, 108, 109, 110, 111, 135
Heywood, James, 99, 101, 103
Hobbes, Thomas, 3, 4
Hodgson, Joseph, 125
Holland, G. C., 131
Home Office, 16, 22, 73, 74, 80, 90, 97
Hooper, W., 10
Horner, Leonard, 96
Houldsworth, Henry, 109
Howick, Viscount, 45, 46
Hume, James Deacon, 19, 84–5
Hume, Joseph, 21

Insurance, life, 7, 15, 154

Jacob, William, 19–20, 26, 28
Jeffery, Francis, 85
Jerrard, G. B., 122
Jones, Richard, 79, 81, 82, 83, 85, 87, 92

Kay, James Phillips, 26, 35, 54, 99, 105–115 *passim*, 127, 133, 145, 147
Kay-Shuttleworth, J. P., *see* Kay, James Phillips
Kennedy, John, 108–9, 110
Kennedy, Col. Shaw, 110, 116, 180
Kerry, Earl of, 65, 106, 112
King, Gregory, 7
Knight, Charles, 21, 85, 94

Laissez-faire, 83, 92, 93, 107–8, 110, 133, 144
Lancaster, Joseph, 141
Langton, William, 105, 106, 108, 109
Lansdowne, third Marquis of, 85, 87

Lansdowne, fifth Marquis of, 4
Laycock, Thomas, 62
Leeds Literary and Philosophical Society, 126, 128
Leeds, Statistical Committee of the Town Council, 126–31
Lemon, Sir Charles, 82, 87, 97, 101
Life-tables, 7, 8, 15, 38–9, 40, 41, 48, 154
Lister, Nathaniel, 94, 101
Lister, T. H., 29, 30, 31, 97
Liverpool Statistical Society, 124, 128
London, Statistical Society of, 9, 16, 19, 24, 27, 50, 66, 70, 73, 77–104, 111, 115, 117, 119, 123, 128, 135, 138–9, 142, 144, 146; publications, 94

McConnell, Henry, 109, 116
McConnell, William, 115, 116
McCulloch, J. R., 11, 21, 24
McGrigor, James, 45
Mackenzie, Holt, 90, 101
Maclean, C. H., 87, 92, 99, 101, 102, 103, 104
Maitland, William, 8
Malthus, T. R., 12, 79, 81, 83, 85, 87, 92
Manchester Literary and Philosophical Society, 109
Manchester Statistical Society, 26, 61, 73, 87, 90, 95, 99, 105–17, 119, 125, 128, 135–6, 138
Mann, Horace, 30, 42, 66–72
Mann, Thomas, 29
Marshall, Henry, 45–6, 47, 49, 50, 52
Marshall, J. G., 126, 127
Marshall, John, 21
Mayhew, Henry, 188
Meadows, James, 115
Melville, John, 103
Merivale, Herman, 101
Miasma, theory of, 49, 52, 54, 56–7, 61–3
Milne, Joshua, 15
Moivre, Abraham de, 8

Moray, Sir Robert, 5
Mortality, London Bills of, 5, 8, 9, 153
Murray, James, 109, 115

National Association for the Promotion of Social Science, 148
National Society for Promoting the Education of the Poor in the Principles of the Established Church, 23
Natural and Political Observations on the Bills of Mortality, authorship, 2-5, 152
Neison, F. G. P., 60, 102, 103, 138
Newbery, Henry, 109
Newcastle Statistical Society, 124, 125-6

Ogilby, William, 85
Oswald, W. D., 103

Peel, Sir Robert, 19, 147
Percival, Thomas, 9
Pett, Sir Peter, 7
Petty, Sir William, 1, 2, 3, 4, 7, 10, 151-3
Philips, R. N., 109, 116
Philips, Shakespeare, 109
Pinney, Charles, 122
Place, Francis, 84
Playfair, John, 11
Playfair, Lyon, 61, 145
Playfair, William, 11
Political arithmetic, 1-7 *passim*, 151
Political Economy Club, 83
Poor Law Commission, 16, 54, 55, 56, 61, 63, 85, 89, 92, 116, 117, 133
Poor Law Report (1834), 57, 83, 84
Pope, Charles, 24
Porter, G. R., 21-7, 66, 68, 73, 82, 84, 87-103 *passim*, 140-1, 148, 175
Price, Richard, 8
Prichard, J. C., 122
Privy Council Committee on Education, 16, 65, 116, 133

Public health, 9, 27, 35-40, 53-64, 99-101, 119, 126-7, 167; relationship to poverty, 35, 36-7, 54-5, 57, 58-64, 72, 106-7, 128, 130, 135, 136, 137, 138-9, 145-6
Public Health Act (1848), 60

Quetelet, Adolphe, 22, 78-9, 82, 83, 84, 89, 158, 171

Rawson, Rawson, 22, 90-104 *passim*, 131, 132, 133, 139, 141-2, 146, 174
Redgrave, Samuel, 22, 74, 90, 94
Registrars of births and deaths, 29, 30, 31, 54
Registration Act (1836), 15, 29, 31, 36, 38, 42, 53-4
Restoration Science, 1-2, 4
Ricardo, David jr., 80
Ricardo, David sr., 21, 81
Rickman, John, 12-13, 15, 65, 84, 156
Roberton, John, 62, 116-17
Robinson, James, 108
Robinson, Samuel, 108
Romilly, Edward, 99
Romilly, Henry, 115, 116
Romilly, Samuel, 13
Rose, George, 12
Rota Club, 3
Royal Commissions: Children's Employment, 102; Employment of Children in Factories, 80, 83, 85, 116; Hand-Loom Weavers, 96, 102; Municipal Corporations, 80; State of Large Towns and Populous Districts, 60-2
Royal Society, 4, 5, 77
Russell, Lord John, 29, 147

Sadler, M. T., 127
Sandon, Viscount, 124, 139
Science, status of, 78
Sedgwick, Adam, 79
Select Committees: Children Employed in Manufactories, 14; Criminal Convictions and Com-

Index

mitments, 14; Education of the Lower Orders, 14; Education of the Working Classes, 55; Friendly Societies, 15; Health of Towns, 55–6, 62–3, 64; Public Documents, 21

Senior, Nassau, 81, 83–4, 87, 92

Sheffield Statistical Society, 131–132

Short, Thomas, 8

Sinclair, Sir John, 10

Slaney, R. A., 55–6, 99

Smith, T. Southwood, 54, 55, 61, 63

Society for the Diffusion of Useful Knowledge, 21, 80, 85

Sociological Society, 149

Somerville, Mary, 87

Somerville, William, 79

Spence, William, 103

Stanley, Lord Edward, 66

Stanley, Rev. Edward, 88–9, 116

Stationary population, problem of, 7, 8, 59–60

Statistics, criminal, 13–14, 22, 24, 25, 26, 72–4, 94, 109–10, 130–1, 139–44; education, 14, 23, 26, 41, 65–9, 94–5, 97, 102, 111–12, 112–114, 121, 123, 124, 125, 139–44; general, 19–21, 22–6, 88–9, 90, 111–12; meaning of term, 9–11, 82, 85–6, 110, 119, 122, 123, 146; religious, 66, 69–72, 115

Stephen, Sir James, 101

Strutt, Edward, 85

Sturges-Bourne, William, 101, 103

Superintendent registrars of births, deaths, and marriages, 29, 30, 58

Sykes, Col. W. H., 79, 80–1, 82, 85, 87, 88, 89, 94, 98, 99, 101, 103, 138

Symonds, Arthur, 73–4

Symonds, J. A., 122

Thomson, Poulett, 21, 26–7, 84, 110–11

Tooke, Thomas, 83, 87, 92, 93, 101, 103

Tootal, Edward, 109, 116

Tremenheere, Seymour, 145

Tufnell, E. C., 85, 87, 92, 144–5

Tulloch, Alexander M., 46–50, 52, 97–8, 163

Ulster, Statistical Society of, 123–4

Vardon, Thomas, 87, 88, 90

Vital statistics, collection and analysis of, 3, 6, 9, 13, 15, 24–5, 29, 31–4, 45–52, 53–64, 96, 97–9, 117; reliability of, 5, 6, 8, 9, 15, 31–4; *see also* Births, Deaths, Public health

War Office, 16, 45, 47

Watson, Joseph, 125

Weight, Rev. George, 70

Weld, C. R., 103

Whewell, William, 78, 80, 87

Whishaw, James, 103

Whitmore, W. W., 85

Wilberforce, Samuel, Bishop of Oxford, 66, 70

Wilks, John, 31

Williamson, James, 127–8, 129, 131

Wilson, David H., 125

Wilson, John, 50–2

Wilson, Thomas, 132, 133

Wood, G. W., 85, 108

Wood, J. R., 112, 115, 116, 125

Zimmerman, E. A. W., 10